Inventing Great

Inventing Great Neck

JEWISH IDENTITY AND THE AMERICAN DREAM

Judith S. Goldstein

RUTGERS UNIVERSITY PRESS
NEW BRUNSWICK, NEW JERSEY, AND LONDON

Library of Congress Cataloging-in-Publication Data

Goldstein, Judith S.
Inventing Great Neck : Jewish identity and the
American dream/ Judith S. Goldstein.
p. cm.
Includes bibliographical references and index.
ISBN-13: 978-0-8135-3884-6 (hardcover : alk. paper)
1. Jews—New York (State)—Great Neck—History. 2. Great Neck (N.Y.)—
Ethnic relations. 3. Great Neck (N.Y.)—History. I. Title.
F129.G694G65 2006
974.7′245—dc22
2005035656

A British Cataloging-in-Publication record for this book
is available from the British Library.

Manufactured in the United States of America

IN MEMORY OF

Chassie Lee Burr

1902–1996

Contents

Acknowledgments

I am most grateful to so many people for aiding in the writing of this book and sharing their histories, memories, and observations of Great Neck. I have relied heavily upon personal interviews with numerous people who generously gave their time to this consideration of Great Neck's history. Among the long list, too long to enumerate, are those who patiently and repeatedly shared their knowledge and thoughts about Great Neck: Rabbi Mordecai Waxman and Ruth Waxman, Rabbi Jerome K. Davidson, Hilda Liff, Wini Freund, Roswell Eldridge, Dorothy Hicks, Jack Fields, and Tex McCrary.

Many professionals, including the staff of the New York Society Library, provided critical access to resources and references. In particular, I would like to thank Risha Rosner at the Great Neck Public Library for her knowledge and patience. My gratitude goes as well to Daniel Sokolow, archivist at the David Taylor Archives at the North Shore Long Island Jewish Heath Systems.

To Sue B. Mercy, Peter Schuck, Neil Flax, Ronald Spencer, Dorothy Hicks, William Tucker, and Barbara Trimbell, who read and thoughtfully edited the manuscript, my deep thanks. Although called into service over a period of many years, few of them expressed exasperation or disappointment over the slow development of the manuscript or my reliance upon their critical abilities to help turn historical material, theories, and even hunches into what one hopes is an illuminating exploration of Great Neck's past.

Inventing Great Neck

Introduction

Great Neck, New York, is one of America's most fascinating suburbs. The community, located at the eastern edge of New York City, developed an intriguing and distinct identity—in large part from its special Jewish history—from the 1920s through the 1960s. As a community, Great Neck has made aggressive claims to national recognition. In the 1920s it was a home for a new celebrity culture of writers, journalists, and Broadway and Hollywood stars, including many Jews who were not welcomed in other communities on Long Island's North Shore. In the 1940s, 1950s, and 1960s, Great Neck witnessed the creation of one of the country's outstanding public school systems, and in the late 1940s it served as the temporary home of the United Nations. In the 1960s, Great Neck was notable for its support of the civil rights movement and student activism; and, from the 1940s until today, it ranks as one of the most significant outposts of suburban Jewish culture, led by distinguished rabbis and marked by the Reform, Conservative, and Orthodox movements. In the process of inventing and reinventing itself, decade after decade, Great Neck has spun out many striking realities and myths—none more forceful than F. Scott Fitzgerald's *The Great Gatsby*—that have attracted and repelled large numbers of people. Drawing attention, through admiration and contempt, has been a Great Neck specialty.

In many ways, Great Neck reflects the tensions, dramas, and dreams common to America's countless suburbs. But it has also pursued its own conspicuous and unique path while transforming itself from a Gentile community to a mixed one and, by the 1960s, to a predominantly Jewish one. *Inventing Great Neck: Jewish Identity and the American Dream* explores individual histories and forces of collective social development over four decades in this unique community. Set against a background of incessant change, both within the community and without, *Inventing Great Neck* focuses on Great Neck's collective ambitions, accomplishments, and failings from the 1920s through the 1960s. Dynamic tensions infuse the history: between the suburb and New York City; between Jews and Gentiles; between domesticity and development; between residential permanence and moving on; between Great Neck and the aristocratic Protestant enclaves to the east on Long Island's North Shore; between an entrepreneurial, business-dominated society and an intellectual, artistic culture; between immigrants and their children; and between blacks and whites.

The historic Great Neck is worth a close look, viewed both from an insular perspective and as part of greater urban and national forces. Like so many other communities in America, Great Neck has served as a safety valve—an escape for the well-to-do and the almost well-to-do from living inside volatile, diverse, urban societies. The quiet, residential community tempted people away from New York City's ethnic and racial cauldron. But the city continued to exert a powerful force on the suburb, through the highly charged currents of industry, finance, race, and religion. Great Neck residents were pulled into the city's networks of work, money, culture, and immigrant family ties. Great Neck's success was tied to commuter railroads and automobiles, dreams of mobility, and the heady prosperity following World War I and World War II. It was a place to regroup; engage in democratic processes at the grass-roots level; and construct social experiments, voluntary organizations, and outstanding public and religious institutions. In the process of trying to create a diversified community of Jewish and Gentile associations, Great Neck provided an important example of ethnic and religious connections marked by early success and then striking failure.

Great Neck is a peninsula, covering 11.4 square miles, approximately sixteen miles from the heart of New York City. For hundreds of years, Great Neck was a gentle landscape, modestly devoted to supplying agricultural produce to the city. In the late nineteenth century, Great Neck became a summer colony—the "Newport of the Sound," it claimed—connected to the city by train and boat. Life in Great Neck approximated that of a new society with the acquired tastes of the British gentry: weekend entertaining, house parties, golf, and liquor. Great Neck, a fiefdom of rich landowners, consisted of a number of small villages. This pastoral satellite of New York was thirty minutes away from the city by train, the first stop beyond the city border. It became a special place where new money could settle—and rent, buy, and speculate in houses and land—and the first point of entry into the solid, golden chain of estates on the North Shore that was the playground of New York's Gentile aristocracy.

F. Scott Fitzgerald moved to Great Neck in 1922, drawn to its exuberant and transient life. At the time, Great Neck had a population of 12,000—including two hundred Jewish families—a few schools; one main street; many churches (but no synagogue); an exploding real estate market; and a potent mix of merchant princes, robber barons, artists, writers, Broadway moguls, actors, actresses, and journalists, including William K. Vanderbilt, Moses Annenberg, Alfred P. Sloan, Herbert Bayard Swope, Walter Chrysler, Henri Bendel, Hiram Bloomingdale, Ring Lardner, P. G. Wodehouse, Oscar Hammerstein II, George M. Cohan, Eddie Cantor, Fanny Brice, W. C. Fields, Paulette Goddard, and Groucho Marx. For three years, Fitzgerald wrote and partied in Great Neck. Jay Gatsby came to literary life in West Egg—the fictional derivative of Kings Point. *The Great Gatsby* and Great Neck evoked America's infatuation with New York City; ambition; Society; the transformative power of vast, newly acquired wealth—and the hollowness of its pursuit—and the convoluted possibilities of Jews mixing with Gentiles.

The 1930s, the Depression years, were vastly different. Great Neck struggled with developments that could not sell, estates that could not be maintained, and stars that jumped ship and moved to Hollywood. Great Neck turned from romance and glitter to selling houses to the middle class. By the late 1930s, banks owning houses in Great Neck were desperate to unload their Depression assets. Gentile families were sought, but the banks were willing to sell to Jews as well. Although many homeowners still refused to sell to Jews, this period marked the first time that non-celebrity Jews found an opening into the Great Neck real estate market. That Jewish population grew slowly within an overwhelmingly Gentile landscape of refined gentility. The creation of the first synagogue, a Reform temple, attracted a generation of Jews who wanted to free themselves from New York's immigrant ghettos and the self-segregation of Orthodox observance and education. In Great Neck, middle-class Jews began to find an accepting place in Protestant America. They confronted the relics of restrictive covenants and letters in the local paper about 'those people from Brooklyn.' With persistent effort, they overcame most of the restricted institutions and anti-Semitic practices and sentiments of Great Neck. The Jewish population sallied into the mainstream with forcefulness and confidence.

Great Neck's future was for middle-class families. The 1940s were Great Neck's pivotal years of ethnic, institutional, and historic transformation, as the suburb developed, in large part to serve the needs of the growing Jewish community, following the Second World War. After the peace the community, looking to its own needs, committed itself to a strong educational system. In 1942, in the first significant step toward improving the schools, the town fathers hired John L. Miller, trained at Bates College and Harvard, as superintendent of schools. In the hallowed tradition of a New England headmaster, he led his corps of yankee teachers with firm values and objectives. Intolerant of anti-Semitism, the school system welcomed students from Jewish neighborhoods in the city, although it was slower to accept Jewish teachers. Good education became the highest priority and drawing force of the community. The nationally recognized system attracted ex-soldiers with growing families, GI benefits for education, mortgages, and demands for a new way of life.

Word spread in the 1940s and 1950s that Great Neck welcomed those who valued education—Jew and Gentile alike. But the balance of ethnic forces in Great Neck began to shift away from the national norm and draw strength away from the Protestant and Catholic churches and parochial schools. Great Neck drew much of its new population from second-generation American Jews and Jewish refugees escaping from Nazi and German-dominated Europe. Gentiles from the upper and middle classes avoided Great Neck and moved to other communities on the North Shore where Jews were not yet welcomed. The positive response of Gentile leaders such as Miller, William Zinsser, a civic-minded proponent of zoning and orderly development; Hal Lanigan, the editor of the *Great Neck News* in the 1920s; and outstanding teachers such as Gertrude Pingree, Dorothy Hicks, and Jack Fields encouraged the Jewish population to feel accepted. Although not everyone moved into or out of Great Neck in response to the changing ethnic and religious profile of the community, its reputation was built, in large part, upon that profile. Tilting toward a Jewish community, as Great Neck did in the 1940s, resulted, by the 1960s, in the sociological phenomenon of tipping.

The Gentile old guard gave way. A Jewish old guard had never existed. When Jews started to move to Great Neck in the 1920s, there was no Jewish presence that required the recognition of a Jewish past or the constraints of social deference to an established Jewish hierarchy. The growing suburb, in fact, reinforced the sense of optimism and social freedom. Immigrant Jews who joined Jewish populations in large cities throughout America had to confront well-established religious and social patterns of assimilation and integration, usually of German Jews. For example, Jews who moved to the South in the nineteenth century had to take account of a painful history that divided families who were part of the Civil War from those who came later. Regional histories such as *A Portion of the People: Three Hundred Years of Southern Jewish Life*, edited by Dale and Theodore Rosengarten, give poignant testimony to the religious, economic, and social complexities that newly arrived Jewish immigrants faced upon entering Southern society.[1]

Great Neck was different: free from the demands and expectations of an established Jewish community, Great Neck Jews developed little connection to or interest in American Jewish life beyond the city. For their history, Great Neck's Jews looked back to the *shtetls* or major cities in Eastern Europe with large Jewish populations, back to Ellis Island, back to New York's Jewish population, numbering 1,640,000 in 1920—but not out to Jews in Charleston, San Francisco, Boston, or Kansas City and other American cities.[2]

In the late 1940s and 1950s, America led the world. New York led the country. Nassau County led the state in its expanding populations. And Jewish Great Neck, in fact and reputation, was a leader in the reconfiguration of America's suburban world. Once again, big money came home to rest in Great Neck. So did the United Nations, on a temporary basis, before its building was completed in New York City. Great Neck grew to approximately 40,000 people. Ninety-five percent of the old estates were developed on plots of one acre or more for a heady mix of clothing manufacturers, real estate developers, lawyers, importers, jewelers, analysts, doctors, and stockbrokers. Despite Great Neck's reputation, the community was not all up-scale. Many middle-income people, including teachers, writers, and labor leaders, moved to modest homes in modest villages. Some families stretched to be there and struggled to show a facade of wealth which barely hid their realities of limited means.

The transformation of the community was completed in the 1960s, when Great Neck diverged from the national norm and the possibility of ethnic equilibrium. Gentiles became the minority. The remnants of the once dominant Gentile community gave up most leadership positions in local voluntary and political organizations. Gentiles retreated into diminishing church congregations and a few social and recreational clubs, which welcomed only a few Jewish members. (A very few Gentile families still refused to sell houses to Jews.) Furthermore, the connection between a decaying and frayed New York City and its prosperous suburban satellite grew tense. Great Neck residents drew back in dread from the city that was engulfed in financial and racial turmoil. Those tensions split Great Neck in the late 1960s, when, after fiery public debate, it rejected a busing plan to educate a small number of black students from Queens. Despite providing large sums for the civil rights movements—as well as sending some of its rabbis and students on Freedom Rides and providing temple platforms for black leaders—Great Neck resisted efforts, within its borders, to improve black lives. Vietnam protests besieged the schools as student activists walked out of classes and burned flags. Civility moved out. Families collided over parental pressures for success, adolescent rebellion, the drug culture, and the compulsive propensity to display wealth. These local changes reflected the disturbances of the broader society in transition. Russell Baker described the precipitous slide into this new social territory:

> The martini hour was ending; marijuana, hallucinogens, and the needle in the arm were the new way. The tinkling piano in the next apartment was giving way to the guitar in the park. People now had so much money that they could afford to look poor. Men quit wearing fedoras and three-piece suits to Yankee Stadium and affected a hobo chic—all whiskers and no creases. Women quit buying hats and high-heeled shoes and started swearing like Marine sergeants. College students, who had once rioted for the pure joy of it, began rioting for moral and political uplift, issued non-negotiable demands, held the dean hostage, and blew up the physics lab. Gangster funerals disappeared into the back of the newspapers, upstaged by spectacular nationally televised funerals of murdered statesmen.[3]

By the 1960s, the social, economic, and ethnic patterns in Great Neck were set: its large population was more than 50 percent Jewish, highly educated, overwhelmingly Democratic, and conspicuously wealthy—although there was also a solid base of middle-class families. Many people, both Gentiles and Jews, perceived the community as too Jewish, even for those Jews who desired a mixed community. Further east on Long Island, new alternatives became available as much of the North Shore diversified, just as Great Neck had done in the 1940s and 1950s. Economic and political factors made it possible for new suburbanites to claim pieces of the great estates. Developers bought them, chopped them up and sold to the highest bidders. Antidiscriminatory laws and the civil rights movement made it increasingly difficult to sustain restricted communities.

Starting in the 1970s, Great Neck had difficulty holding on to its established identity, connections, and history. Almost all of the estates were gone. In most of the community, hills and farms were covered cheek-by-jowl with houses. Traffic choked the roads and nearby highways. Developers built office buildings and new apartment houses. Commuting was no longer essential. Middle Neck Road, long the central artery of Great Neck's small commercial life, began to look like just another commercial strip. Great Neck still attracted young, well-to-do families and was even home to a few entertainers such as Alan King. But it invited ridicule and distaste for its brazen ways and lavish spending. Public schools were closed because of the shrinking student population. Two high schools split the former unified identity of the community.

The influx of Sephardic Jews—wealthy, Orthodox and separatist—brought new strains. The Jewish community was split by complex class and religious divisions when the Orthodox community—consisting of Iranian and Syrian Jews as well as those from Ashkenazi backgrounds—grew dramatically, established day schools and synagogues, and closed their stores on Saturday, the Jewish Sabbath. In the 1920s, the first generation of Great Neck Jews had reversed the traditional American process of division within the Jewish community: Great Neck's Jewish base was Reform. Fifty years later, with the growth of the Orthodox population, the unified and harmonious relationships among the Jewish population, nourished for decades by Rabbis Jacob Rudin, Mordecai Waxman, and Jerome K. Davidson, began to fray.

This study of Great Neck's development, emphasizing both its ethnic and religious transformation and the impact of its Jewish population, invites four major questions. Why write about Great Neck instead of other outstanding communities with significant Jewish populations, such as Scarsdale in Westchester, Newton and Brookline in Massachusetts, or Shaker Heights in Ohio? Can one legitimately write about a community in terms of its collective spirit, goals, and accomplishments? Why start in the 1920s? And why close the study in the 1960s instead of 2005?

The answers seem clear to me. No other suburban communities with large Jewish populations match Great Neck's combination of size, advantageous geographical position as a New York City suburb, rich literary evocations—especially through the writing of F. Scott Fitzgerald—and aggressive development and promotion of image and assets. Not unlike thousands of other American communities, Great Neck was in the business of selling itself. But few communities did so with quite the same combination of stereotypically Jewish qualities such as aggressive brashness and conspicuous success.

To match Great Neck's size, the relatively small town of Scarsdale would have had to attach itself to Rye, Harrison, Larchmont, or a few other Westchester communities. Of course, this never happened. Newton and Brookline were close to Boston and Shaker Heights to Cleveland, but neither of those cities had New York's singular, seductive mix of Broadway; the garment trade on Seventh Avenue; the Jewish Lower East Side; Greenwich Village; Wall Street; the Metropolitan Opera; the Museum of Modern Art; and the Dodgers, Yankees, and Giants. No other American city could challenge New York's combination of economic power and social and cultural dominance—always bursting with new people and ideas—even as the city was entering its painful period of noticeable decline in the 1950s.

Great Neck created a distinctive collective voice. Like other suburban communities, Great Neck, sometimes through bitterly contested local elections, settled upon tax policies, school budgets, and zoning issues. But going beyond the recognized records of expenditures, politics, and organizational activities, the fortunate social historian can turn to the rich inventory of writers, such as F. Scott Fitzgerald and Edmund Wilson; entertainers, including Eddie Cantor; and journalists, such as Bayard Swope, who left indelible impressions from their time in Great Neck. Their writings and activities mark the spirit and yearnings of individuals who gave the community a lasting tone that illuminates Great Neck's past and still haunts its future.

Finally, the reasons for the particular time frame of this study: beginning in the 1920s and ending in the 1960s. The opening decade seems easy to explain. Only in the 1920s does Great Neck emerge as a place that attracts attention in the city: visited by celebrities, talked about, admired and resented—the object of both envy and scorn. Until the 1920s, Great Neck was just another Long Island community: Gentile, quiet, and self-contained. The post–World War I euphoria and prosperity put an end to Great Neck's obscurity. Fine homes, well-known personalities, easy access to and from the city, good parties, and a multiplicity of golf courses promoted Great Neck as the place to be. It was the hot spot for the fast crowd, including Jews who could not easily find social acceptance in other North Shore communities. A few Jews soon meant more Jews. And more Jews meant fewer Gentiles. The suburban version of America's convoluted ethnic and religious interactions—the social dynamics of attracting some and repelling others—began for good in the 1920s.

But why end in the 1960s? This is a more complicated matter. Certainly, Great Neck will continue to challenge the social historian in regard to the decades from the 1960s to the present—another period of significant community transformation. It is my belief, however, that a combination of factors gave Great Neck's earlier development a unique distinction and drama. From the 1920s to the 1960s that combination—and it is the mix of factors that is crucial—consisted of ethnic and religious interactions in the new suburban arena of competing values and identities; Great Neck's compelling connection to New York City through work, culture, and the immigrant family; the idealized view of protected, cohesive families living in single homes on tranquil streets; Great Neck's exuberance in building fine schools, hospitals, and a variety of organizations in the period when America, the suburbs, the economy, and the family—with women at home in service to their husbands and children—were ascendant; and finally, the confidence of American Jews about eventually entering the upper reaches of academia, the professions, and American cultural life as anti-Semitism loosened its national hold.

By the end of the 1960s, many of these factors had changed. Great Neck had given up on achieving any balance between Gentiles and Jews. With a Jewish population of over 50 percent, acceptance was no longer in question. The churches were in deep financial and demographic decline. The growing population necessitated the building of a second high school, which resulted in a degree of competition and differentiation between Great Neck South and Great Neck North. A different kind of split resulted from the expanding presence of an Orthodox Jewish community: the educational system that had once united the community was of no interest to Jews who favored a parochial and not a secular, public education. And Great Neck no longer honored the connection between the suburban oasis and the city. As racial unrest and financial instability plagued the city, Great Neck loosened the close ties of urban-based work, culture, and family. Another major development involved the feminist movement. Community organizations that had profited from the vital attention and unpaid labor of Great Neck wives—wives who had no other place to direct their energies and ambitions—started to decline as women demanded opportunities in the workplace. Finally, the demands of students in the Vietnam era shattered the image of stability in the schools and the confidence of teachers and parents. The educational system was no longer a hallowed, revered, and sure source of social control and order. From the late 1960s on, teachers who experienced the change looked back wistfully to a golden era of respect, recognition, and community support that characterized the earlier period. Nearly seventy years ago, Fitzgerald condemned the Great Neck-inspired world of West Egg for its meaningless and tragic spirit: a "raw vigor" that "herded its inhabitants along a shortcut from nothing to nothing." He was wrong about Great Neck: it didn't burn out. From the 1920s on, Great Neck produced generations of families that broke into the dynamic and rich realization of the American dream: wealth, acceptance, recognition, and substantive achievement. Great Neck led the ascendancy of middle-class America, especially middle-class Jewish America, in staking out new territory in suburbia. Critics, including Lewis Mumford, Kenneth Jackson, Lizabeth Leibowitz, and many others, have examined the broad implications of the pre- and post-World War II suburban revolution. Without focusing specifically on Great Neck, they condemned the isolation, racial and gender inequalities, smugness, and self-gratification of suburban life. Great Neck is a good example of much of what they decry about suburban life. But more importantly, Great Neck should be known for its distinctions: its special mix of intellectuals, achievers, and the socially conscious who transcended the bland, mediocre, and self-serving contentedness of much of suburban life.

On the edge of America's greatest city, for a few decades Great Neck symbolized opportunity and aspiration, mixing Jews with Gentiles and educating fine minds. From the 1920s through the 1960s, there was a special chemistry that drew different kinds of people, Gentiles and Jews, with different motives, to the suburb: intellectuals and businessmen, the European-born, the American rural- and urban-born, the refined and uncouth, all wanting to acquire a part of Great Neck's special wealth and promise. Great Neck, fiercely entrepreneurial and educationally and culturally acquisitive, created a distinguished, Jewish-led society. *Inventing Great Neck* is Great Neck's story.

On the Map

DISCOVERY

Eddie Cantor, the Jewish comedian, singer, and star of vaudeville, Broadway, and Hollywood, built his dream-home in Great Neck, New York. In 1928, on the verge of moving into his pseudo-English mansion on Long Island's North Shore, Cantor was in a state of reflective happiness. He tucked his memories—the painful ones of the poverty and torments of his Lower East Side childhood and the anti-Semitic persecutions of Eastern Europe—safely into the past. In the residential company of other celebrities the thirty-six-year-old star and his family were ready to move away from the city into permanent domesticity in Great Neck.

Spirited, fast growing, and forward looking, Great Neck eagerly bent to America's latest social, economic, and cultural forces. The setting blended the sweet pleasures of beauty and tranquility with vibrant echoes of New York City, just a short distance away by train, boat, or car. A strong spirit of opportunity and daring pervaded the place. Residents could sense the excitement of creating a society of the high living and achieving, a special community that attracted the rich and renowned. In Great Neck, they could also find a special social twist as the community boldly veered away from its neighbors on the North Shore. It was one of the very few suburban hot spots in America that accepted, and sometimes even welcomed, Jews into its world of middle- and upper-class values, traditional New England and pseudo English country life. For Eddie Cantor, Great Neck offered the optimistic, restless volatility of an inclusive, wealthy community that enjoyed the stimuli of Broadway, Hollywood, and high society.

The moment was right for Cantor to make his move. Postwar America was fixated on success and the unconventional doings of the rich, the nouveau riche, and the famous. Postwar Great Neck, competing for residents and wealth, sought attention and notoriety. Cantor had an inspiring story to tell, one that, for the moment, reached a climax in Great Neck: from poor to rich, from immigrant to star, from ghetto to Gold Coast, from renter to homeowner. The son of poor, Russian Jewish parents, Cantor had triumphed on Broadway, in Hollywood and now, in 1928, in Great Neck. What fortuitous forces pushed him from despair and desperation— orphaned and impoverished as a boy on the Lower East Side—to fabulous Broadway success as a young man? In 1928, after triumphs on the stage and screen in *Kidd Boots* and *Whoopee,* Cantor gave the public his story: *My Life Is in Your Hands.* For the first time, Cantor had money and time for the seemingly gracious, charitable life of the gentry. "And so, engaged in welfare work, secured by sound investments and surrounded by a goodly family, the life of the early Henry Streeter is complete."[1] Unrushed and unperturbed, he wrote in his memoir about the paradisiacal pleasures of Great Neck. "I step out on the lawn. Opposite my house is one of the most magnificent estates in Great Neck. I cross the road and approach its stone gateway. There is a small sign near the entrance reading, 'Nathan S. Jonas.' As I walk up the wide gravel path I gaze at the unfolding garden plotted majestically across the plain of green and tinted with mellow colors in the last gleams of sunset."[2]

Assuming the voice of the third-person observer, Cantor wrote: "The slum boy of the tenement is learning all about trees and flowers and nature. . . . Four years ago this wonder garden was a cornfield. Beyond it were barren tangles of weeds. Now," Cantor continued, "a stately castle rears its armored head upon the hill. It is the story of a modern pioneer, a pilgrim of the twentieth century whose wheels of industry are pushbuttons and who accomplishes overnight what it took backwoodsmen many generations to perform."[3]

That pioneer and pilgrim, Nathan S. Jonas, was also Cantor's banker and financial advisor. Jonas, the Jewish mentor, philanthropist, and investment advisor, brought Cantor into bucolic, peaceful Great Neck, with its rich land investments and speculation. Proud and confident, Cantor recounted one pertinent tale of Great Neck enrichment and putative largesse. In 1923, Jonas, the president of the Brooklyn-based Manufacturer's Trust, had bought 175 acres (for $1,650 an acre) close to William K. Vanderbilt's estate in the Lakeville section of Great Neck. Instead of building his mansion on the property, Jonas and some friends developed the Lakeville Golf Club. "It is regarded," Cantor wrote, "as one of the most beautiful and exclusive country clubs in America."[4] Even more impressive to Cantor was the fact that Jonas had had to pay four times the original price to buy more land for himself. Subsequently, Jonas sold Cantor ten acres across from the golf club. By 1928, Great Neck property was selling at $10,000 an acre. "I have often wandered with Jonas," Cantor mused with heartfelt hyperbole, "over his fifty-six acre estate adjoining the club and shared the joy he takes in this self-made retreat from the business world. Here the banker and the actor go far back to primitive rustic life, but it is idealized and you can detect the magical touch of power and gold in every flower of the garden and every string bean on the farm. Instead of waiting hundreds of years for saplings to sprout and grow into mighty trees, they rise here in full bloom within the span of a week. Space and time are the slaves that tremble under the wand of wealth."[5]

"Trembling" was a bit excessive. Like the rest of the North Shore, Great Neck had been accustomed, since the late 1800s, to the transforming impact of the rich and the "wand of wealth." But Great Neck was pulsating with something that was equally strong and valuable: American idealism and the fervent spirit of a growing community. Despite the hyperbole, Cantor described poignant and real things that he saw right in front of him: the power of individual and communal aspiration, the pleasure of landscape and the creative transformation of nature, the promise of family happiness and well-being, and the expectation of religious tolerance.

Great Neck carried the bold standard of success and wealth as well as the ostentatious promise of much more to come. Abundant hopes and vital connections infused the boosterism of a thriving community. Its publicists, especially Hal Lanigan, the editor of the *Great Neck News*, touted the special aura: Great Neck, close to, but safely removed from, the chaos of the city, offered a stable American community for prosperous families; Great Neck, within sight of the greatest city in America, thrived on proximity and easy access; and Great Neck, so hungry for success, provided unusual openings for Jews in America's rigid social and religious order. Eschewing modesty, Great Neck set immense challenges for itself: attract more of the wealthy, build more mansions, grab the celebrities and defy the social separation of Gentiles and Jews.

Development, wealth, star-status, and persistent publicity were the crucial ingredients for attracting more residents and shaping an irresistible, high-priced, cosmopolitan image of Great Neck in the 1920s. Conspicuous theatrical connections with New York City, Chicago, and Hollywood were essential. News and image building, centered on Great Neck, came from New York City papers, national journals, and two local weeklies. Names—lots of names—provided the litany of success and drew the interest of Great Neck's established residents and investors as well as prospective residents and would-be investors.

The town reveled in news, from inside and without, of its famous, wealthy Gentile and Jewish residents: businessmen such as Moe Annenberg, August Heckscher, Harry F. Sinclair, Walter P. Chrysler and Alfred Sloan; Broadway celebrities such as Tom Meighan, Ed Wynn, Oscar Hammerstein II, George M. Cohan, and Groucho Marx; and journalists such as Herbert Bayard Swope and Ring Lardner. The *Great Neck News*, started in 1925, dedicated itself to the peripatetic schedules of famous hometown residents. The paper tracked their trips away from New York and, in the case of the entertainers, their appearances on the national theater and movie circuits in Chicago, Hollywood, and Broadway and, most significantly, their returns to Great Neck. The *New Yorker* magazine also acknowledged Great Neck's significance. Edited by Harold Ross and generously underwritten by Raoul Fleischmann, the upstart, weekly magazine explored new terrains of irony, humor, literary snobbery, entertainment, and stylish probing into prominent personalities on the make. Walter P. Chrysler, the newly rich automobile maker from Kansas and a Great Neck resident, was the subject of a 1927 *New Yorker* article: "He, a country boy," the feature stated, "has reached the heights from which he can dispense advice and help to those who are below him."[6] This was good copy for another American tale of rags to riches. Equally important was Chrysler's style and signs of wealth. "Certainly, there is ostentation," the *New Yorker* writer observed. "His palatial home at Great Neck is the typical residence of a leader in the Sanhedrin of the successful. There is an air about it which says the contractor was told: 'don't worry about the expense, old boy; go the limit.'"[7]

The *New Yorker* signified that Great Neck, with its population of approximately 200 Jews—Cantor, Marx, Annenberg, Hammerstein, et al.—was a different kind of suburban community. The "Sanhedrin of the successful!" Who could have missed the titillating reference including the Semitic alliteration? Other *New Yorker* pieces, however, were subtler about the presence of Jews and Gentiles. John Held, Jr., for example, a caricaturist par excellence of the 1920s, was the *New Yorker*'s inspired social cartographer. "In and About Great Neck: Pictured from the Description of a Week-End Guest—And What a Week-End," appeared in July 1927. Held, who lived in Westport, Connecticut, regarded Great Neck as the epicenter of the *New Yorker* weekend and an ideal subject for the new magazine.

On his own quixotic scale, Held drew the rich peninsula of Great Neck and Port Washington, including Sands Point, jutting out into Long Island Sound, and divided by Manhasset Bay and Hempstead Harbor. Little Neck Bay to the west was not shown. Held's tantalizing view of Great Neck spread east to the Gold Coast of the North Shore of Long Island, although it didn't extend all the way to the Morgans in Glen Cove or the Fricks and Phippses in Westbury. In homage to Great Neck, Held viewed the peninsula as an integral part of the North Shore. Its 600 estates, in holdings of from fifty to 2,000 acres, mimicked the luxurious realms of the English aristocracy: lordly domains of mansions, manor houses, village churches, polo fields, hunts, race tracks, golf courses, private docks, private motor ways, gardens, specimen trees, and multitudes of servants and service people.

The map was a one-dimensional concoction of delicious distortions and insinuations. Held placed dollar signs around the borders of his Great Neck map. Bootleggers' ships floated on the waters off "Kings Pernt" and Sands Point. Held dropped a few sardonic captions around the map for further edification: on the Long Island Sound, "These ships are breaking the Law for the rich man, while the poor has to drink perzon;" at the home of Harry Alexandre, "Here danced the Prince of Wales;" and with the Meadow Brook Hounds, "hunting up and down the bay or baying up and down the hunt." A few traditional icons showed up: one church in Great Neck, a squiggly line for the Long Island Railroad running through Great Neck to Port Washington, some train stations along the line, yacht clubs, hunt clubs, and golf clubs. Held's map offered a profusion of famous society names that filled up the territory from Great Neck to Port Washington. Reflecting the *New Yorker*'s subversive social tone and tastes, Held's pen gave equal weight to Jewish and Gentile names.[8]

Held was well equipped to make satiric maps for the *New Yorker*. In fact, he had training as a cartographer, first on an expedition to Central America for the Carnegie Institute and then mapping German U-boat positions for the Navy during World War I. But now, in the sexually liberated 1920s, he was charting the hard-drinking and giddy doings of the restless rich who moved among favored spots up and down the East Coast and looked aghast at the rest of America that couldn't, or didn't want to, keep up. Held was highly touted, enjoying success as the premier draughtsman of Prohibition days and the Jazz Age. Held played with the geography of social change and aspiration, caricaturing city spots as well as the weekend watering holes of the wealthy. "Great Neck" was one of his maps in a series that frivolously depicted cities, town, states, and sporting spots: Saratoga Springs, Florida, Hollywood, New England winter sports, rivers for trout fishing, and New York City.

The full-page *New Yorker* cartoon confirmed an essential fact: Great Neck had emerged on the satiric social map as a coveted place of money and fame. Of course, Held left out crucial information about the peninsula. He gave no indication of the topography nor of the subtle beauty of lush, varied terrain framed by the bays to the east, north, and west. Held's map ignored the historic imprints of the Indians, the Dutch and English settlers, the farms, estates of the late nineteenth century, and the hotels for summer excursions. He showed no interest in the constellation of institutional, commercial, and political entities: schools; churches; numerous residential developments; banks; real estate agencies; the roads on the peninsula; the enclaves of Irish, Polish, and black residents; nor the interlocking political and administrative jurisdictions of incorporated and unincorporated villages, schools, parks, and water districts. The caricaturist even omitted certain significant names on the roster of the rich: William K. Vanderbilt and Roswell Eldridge in Great Neck and Payne Whitney in Manhasset. And finally, Held gave no indication of social tensions and prejudice—for which he would have had to include the city with its millions of Jewish immigrants and the multitude of North Shore villages where Jews were not welcome to live.

The most significant omissions lay to the west. Implicitly, Held's map was one of separation. He deliberately ignored the geographical connection between the sparsely populated villages of Great Neck and New York City as the industrial, financial and mercantile center of American life. In Held's world, Great Neck, in the town of North Hempstead and in Nassau County, had no connections to the west, to the border lines of Queens County, then on to Kings and New York Counties. Manhattan, critical to the amassing of names and the creation of wealth and culture, existed only by implication as the place from which one fled for the weekend retreat. Nor did Held look to the continent beyond, to the midwestern and western states such as Utah, where Held grew up, or Fitzgerald's Minnesota, Lardner's Michigan and Swope's Missouri. Held defined Great Neck in the 1920s as part of the Gold Coast, home to its own special cast of characters, awash in success. In no way, however, did the map show how Great Neck had burst into notoriety and differentiated itself from its neighboring communities. Nor did it even hint at Great Neck's quiet, unremarkable past, which reached right up to the 1920s.

To chart that history, one would need to create multiple maps and super-impose them, one on top of other, like an architect's set of plans. The first few would focus on the history of nomenclature and possession. Through the seventeenth and eighteenth centuries, Great Neck's name changed many times: first it was called Wallage, then Matthew Garrison's Neck, Madnan's Neck, and, finally, Great Neck.[9]

The first inhabitants were the Mattinecock Indians, who fished rich waters and farmed fertile land. They were pushed aside by Dutch and English settlers who established farms and pastures for cattle. In a tangle of competing land patents and claims of control, local governance and alle-giances seesawed back and forth between Dutch New Amsterdam and the English-dominated town of Hempstead. The English won out in the mid-1660s when the area became the possession of James, Duke of York. Large farms, saw mills, and gristmills were established on the Great Neck peninsula. The landowning population was small, as was the labor force that included a few slaves in the late 1700s.

Differences preceding the Revolutionary War caused a split between the northwestern areas of Long Island and the communities to the south and east. In 1775, several communities, including Great Neck, broke away from Hempstead with its strong Tory sympathies and formed the town of North Hempstead. During the war, after the Continental Army lost Long Island, English forces occupied and intermittently pillaged livestock and crops in Great Neck and areas around it. With the end of the war, Great Neck reverted to a peaceful existence. During the next hundred years, it was the quiet setting for burgeoning estates, farms, and increased trade with villages on Long Island and New York City across the Sound. Great Neck, which had had a small number of slaves in the seventeenth century, easily conformed to the statewide abolition of slavery in the late 1820s.

Another series of historically illustrative plans would show Great Neck's isolation from nineteenth-century industrial, urban America. Through-out the late 1800s, Great Neck was little affected by the tumultuous trans-formation of urban and industrial life to the west. Its population remained small—only 1,600 on the eve of the twentieth century. Its land values slowly moved upwards as wealthy families moved to Great Neck. During the

Gilded Age after the Civil War, many farmers sold their properties to New York residents who aggregated holdings for summer and weekend use. William Gould Brokaw, a wealthy manufacturer of men's clothing, and W. R. Grace, the shipping mogul and former mayor of New York City, were two of the most distinguished men who built fine houses and gardens and planted trees to embellish the former landscape of farms. Amusement areas and hotels attracted daily visitors, who came by boat across the Sound to escape the city's stifling summer heat.

In the summer months, people, along with freight, produce, and animals, went by steamboat to and from the city. The boat stopped at Sea Cliff, Glen Cove, Sands Point, Steamboat Landing in Great Neck, Whitestone, and finally at Manhattan at Twenty-third Street and Peck's Slip near Wall Street. Commuting men went to work on the 7 a.m. boat and returned late in the afternoon to wives and servants waiting in handsome carriages. Despite the opening of a rail line from Flushing to Great Neck in 1866 (backed by some of the largest landowners on the peninsula) and its extension to Port Washington in 1898 (by a subsidiary of the Long Island Rail Road), life on the peninsula remained oriented to Long Island Sound with its steamboats, side wheelers, and yachts. By the turn of the century, the train took passengers to Hunter's Point in Long Island City where they took a ferry across the East River to Manhattan.

Commercial shops and institutional life developed in slow motion: schools, a library, a post office, dry goods stores, grocery stores, peddlers, a fire company in 1900, the first bank in 1906, electricity in 1910, sidewalks along Middle Neck Road—the main road—and a park district to encompass most of the peninsula in 1916. Churches were established along Middle Neck Road at its northern end: the Catholics built St. Aloysius in 1876 and the Episcopalians founded All Saints in 1886. At the other end of Great Neck, near the station, three more churches were founded: St. Paul's Episcopal Church, the Community Church, and the Methodist Church on the top of Spinney Hill. Generally, rural domesticity, isolation, and little development continued to characterize Great Neck until Pennsylvania Station opened in New York City in 1911. In the Nassau County Atlas for 1914, many of Great Neck's streets still were identified generically as First Avenue, Second Avenue and bisected by First Street and Second Street. The population was 3,600 with approximately 700 in the schools. The community was indistinguishable from Douglaston to the west in Queens or Port Washington to the east in Nassau County. Until the late nineteenth century, Great Neck, along with large portions of Long Island, was simply not part of the wild American entrepreneurial grab for raw materials and instant wealth. Political parties paid little attention to the small population. No individual sought to turn the area into a private duchy. In a small community, people knew every tradesman, house, and farm. They watched as properties were amassed and then divided, passing from farmers to summer people and then, with increasing frequency, to developers.

Until the turn of the century, distance and inaccessibility protected Great Neck from New York City's industries, immigrants, and geographical aggrandizement. Bloated with energy, wealth, and a population of millions, New York City absorbed Brooklyn, Staten Island, the Bronx, and Queens in 1898. With consolidation, New York remained America's largest and most vibrant city, with vast producing and consuming markets. At last, the city gained the resources to modernize its transportation networks, residential markets, and educational systems. But the communities to the east and south on Long Island wanted little part of that glory and transformation. In 1899, the undeveloped eastern part of Queens, eager to remain apart from the city, organized itself into Nassau County, consisting of 272 square miles. Great Neck was the first area on the city border in the new county.

DEVELOPMENT

The new boundaries were set, but they could not preserve Great Neck's remoteness and unaggressive pace of development. Within the first few years after the turn of the century, engineering feats resulted in railroad tunnels under the East River and Hudson River and the completion of the magisterial Pennsylvania Station in 1911. These striking improvements, along with the development of the automobile, jolted the Great Neck peninsula out of its ordinary, uneventful ways. Now, the trip to the city could take under an hour. The subways in New York did the rest. By the 1920s, the Long Island Railroad (LIRR) fed into subway lines that connected to Seventh Avenue—Broadway and the garment area—Brooklyn, Harlem, the Lower East Side, and the Bronx. Motor roadways and railroad tracks brought the peninsula, only sixteen miles from Manhattan, into the orbit of urban America. Long Island, rural, quiet, and rich in beaches and shorefront, irresistibly presented itself as an alternative, for permanent living or weekend visits, to the city's heat, noise, congestion, and mixed populations

In the first decades of the twentieth century, the rich reveled in Long
Island's charms, not the least of which was the money made by selling
their estates, or parts of them, for residential suburban enclaves. Before
Penn Station was completed, Long Island had lagged far behind Westchester and New Jersey in suburban growth. By 1910, when Penn Station
was about to open, developers descended on Long Island's virgin lands
and sculpted farms and large holdings into upscale residences. At first,
the Great Neck developments had to be close to the railroad station. Before
cars were commonly used in the 1920s, most commuters needed to walk
to and from the station for the ride to the city that took, depending on
the number of stops, from twenty-eight to fifty minutes. By the second
decade of the century, over sixty trains stopped in Great Neck, with the
last one leaving the city at two thirty in the morning.

Hundreds of houses imitating Spanish, English, Italian, and Colonial
styles, costing from $5,000 to $100,000, sprouted from Great Neck's land.
Several held interior treasures of fine metal, wood and glass detailing, such
as the Kensington home built by Joseph Dujat, a distinguished designer
of architectural ornamentation. The houses formed enclaves with borrowed or bucolic names such as Kensington, the Great Neck Estates, Great
Neck Hills, Russell Gardens, University Gardens, and Kennilworth. Family names, associated with Great Neck farms and estates, such as Deering,
Mitchell, Hicks, and Allen, that dominated the eighteenth and nineteenth
century maps of land ownership, often dwindled down to street signs.
These constituted Great Neck's homage to the past. Elsewhere, reference
to the English landscape, through street names and architectural styles,
was appended to the landscape.

The developments of the first two decades differed in amenities and
styles: some, such as Kensington, were laid out in a grid of handsome
streets, with added amenities such as bathing clubs; others, such as the
Great Neck Estates, were located on winding, botanically-named streets.
In addition, four golf clubs in Great Neck reworked the landscape as a
sign of the community's mania for the genteel sporting life. As the population grew, villages incorporated to maintain control over zoning and local
governance. The peninsula was divided into a patchwork of incorporated
and unincorporated villages, although they joined together in one school
and water district.

Sustaining the momentum of residential success—selling the community of year-round domesticity with houses, schools, and churches—became the business of entrepreneurial battalions. Whatever the specific shape

and visual tone of the homes and sporting amenities, real estate investors, developers, and agents sought to lure buyers to an idyllic American way of life: to rescue them from urban turmoil, immigrant diseases and discordant noise. Great Neck boasted of its quiet, verdant, house-oriented, pseudo-English existence. Like so many other suburbs, Great Neck lured residents who yearned for the ideal of family life—a life in the middle or upper class, socially secure, ordered, and controllable.

Yet, Great Neck's boosters had to strike a delicate balance between the peninsula's connection to the city and its promised differences. Great Neck's emerging culture drew away from the city but never distanced itself too much from prized urban assets of friends, work, and entertainment. This was the key to Great Neck's immediate and rapid success. Ring Lardner, the sardonic and incisive writer and playwright, captured the contradiction when he called Great Neck, his new hometown in the 1920s, "Wonder City." Great Neck, the suburb, used New York City as the visual, spirited, and easily accessible backdrop for a new way of living. From the shores of Kings Point to Great Neck Hills, near the railroad station, one could glimpse the skyscrapers of the city. The city was in view, but not too close, separated by the sound and the flatlands of Queens which still mixed large tracts of undeveloped land with lower-class housing. By the 1920s, traveling into the city was relatively easy by train or by car.

Big Names

The connection to the city—the place of work, excitement, wealth, and culture—was essential to Great Neck's allure. Just east of the city line, just west of the full spread of the Gold Coast, Great Neck became the spirited meeting ground for those who moved in two worlds and sought to make new rules for each. By the 1920s, the former North Shore playground of the rich and staid attracted fast-paced theater directors, actors, actresses, journalists, and writers. Often, the stars amused and attracted the rich. The rich, naturally, delighted the stars. The rich and the stars—and sometimes they were one and the same—were a developer's dream in the suburban setting close to the city.

Great Neck offered a seemingly safe investment in domesticity through home and community, as well as a way to exhibit personal success, manipulate reputations, and rework social lines. High-class development propelled the peninsula to fame and success. Selling houses, names, real estate—homes, land, clubs, and small businesses—meant continuing to attract big names away from the city. The bait was the profitability of an expanding community with local banks; theaters; churches; golf courses; newspapers; and public, parochial, and private schools.

Herbert Bayard Swope, already into his fourth year as executive editor of Pulitzer's *World,* in 1924 the highest paid and most influential newspaper editor-in-chief in America (with an annual salary of $44,000), made his summer and weekend home in Great Neck. In the celebrity world, Swope was the biggest asset a place could have: a brilliant, Pulitzer Prize–winning reporter; bon vivant; stunning conversationalist; and friend of the mighty and rich. He was also a walking metaphor for Great Neck's daring social experiment. Ignoring traditional barriers of class, religion, and race, Swope made himself the center of the new suburban constellation of celebrities in Great Neck: the new rich, the old rich, stars of the stage and movies, journalists, and writers. Despite his background as the son of a Jewish watchmaker in St. Louis, by the force of his personality Swope rose majestically, and fashionably, above his modest background and America's anti-Semitic social and economic barriers. As a community, Great Neck was trying to do the same: to push aside the traditional barriers built on social separations.

No one was better connected than Swope to the intricate heart of New York though its press, writers, financiers, socialites, and sporting rich. He employed and befriended the best writers, such as Franklin P. Adams, Walter Lippmann, Frank Sullivan, James Wolcott, Haywood Broun, Ring Lardner, E. B. White, and John O'Hara. Under Swope's forceful direction, the *World* charged ahead of the *New York Times*, *Herald Tribune,* and *Telegraph, Daily News*, and *Mirror*, beating the competition on the low and high end of the city's newspaper world. He created the op ed page for the *World* that, according to historian Frederick Lewis Allen, was "the most lively and readable page in any newspaper in the country."[10] Why an op ed page? "Nothing is more interesting than opinion when opinion is interesting," Swope said.[11] He was innovative and courageous with hard news, as well. In a series of twenty-one articles, he pursued the Ku Klux Klan.[12] He hired the first black columnist to work for a white paper.[13]

Swope had grown rich from investing in the stock market, under the aegis of his friend Bernard Baruch, and from backing theatrical productions such as the *Ziegfeld Follies*. Swope met the wealthy and famous on their own ground—especially at the racetrack, as a fellow owner of racehorses and a fervid gambler. Filled with the latest news, gossip, and tips about people, plays, events, horses, and stocks, he played with politicians, writers, gangsters, and grandees. Swope and his beautiful, acerbic wife Margaret, known as Pearl to Swope, and some of their closest friends, set tastes and trends. The North Shore was the mock-English playground for golf, sailing, polo, hunting, racing and croquet. His stature, friends, and interests brought him into the socially exclusive clubs. By the late 1920s, he belonged to eighteen clubs, including the Turf and Field Club at Belmont Park, Soundview Golf Club in Great Neck, and the Casino at Sands Point. As a Jew, however, he couldn't make it everywhere. Swope never got into the Racquet Club in the city. He was forced to withdraw his name when his candidacy was opposed, possibly for reasons of prejudice or for the enemies he had made in the newspaper world.

If Swope couldn't break into all the clubs, he could mix elsewhere, especially in Great Neck, with the old guard of the WASP elite. The Swopes were famous for their formal and informal gatherings of guests in New York and Great Neck. "The Swopes' country establishment, like their one in town, resembled a public place of entertainment," E. J. Kahn, one of Swope's biographers, wrote. "Shakespeare-spouting poets and, when it came to that, Shakespeare-spouting pugilists might be seen there, milling and churning among Senators, polo players, professional gamblers, Supreme Court Justices, and horsy debutantes; the house was like a decompression chamber between social extremes."[14] Just like Great Neck.

Swope was adept and assiduous at bunching the famous and powerful, as well as the gifted hangers-on. Some were there just to amuse the others and some were there to make business deals. Swope was a facile matchmaker and rainmaker, melding the wealthy and socially superior with writers, theatrical producers, directors, ambitious actors, and seductive actresses. Noel Coward, the imposing talent, purveyor, and impostor of British chic and class, thought that the Swopes had the "only household in America where visits could be compared to weekends in an English country house." Raoul Fleischmann, who staked the *New Yorker*, paid the Swopes the ultimate compliment. He sighed, "When I die, I hope it's at the Swopes'."[15]

Swope's hospitality attracted notables such as Bernard Baruch; George Gershwin; Robert Moses; Irving Berlin; Harpo Marx; F. Scott Fitzgerald; Edna Ferber; George Kaufman; August Belmont; Fanny Brice; Ethel Barrymore; Oscar Levant; Ralph Pulitzer; Ruth Gordon; Leslie Howard; the Doubledays, Mellons, Vanderbilts, Whitneys, and Harrimans; Walter P. Chrysler; Otto Kahn; Harry F. Sinclair; Charles M. Schwab; and Herbert's brother Gerard, who was president of General Electric. They amused each other with games, drinking, gossip, and stinging talk. Pearl Swope was beautiful, charming, and sharp tongued. "It was," Pearl Swope commented, "an absolutely seething bordello of interesting people."[16] "There may have been parties that were more lavish and imaginative," Allen wrote, "but there were never any parties that were more fun than the parties of the 1920s, and if any hostess could be called their progenitor, it was Margaret Swope. . . . To the musical accompaniment of a promising pianist named Gershwin, Margaret mixed, mingled, and juggled with a dexterity that would have put a prestidigitator to shame. What was later vulgarized as Cafe Society started spontaneously at Chez Swope."[17]

Friends flocked to the Swopes' in New York and Great Neck. "As in the tradition of some of the statelier English country houses," Kahn wrote, "the Swopes gave their guests considerable latitude, even dispensing with such customary American amenities as introducing them to one another. Conventional introductions were generally superfluous; everybody was supposed to know who everybody else was."[18] Usually, they did. When the Swopes opened their homes to Ruth Gordon, the actress, she felt as though she had been sucked into heaven. "We showed up every night," she wrote. "Where else was better? Where else was as good? At Swopes' you belonged. If you didn't, you didn't get in twice. There were few outsiders. Everybody in was tough. Everybody could take it. And did. And everybody could give it out. And did."[19]

The house that served as backdrop for the theatrical entertaining of the Swopes was located on East Shore Road, looking east to Sands Point. "The Great Neck house was a peaked three-storied edifice that stood impressively on the top of a hill overlooking Manhasset Bay," Allen wrote. Swope and his friends played croquet on the large lawn; others swam or picnicked and looked out over the Bay from the house. Pearl Swope, Allen observed, "was the stage manager of idyllic weekends that adroitly combined an informal simplicity with underpinnings of luxury that were to become legendary."[20] But it wasn't the house or the setting that drew them. It was Swopes and company. "By three o'clock." Gordon recalled, "when people drove down from New York or over from Oyster Bay or Glen Cove or across from Locust Valley or up from Smithtown or around from Sands Point, the host and hostess and house guests were mostly awake. Lunch was at the great oblong Chippendale which every summer traveled from West 58th Street to the Great Neck dining room."[21]

Breakfast, lunch, and dinner for the multitudes were served loyally and elegantly by the long-suffering staff of servants. They had become used to unpredictability and instant crowds of people for dinner. In a matter of minutes, the list of recently invited guests could shoot from twenty to fifty-five. The Swopes' principal maid, Mae Fielding, who was black, was apparently known throughout Great Neck and the North Shore as Mae Swope. She descended on suppliers and merchants any hour of the day or night, Sundays and holidays included, when provisions were suddenly needed. Ruth Gordon remembered the frenzied routine of pursuit. The chauffeur sped away in the Buick, she wrote, "Mae besides him, her black straw 'day-off' hat pinned over her organdy cap, the organdy streamers flying in their own breeze. . . . They headed for Port Washington. Some people's address book is for friends, Mae's was for the trades people's home addresses. She was off to rout butcher Hewitt from his Sunday afternoon nap and help him open his store."[22]

The tempo was set by Broadway openings, newspaper deadlines, croquet games, the race track, the LIRR, the penchant for late lunches and late dinners, and the imperial schedules and socializing of the Swopes who went everywhere, were wanted everywhere, and invited guests all the time. The actress Ruth Gordon was one of the twenty-odd family members, guests, and servants who regularly were in the Swope entourage. During the weekday nights, Pearl Swope and Gordon would get in the car and drive to the Great Neck train station. "We drove up the back road," Gordon wrote, "winding through the pine woods, past sleeping Great Neck houses, down into the closed-up village. When we got to the one bright spot, the Great Neck Long Island Rail Road station, it was five past three A.M. Pearl drove under the trestle and pulled up at the platform down the track. Swope was always on the last car."

> Soft salty air off the Sound. No one on the platform and being down at the station in sleeping pajamas lent a dash. Lights showed under the bridge from Bayside, there was rumble, more of a rumble, then came the engine with a line of bright empty cars. The conductor got off, then Swope. He strode down the platform, all the morning papers under his arm, a magazine or two, elegant light brown felt hat set on his red hair at just the right dazzling tilt. Blue shirt, with its gold collar pin, Sulka tie tied just great, dashing chalk-striped blue suit or dashing some other one, elegant polished brown made-to-order shoes, he strode along swinging a stick, as though it were mid-afternoon. He kissed Pearl and me, then climbed in back.
>
> 'Want to drive around?' asked Pearl.

'Sure. Where does Leslie [Howard] live?'
Pearl headed under the trestle down Middle Neck Road.
'Kings Point?' asked Swope.[23]

Hours before sunrise, the Swopes and Ruth Gordon drove off to take a look at the Great Neck house of their Broadway friend.

West Egg

Yet for all the panache, access to great names, clubs, and wealth, there was a dark side to Swope that cut deep. Swope's power, influence, routines of spirited play, and consummate matching of favors and friendships did not always suffice. To his friend Sherman Morse, Swope wrote plaintively in his forties: "As I grow older I find myself fiercely desirous of the love and good will of my friends—God! how few they are. What a lonely life we lead between birth and death. How few there are whom we know and who know us. . . ." Recently, "I have gone through periods of heavy despondency. I can find no reason at all for this. Were I able to discover the cause it would resolve itself into a simple case of worry and one could wave it away. But everything is going well. The paper is doing well. I never had more money. Pearl and the kids are beautiful. My home life is ideal, yet I am overpowered by a sense of futility; I have always before me a sense of the grave ending all. You could help cure me of this."[24]

Did anyone detect Swope's lonely side of longing? Did F. Scott Fitzgerald see it—that young, talented, ambitious, socially insecure, handsome literary chronicler-of-the moment who aspired to turn his stories into Broadway plays and movies? Despite his alcoholic binges, did the novelist sense that something was amiss with Swope in the feverish partying and play on East Shore Road? Fitzgerald's *The Great Gatsby* tore the thin cover off Great Neck's social giddiness, implausible aspirations, and high-risk experiment of mixing old and new money, Gentile and Jew.

In 1922, when Fitzgerald and his wife Zelda first rented a house in Great Neck Estates, as the author of the best-selling *This Side of Paradise*, Fitzgerald was one of the trendy famous. In fact, he was, for a short time, a star of sorts at Swope dinner parties. "Fitzgerald, followed by a crowd of admirers," Allen wrote, "would wander . . . to the gazebo, where the group would ensconce themselves with a couple of bottles of Swope's excellent bootleg whisky. (Swope would serve nothing unless it first had been tested at a laboratory to make certain that it was drinkable). The revelers never brought their dishes back. Sometimes, they would not even bring themselves back, but would curl up in the gazebo or the garden and go to sleep. Fitzgerald was famous for having slept on every lawn from Great Neck to Port Washington."[25]

The Fitzgeralds, however, didn't last forever as Swope invitees. Fitzgerald and Zelda, Scott's unstable and often manic wife, were disinvited. It wasn't Scott's drinking, however, that ended the fun. There were limits and rules to the drinking and sexual play that Pearl Swope set at her homes. "It was Zelda Fitzgerald," Allen wrote, "who committed the ultimate offense as far as Margaret was concerned." Zelda went after Pearl's shy young brother. "A few drinks convinced the beautiful Zelda that he had to be brought out of his shell, and that she was the one to do it. At first it was amusing to watch him become shyer as she became bolder. But the fun and games stopped when she tore off all her clothes and chased the terrified adolescent upstairs, where he locked himself in his room while she pounded on the door. That was it for Margaret. Zelda was out. 'Not with my brother, sister! Not in my house, Mrs. F.!'"[26]

Pearl Swope threw them out, but not before the writer had found a setting for loss buried under tasteful frivolity. Swope put Great Neck on the map in the 1920s as the place to be, especially for journalists and entertainers. But it was F. Scott Fitzgerald's novel *The Great Gatsby,* begun in 1924 while he was living in Great Neck, and published in 1925, which placed the peninsula high in the literary galaxy of America's longing and aspirations. He created the fictional mystique of the bay that symbolically separated the world of aspirants from those born to superiority and wealth. At Swope's house on the Great Neck peninsula, Fitzgerald looked across Manhasset Bay to veritable estates and stellar old-guard names in Sands Point on the Port Washington peninsula. In *The Great Gatsby,* his imagination refigured the two into West Egg and East Egg.

In Great Neck, Fitzgerald was riveted to the hard-edged essentials of class, prejudice, and tragedy. "It was a matter of chance," Nick Carraway, the novel's narrator and conscience, observes "that I should have rented a house in one of the strangest communities in North America. It was on that slender riotous island which extends itself due east of New York— and where there are, among other natural curiosities, two unusual formations of land. Twenty miles from the city a pair of enormous eggs, identical in contour and separated only by a courtesy bay, jut out into the most domesticated body of salt water in the Western hemisphere, the great wet barnyard of Long Island Sound." Nick Carraway and Jay Gatsby lived in the "less fashionable" West Egg, across from "the white palaces of fashionable East Egg" that "glittered along the water."[27]

Between the two lay the raw places of romance, disappointment, class and religious differences. "Let me tell you about the very rich," Fitzgerald wrote in a short story, "The Rich Boy," published in 1926. "They are different from you and me. They possess and enjoy early, and it does something to them, makes them soft where we are hard, and cynical where we are trustful, in a way that, unless you were born rich, it is very difficult to understand."[28] Anson Hunter, Fitzgerald's protagonist, was born to great wealth, used to deference and devoid of the "mist" of "idealism" or even "illusion." "Anson," Fitzgerald observed, "accepted without reservation the world of high finance and high extravagance, of divorce and dissipation, of snobbery and of privilege."[29]

For generations, that world of "divorce and dissipation" had been wrapped behind the walls of upper-class exclusivity. In the 1920s, it spread to all classes in America, in spasms of new styles, social mobility, and sexual freedoms. Fitzgerald was inexorably drawn to the social chaos, nurtured in the postwar decade of prosperity and Prohibition. It was Fitzgerald's fate to be both "reckless participant and dispassionate observer," as he journeyed from St. Paul to Princeton, New York City, and Great Neck.

By his own account, Scott and Zelda moved to Great Neck with their young daughter to find the middle ground between the exhausting, spirited city and the dull security of the Midwest. (Nick Carraway echoed the need for escape from the Midwest. "Instead of being the warm center of the world the Middle West now seemed like the ragged edge of the universe—so I decided to go East.")[30] The Fitzgeralds hired a staff for their newly built rented house in Great Neck Estates—their "nifty little Babbit home," Zelda said.[31] They joined one of the golf clubs where Zelda frequently played. They went in and out of the city at will—both attracted and repulsed by its punishing pace and, in Fitzgerald's words, its "Bacchic diversions, mild or fantastic."[32] They gave parties, like Swope, for their literary friends: Edmund Wilson, John Dos Passos, Rebecca West, and Ring Lardner. They had drunken escapades, destructive sprees, and cruel fights.

Wilson captured some of the wicked fun in his comic piece, "The Delegate from Great Neck." The imaginary conversation between Van Wyck Brooks, the renowned critic of American literature, and Fitzgerald, the hustler-writer of the younger generation, ended when Fitzgerald invited Brooks to visit in Great Neck.

We're having a little party," Fitzgerald boasted. "Maybe it would bore you to death—but we're having some people down who ought to be pretty amusing. Gloria Swanson's coming. And Sherwood Anderson and Dos Passos. And Marc Connelly and Dorothy Parker. And Rube Goldberg. And Ring Lardner will be there. You probably think some of those people are pretty lowbrow, but Ring Lardner, for instance is really a very interesting fellow: he's really not just a popular writer: he's pretty morose about things. I'd like to have you meet him. There are going to be some dumb-bell friends of mine from the West but I don't believe you'd mind them—they're really darn nice. And then there's a man who sings a song called, *Who'll bite your Neck When my Teeth are Gone?* Neither my wife nor I know his name— but his song is one of the funniest things we've ever heard!"[33]

In the beginning, in 1922, Great Neck was fun, full of high hopes and all the right people. "Great Neck is a place," Fitzgerald wrote a cousin, "for celebrities—it being the habitat of Mae Murry, Frank Craven, Herbert Swope . . . Samuel Goldwyn, Ring Lardner . . . Jack Hazard, General Pershing. It is most amusing after the dull healthy middle west."[34] A year later, life was a bit sour. "This is a very drunken town full of intoxicated people and retired debauches [plus sign for and] actresses," he wrote to a Princeton friend.[35] Zelda recalled: "In Great Neck there was always disorder and quarrels: about the golf club, about the Foxes . . . about everything. . . . We gave lots of parties: the biggest one for Rebecca West. We drank Bass Pale Ale and went always to the Bucks or the Lardners or the Swopes when they weren't at our house. . . . We drank always . . . there were always too many people in the house."[36]

In addition, the Fitzgeralds faced painful professional and financial failure. Since moving to Great Neck, Scott had written a few stories, articles, and one play. Ignominiously, it closed after the first performance in Atlantic City. Neither the producer Sam Harris, nor the lead actor Ernest Truex, both Great Neck friends, could turn *Vegetables* into Broadway material. Deeply in debt in the late fall of 1923 and winter of 1924, Fitzgerald forced himself to write seventeen salable short stories (of embarrassing quality, he thought) and worked on his third novel. He even made money from his panicked exasperation at living beyond his means in Great Neck. The *Saturday Evening Post*, in April 1924, published "How to Live on $36,000 a Year."

In his comic confessional on money, Scott admitted to his readers that debt wasn't a new thing for Zelda and himself. But this time it was different: for the first time they had plotted their course with a budget. "We had, however, reckoned without our town," Fitzgerald acerbically wrote of Great Neck. "It is one of those little towns springing up on all sides of New York which are built especially for those who have made money suddenly but have never had money before."[37] A special breed of merchants made the town "the most expensive one in the world."[38] Still, he thought they could handle it: he worked on a novel, anticipated royalties from *Vegetables*, and borrowed from his publisher. Then disaster: the play failed on opening night and the Fitzgeralds were $5,000 in debt. "But one satisfaction nobody could take from us. We had spent $36,000, and purchased for one year the right to be members of the newly rich class."[39] Then, he wrote, they rushed to economize. Well, that was no answer. "We can't. We're too poor to economize. Economy is a luxury. We could have economized last summer—but now our only salvation is in extravagance."[40] Hard work helped, too. Writing one story after another, Fitzgerald pulled them out of the hole. A reprieve was at hand. "It took twelve hours a day for five weeks to rise from abject poverty back into the middle class."[41]

But they couldn't keep it up—or keep up. Fitzgerald's self-mocking couldn't save them from their recklessness, financial irresponsibility, alcohol, and mental illness. Nothing was really going right in Great Neck. In retrospect, Fitzgerald observed, "we were no longer important. The flapper, upon whose activities the popularity of my first books was based, had become *passé* by 1923—anyhow in the East. I decided to crash Broadway with a play, but Broadway sent its scouts to Atlantic City and quashed the idea in advance, so I felt that, for the moment, the city and I had little to offer each other. I would take the Long Island atmosphere that I had familiarly breathed and materialize it beneath unfamiliar skies."[42]

He did just that. In France, in 1924, Fitzgerald finished *The Great Gatsby*. The novel, published in 1925, received mixed reviews and failed to sell as well as *This Side of Paradise*. Many critics focused on Fitzgerald's evocation of dissolute Long Island. The Englishman Shane Leslie wrote: "I think this is a marvelous picture book. It brings back to me the world of Long Island like an Arabian Night mixed with a subway sound [*sic*]. I can see the exact big mansion and the flow of guests and the riotous hospitality and the greenlight blinking on the pier and I can hear the foghorn bleating like a ghost suffering vivisection all night. Long Island cannot have an Epic because it's [*sic*] inhabitants are not sagalike or heroic—only locusts and fireflies that float in an ephemeral radiancy. But this is a wonderful idyll of Long Island—How well I remember the Ash heap off Flushing."[43]

H. L. Mencken, however, thought *The Great Gatsby* inferior to *This Side of Paradise*. The scornful critic wrote that Fitzgerald's prose was much improved, but the new novel lacked depth and interesting characters. "The scene," Mencken wrote, "is the Long Island that hangs precariously on the edges of the New York City ash dumps—the Long Island of gaudy villas and bawdy house parties. The theme is the old one of romantic and preposterous love—the ancient *fidelis ad urrum* reduced to macabre humor. The principal personage is a bounder typical of those parts—a fellow who seems to know everyone and yet remains unknown to all—a young man with a great deal of mysterious money, the tastes of a movie actor and, under it all, the simple sentimentality of a somewhat sclerotic fat woman."[44] Mencken fixated on the social and cultural dynamics. "The Long Island," Mencken wrote, that Fitzgerald "sets before us is no fanciful Alsatia; it actually exists. More, it is worth any social historian's study, for its influence upon the rest of the country is immense and profound. What is vogue among the profiteers of Manhattan and their harlots today is imitated by the flappers of the Bible Belt country clubs week after next."[45]

Since 1925 when Leslie and Mencken issued their judgments, scholars and literary critics have analyzed Fitzgerald's every word, source, inspiration, conflict, and action relating to *The Great Gatsby*. In the process, they have foraged over Great Neck's temper and terrain to ascertain how it stimulated Fitzgerald's imagination and drove his craft to produce the superlative novel. Which Great Neck entertainers, they asked, which journalists, socialites, and gangsters matched Fitzgerald's fictional characters? Which Great Neck house was Gatsby's model? Which parties? What Great Neck sources and stories did Fitzgerald draw upon to cast the plot and personalities?

The critics and scholars have successfully answered many of the questions relating to Great Neck influences on Fitzgerald. But what about the reverse impact? What did Fitzgerald's impressions and judgments mean and reveal about Great Neck's character and history? In fact, nothing good. A torrent of unflattering judgments, not specific to Great Neck, but unmistakably inspired by it, fueled the novel. Born outside the true Gold Coast, up-start dreamers and romantics, Fitzgerald made clear, could not enter the precincts of the rich. In fictional terms, Gatsby couldn't win Daisy and West Egg couldn't rival East Egg. So close, but so far away. Fitzgerald revealed that Great Neck was already different from the communities of established wealth and social superiority east of Manhasset Bay. It wasn't really a matter of better or worse; Fitzgerald didn't really think that the rich were finer people. No, it was only that the rich, and their entourage, could lie, cheat, use other people, and still remain on top, no matter what they did. "They were careless people," Fitzgerald wrote about Tom and Daisy Buchanan, and "they smashed up things and creatures and then retreated back into their money or their vast carelessness, or whatever it was that kept them together, and let other people clean up the mess they had made."[46]

A second harsh Fitzgerald judgment: the rich on the other side of the Bay regarded the arrivistes to the west—entertainers and others of that ilk—with the insiders' insidious contempt. (The Great Neck old guard, however, such as the Graces, Hewletts, Eldridges, Morgans, and Phippses, didn't seem to count with Fitzgerald. They hardly competed for his attention with the theatrical crowd.) Mansions, money, and the partying crowd might temporarily attract and amuse the rich from across the Bay, but not for long. Aspiration, while noble, was hopeless for Gatsby and West Egg. The rich from elsewhere would survive and reign, no matter what; the upstarts would fail, no matter what. Daisy, Nick related, "was appalled by West Egg, this unprecedented 'place' that Broadway had begotten upon a Long Island fishing village—appalled by its raw vigor that chafed under the old euphemisms and by the too obtrusive fate that herded its inhabitants along a short-cut from nothing to nothing."[47]

And finally, a last and equally pessimistic Fitzgerald judgment that again pointed specifically to Great Neck's social world: Jews were crude, ugly, uneducated, and untrustworthy. Meyer Wolfsheim, Fitzgerald's Jew in *The Great Gatsby,* carries the stench of anti-Semitism. Nick met him for the first time in a restaurant on Forty-second Street. "A small, flat-nosed Jew raised his large head and regarded me with two fine growths of hair which luxuriated in either nostril. After a moment I discovered his tiny eyes in the half-darkness."[48] Meyer Wolfsheim, the bootlegging, gambling friend of gangsters, is the source of Gatsby's money. Wolfsheim corrupted Gatsby and even the country at large. Nick was staggered to learn that Wolfsheim rigged the 1919 World Series. "It never occurred to me," Nick observed, "that one man could start to play with the faith of fifty million people—with the single-mindedness of a burglar blowing a safe."[49]

For Fitzgerald, Broadway was the crux, the pivotal connection. In Fitzgerald's fiction, Broadway begat West Egg. And in Fitzgerald's everyday world, people associated with Broadway, such as Sam Harris, Sam

Goldwyn, Oscar Hammerstein II, Ed Wynn, and even Swope, begat Great Neck. There were Jews on Broadway, Jews in Great Neck, and the pivotal Jew in Gatsby's tragic life. Wolfsheim boasted to Nick that he had made Gatsby. "'I raised him up out of nothing, right out of the gutter. I saw right away he was a fine-appearing, gentlemanly young man, and when he told me he was an Oggsford I knew I could use him good. I got him to join up in the American Legion and he used to stand high there. Right off he did some work for a client of mine up to Albany. We were so thick like that in everything'—he held up two bulbous fingers—'always together.'"⁵⁰ Of course, Wolfsheim didn't live in West Egg; in fact, he wouldn't even visit for Gatsby's funeral. But Wolfsheim was Gatsby's shortcut from "nothing to nothing," in Daisy's sardonic words. And Great Neck, in Fitzgerald's world, was the actual shortcut from "nothing to nothing," for the arrivistes—so many of whom were Jews.

Fun, Fame, and Family

But none of this mattered to the Great Neck of the moment. In 1925, the writer's probing judgments only got through to the cynical few. Who in Great Neck believed in the possibility of Fitzgerald's futile social trajectory—starting with nothing, making something, and then ending, years later, with nothing? Mighty promises were in the soul of America in the 1920s. Starting from poor and undistinguished stock meant little in the age of prosperity and giddiness. In Great Neck, Midwesterners and immigrants from the Lower East Side got close to the so-called American aristocracy. Fitzgerald's voice of doom—from "nothing to nothing"—couldn't compete with the developer's call for a new house, garden, and golf club on the Gold Coast of celebrities. Bad impressions, even a place marked by the presence of many Jews, had no impact on the speculative mania of development that gripped the country and Great Neck, in particular. Great Neck squirmed a bit over Fitzgerald's novel, but rapidly turned to a flattering picture of itself, away from the innuendoes and distortions. Fitzgerald was safely in France and no longer another famous local.

The *Great Neck News* had a very different story from Fitzgerald's to tell: it had nothing to say about Gatsbyesque yearnings and anguish in Great Neck. To the contrary: from the vantage point of the paper, Great Neck was a pioneer in suburban prosperity. It radiated as a solid investment, as a salable community. Editor and chief writer Hal Lanigan was ready to cash in on the town's astounding growth, escalating land prices, expanding businesses, civic pride, and connections to the city. The *Great Neck News* was one of two local newspapers, and Lanigan was the number-one booster for the community-in-the-making. He sought to reconcile stardom and domesticity, old wealth and new, community stability and individual mobility in his adopted hometown.

Lanigan gave little consideration to the *North Hempstead Record and Long Island Globe*, the established paper for the area that was published in Manhasset. In the mid-1920s, the eight-page *Record*, dominated by Great Neck activities, concerned itself with the customary terse and factual local news: weddings, schools, churches, roads, sewers, litigation, wills, the Women's Club, Garden Club, the Great Neck Playhouse, and the library. There were no editorials boasting about Great Neck's achievements and hardly any columns to replicate the big city papers. The *Record* did gather little notes on the exotic comings and goings of Great Neck residents, including some of the locally based stars and socialites. "Mme Olga Petrova of Kings Point," the *Record* noted, "accompanied by a pet cat insured for $10,000, sailed on Friday on the S.S. Tuscania on a two month cruise of the Mediterranean."[51]

But Lanigan doted on celebrities as part of the new Great Neck: a dynamic, expanding, happiness-producing, star-packed community. According to the *Great Neck News*, families, houses, gardens, and golf clubs inspired the culture of clean living. Lanigan's manifesto of suburban bliss depended on a new element: celebrity domesticity. Not only would life be better in the splendid suburb, according to Lanigan, but he promised his readers—especially the many who were raised in provincial America, had migrated to the city, and now needed release from its hold—that they would find good news and family-based optimism reflected in his local pages. At the same time, they would enjoy a tasty replica of a big-city paper in the weekly columns and reviews about sports, music, even architecture, and a page of humor by the well-known writer and actor John Hazzard.

Having learned his trade at the *Philadelphia Public Ledger* and *St. Louis Globe-Democrat,* Lanigan was a believer in the power and profitability of newspapers. With 10,000 copies in the inaugural run, the *Great Neck News* sought out an audience that stretched from Douglaston Manor in Queens to Port Washington. Great Neck, however, was the obvious center of his revenue and hopes. Papers, Lanigan proudly told his readers in his first editorial, "represent one of the most powerful agencies in all American public life. They preach to people who never enter a church. They teach folks who were denied the opportunity of school and university. They supply the mental food upon which the souls of men and women are fed and healed."[52]

Lanigan's mental food for Great Neck was an idiosyncratic mix of fame, fun, and family values. Fame came first, but family and recreation—and the two were inextricably tied in promoting domesticity—were requirements in Lanigan's Great Neck. The editor drew up long lists of the famous in Great Neck as an indiscriminate local reworking of Mrs. Astor's legendary 400. Across its pages, the *News* spread interviews and photographs of important Great Neck residents at their homes, preferably with their families. Week after week, the front page featured large pictures of Great Neck celebrities playing golf at one of the local private clubs or, in the summer months, women in bathing suits around a swimming pool. (Out of season, Lanigan pursued and photographed Great Neck residents on vacation in the newly developed resort of Palm Beach.) Equally plentiful were pictures of children, from tots to teens, posing at birthday parties.

To sell Great Neck's exalted image of itself, Lanigan focused heavily on the giants-in-residence of industry and the press, such as Chrysler, Annenberg, Sloan, and even Harry F. Sinclair of Teapot Dome fame. Scandalous or not, their stature as wealthy men was assured. The paper's more challenging task, however, was marketing Broadway actors, actresses, writers, and composers as just fine people—good neighbors and community folk. Somehow, it had to ignore the fact that many of the celebrities-in-residence were hard-drinking and fast-playing. Although Lanigan chose not to see or write about dissipation in Great Neck, it was hard to miss. Ring Lardner gleefully described the Great Neck scene to Fitzgerald, who was in France. "On the Fourth of July, Ed Wynn gave a fireworks party at his new estate in the Grenwolde division. After the children had been sent home," Lardner reported to Fitzgerald, "everybody got pie-eyed and I never enjoyed a night so much. All the Great Neck professionals did their stuff, the former chorus girls danced, Blanche Ring kissed me and sang, etc. The party lasted through the next day and wound up next evening at Tom Meighan's."[53]

Despite the wholesale departures from sobriety, Lanigan persisted in presenting domesticated stars as wholesome family figures. In this campaign, the paper turned most often to Eddie Cantor, Groucho Marx, Sam Harris, and, especially, Gene Buck. One of Ziegfeld's most important composers and lyricists, Buck lived with his "charming family" in a $100,000 home in Kensington. "The Yale Bowl—with lamps," was the way Ring Lardner referred to Buck's living room.[54] "Yes, he is 'of the stage,'"

Lanigan wrote, "and wonderful Great Neck in its wonderful development does not want to lose track of the fact that to a huge extent it has been the ladies and gentlemen of the stage who have come out to Great Neck to live who have aided no little—almost immeasurably, in fact—in keeping the community simmering upwards." (Of course, Lanigan didn't write that Buck was one of Fitzgerald and Lardner's favorite inebriated friends). When it came to the entertainers, however, distinctions were crucial. "Great Neck," Lanigan explained, "is never going to be another Holly-wood. Not a chance! The many folk of the stage who have bought and built here and have always been so finely active in raising funds when the call went out, are a much different type than those rattle-headed, silly nuts and nuterinos that form Hollywood's movie colony. No murders here; no disgraceful orgies; no wild motoring."[55]

At the outset, Lanigan also wooed Great Neck's old guard and clergy to attract as many subscribers and advertisers as possible. He wrote articles about the families that had lived on the peninsula before the boom years. Christian clergymen, such as the Rev. Kirkland Huske of All Saints Episcopal Church, were interviewed and profiled. But six months after starting the paper, Lanigan stopped courting the clergy: they gave him no news, and he then gave them no attention. Even more distant were most of the older, established residents, the old guard consisting of large-property owners and local businessmen. Lanigan openly chastised them for failing to take pride in his booming "Wonder City" and urged them to switch their allegiances from the rival paper. The *News*, he wrote in an editorial, "triumphed with but very, very, very few of the old residents of Great Neck subscribing. And very, very, very few of the old storekeepers advertising with us."[56]

The editorial drew fire, but the lines were drawn. Lanigan was on the side of the new breed of residents and newcomers such as Heckscher, Chrysler, and Nathan S. Jonas who supported growth, paid for community organizations, and liked the bally-hoo of the paper. "We mean," he wrote, "the gentlemen who came and bought or built here in the past decade or so—have used Great Neck only for their home. . . . The old-timers are the gentlemen who were born and reared here, and their fathers and their fathers' fathers before them. . . . Through the wealthy New Yorker coming out here to reside and the establishment of wonderful golf clubs, property values have soared and the old settlers have reaped the reward. And they've banked it and when the call goes out for funds for civic uplift it's the . . . newcomers . . . who pony up."[57]

Lanigan's dismay reflected financial disappointment as well as startling social changes. Much of the old guard didn't like the new Great Neck: developments that chopped up the landscape, the growing and religiously mixed middle and upper classes; feverish commercial activity; classless and, often, tasteless Broadway figures. Many of the long-established families simply took flight, a profitable flight that pleased them as well as developers who grabbed up properties for house-hungry and golf-loving families who became the heart of suburban life. In every section of Great Neck, the pastoral terrain of farms and estates turned into colonies of single-family homes. Captain Frederick F. Russell transformed his fiefdom into the Russell Gardens of houses, elaborate landscaping, bridle paths, tennis courts, a polo field, and swimming pool; the Mitchell estate became Kennilworth; the Booth holdings turned into Broadlawn; the Brokaw estate became Nirvana Gardens; and Lilius Grace's property emerged as Gracefield. William K. Vanderbilt gradually divested his Great Neck holdings: the first parcel became Glen Oaks Golf Club: the second, Deepdale Golf Club on Lake Success and Lake Surprise. Finally, by the late 1920s, Vanderbilt sold the remnants of his estate and moved from Great Neck to Centerport.

In the midst of this frenzied remaking of Great Neck, the *News* staked its future on selling the right kind of residential, commercial, and institutional development. The schools were easy to tout as symbols of salutary growth. The paper proudly reported on the opening of a second elementary school for children in and around Kensington, as well as plans for building a new high school for the expanding population. Administrative and economic changes were more complicated. The *News* endorsed strong zoning laws, holding developers to aesthetic and proper business standards, the incorporation of all the villages on the peninsula, and a master plan. These were concerns of the Great Neck Association and its president, William Zinsser: "Today all of Great Neck is running riot as far as real estate developments are concerned," Zinsser wrote to the *News*. "There is no aesthetic plan which any developer could fit into had he the wish to do so. Streets are laid out only to fill immediate needs or because the maximum number of building lots can be checker-boarded with such a layout."[58]

Alas, sometimes it took a while for the *News* to find its bearings in the development area. At first, in 1925, Lanigan fought against apartment houses that would make Great Neck look like Queens. Within a few months, however, he changed his mind, possibly swayed by expensive advertising in the *News,* and supported the building of high-class apartments, embellished with European amenities. There was no flip-flop, however, about the danger of state parks in Nassau County: these would bring "the mob" and "hoodlums" to the North Shore. If the people who went to Coney Island needed more parks, Lanigan advised, they should be placed in remote areas, "with no private lawns ruined and no beach fronts abused."[59]

Advocacy was one thing, negative news was another. Reluctantly, from time to time, Lanigan plunged into the darker realms of human life. Death, for example at the hands of the "Grim Reaper."[60] A few obituaries appeared in the paper, including ones for Payne Whitney, owner of Greentree in Manhasset; Roswell Eldridge of Saddle Rock; and Mrs. Florence Brokaw Satterwhite of Martin Hall on West Shore Road. Bootlegging was also another irritant, which the paper felt compelled to report, especially police raids on Great Neck's "stills and accessory equipment" which were conveniently located on the porous shores of Long Island Sound and Manhasset Bay.

In the bad news department, some things had to be ignored—such as the Ku Klux Klan. While Lanigan failed to write about a three-day KKK gathering in Great Neck in September 1925, the rival *Record* featured the story on page one. From the local KKK headquarters on Steamboat Road, the paper reported, 300–400 members from all over Long Island, accompanied by bands and floats, marched down Middle Neck Road—in full "Klan regalia, but none were masked." Most of the spectators were "deeply impressed," emitting an "air of grim seriousness about the whole affair." The *Record* reported that many of the leaders rode on horseback and "wore holsters in which were seen dangerous looking weapons." But, all in all, it was a "fine parade" and "meeting" with 3,000 to 4,000 supporters.[61]

The *News* wanted none of this. It would not indulge, or even include, any "unsavory or sensational news" that would undermine the carefully crafted impressions of propriety and prosperity. The *News* would ensure that good names "be spared; women and families not be brought into any existing unpleasantness and all wrongs righted without names or reputations hurt."[62] "In Our Set, by Hal" was Lanigan's weekly column for plugging the stars and charting their travels and triumphs, while keeping the record clean.

Another Lanigan ploy was to feature silly tidbits of writing, designed specifically for local consumption, from notables of the set, such as Groucho Marx, Ring Lardner, and Oscar Hammerstein. Most frequently,

Lanigan prevailed upon Marx to turn his wit on local feuds and problems, such as the site of the new high school or the rebuilding of the old rattling Grace Avenue Bridge. "What a bridge it is!" Groucho told the *News*. "It swings its palsied span o'er the Long Island tracks with all the steadiness of an octogenarian crossing Times Square during a blizzard. Architecturally it is reminiscent of the horror period in American art—a period that gave us iron deer on lawns, corsets for women and copper bathtubs. Bridges are like men—the more insignificant they are, the more noise they make."[63]

Once in a while, however, even "In Our Set" presented a view that clashed with Lanigan's investment-driven, idealized image of Great Neck. Fitzgerald, in absentia, presented one such test. At first, Lanigan welcomed the theatrical version of *The Great Gatsby* on its pre-Broadway run. "For it is of this vicinity," Lanigan observed, "that Fitzgerald wrote in his bizarre characters that saunter and stagger and race through the pages of his exceedingly human novel. And there are characters aplenty in this cross section of life . . . that live at the fanciful 'West Egg' of the book and play who would be recognized on Middle Neck Road."[64]

On opening night in January 1926, at the Great Neck Playhouse on that same Middle Neck Road, the local Great Neck audience apparently was not impressed. After scant applause there was no curtain call. Although Lanigan praised the performance of Florence Eldridge, who lived in Great Neck, and James Rennie, he tried to obfuscate and defend Great Neck's reputation against Fitzgerald's fiction. "Naturally," Lanigan wrote, "the pen picture he drew of our urban life was mythical, for a mythical person, to a very big degree, was 'Gatsby'—he unknown, his villa unknown, his guests unknown."[65]

Worse was to come when the play opened on Broadway. Great Neck, America's latest "Wonder City," became the eye of the storm. The critic Alexander Woollcott identified Great Neck as West Egg. The *News* retorted: "WEST EGG NOT US." In his denial, Lanigan wrote: "Mr. Fitzgerald formerly resided in Great Neck and he wrote his novel when among us. Several of the New York critics, noticeably Alexander Woollcott of the 'World,' is [*sic*] trying to pin West Egg, the locale of the three thunderous acts of 'The Great Gatsby,' on Great Neck. They're simply guessing. The night revelry on GATSBY'S estate is just one of those things of which the playwright takes liberties. It's a most exaggerated scene."[66]

Two years later, Lanigan was even more incensed over accusations, from an undisclosed source, that the *News* was unfriendly towards Jews in the community. "This is as rotten a rumor as was ever circulated." Next to the denial, Lanigan placed a picture of Rabbi David Goodis, the temporary leader of Great Neck's Reform Jewish community of one hundred members that planned to build Temple Beth-El. On the eve of Yom Kippur in 1928, with services scheduled at the Community Church, Lanigan tried to defuse the concerns of his Jewish readers. "To begin with, THE NEWS is for every race and creed. As for the Jews of Great Neck and the plans they are working on—we're behind them 100 per cent. We've got pals among the Great Neck Jewry by the dozens. . . . Through being kept pretty busy we don't go out often. But when we do it's at the home of Jewish friends almost once out of every three times." Lanigan cited his friendship with the banker Nathan S. Jonas. "And as for other Jewish folk who haven't Mr. Jonas' wealth, or are only in the medium class . . . we know dozens upon dozens whom we like equally as much as we like Irishers, the Scotch, the English and the rest. So that's that!"[67]

That was that—for the Jews and for the old guard as well. Reflecting the optimistic and welcoming tone of the *News,* the growing Jewish community sensed that Great Neck was a good place to touch the holy ground of American assimilation. Ambitious, prosperous, and confident in their new surroundings, many of the Jews in Great Neck drew together to form a congregation to establish a local place for Jewish observance and education. They committed to building a Reform temple and radically departed from their Orthodox backgrounds. When Rabbi Goodis was installed as the permanent rabbi of Temple Beth-El in November 1928, two hundred people attended the service at the Community Church. The *News* reported that the Rev. Huske, the Episcopal minister of All Saints, gave the benediction and a cellist, tenor, and organist provided the music.[68] A few months later, the *News* proudly joined the rabbi with Great Neck's Christian clergy. Goodis was a "gentleman," a "scholar," and "as upright and as clean a man, as we have seen in our life, we are confident and we're duly honored that we know him. Dr. Goodis is as likeable as HUSKE, FARNHAM, BENNETT, DONOVAN OR DOLYLE. And as dapper as MACKENZIE, too, we might add."[69]

Jews, especially the ones in the theater, reveled in Great Neck's success: away from Broadway and the cinema studios in Astoria, Queens, but not too far away. Away from the Lower East Side, but not cut off completely. Great Neck was America—with its quaint charms, small center, quiet streets, handsome homes, modest churches and schools, mixing of old and new, and promise of a social landscape of neighborly, domestic bliss. For

Indeed, exclusivity was a powerful but complicated economic and social force. The efforts towards racial exclusiveness, which originally meant particularly the exclusion of both Jews and blacks, did not hold firm for Jews in Great Neck. In fact, the community became nothing less than a highly charged suburban center of mobility for Jews pursuing something better, something more Gentile and established, in a new place—drawn once again to the magnetic force of moving and moving up.

The push for social ascent and exclusivity, most pointedly in retreat from urban centers with millions of people—especially lower-class immigrants and blacks—lured the ambitious and successful Jews to suburban life. Aspiration and achievement, the American requirements for rearranging one's life and standing, took Great Neck from collective obscurity to community fame. In the 1920s, everything in Great Neck bespoke the new, the successful, and the wealthy, especially in the eyes of Jewish immigrants and their children from Manhattan, Brooklyn, the Bronx, and Queens. Great Neck's prominence derived from new wealth—and new ways to show that wealth—as well as new civic, educational, religious, recreational, and social organizations. Great Neck, with its particular gusto, showed them off with pride: residential developments, with the latest technologies dependent on gas and electric lines; churches; plans for a million dollar high school; golf clubs; a temple; active civic improvement organizations; a library; a park district; and a women's club.

All of this looked marvelous to those invested in the community's collective success. However, the escape to the suburbs represented another failure of civilization to the young social, architectural, and aesthetic critic Lewis Mumford in 1921. As a vociferous judge, both of America's urban and suburban creations, he despaired. "The great modern city, for the most part, does not create a common bond but a common repulsion. Suburbia—that vast and aimless drift of human beings, spreading in every direction about our cities—large and small—demonstrates the incapacity of our civilization to foster concrete ways and means for living well. Having failed to create a common life in our cities, we have built suburbia, which is a common refuge from life, and the remedy is an aggravation of the disease."[3]

Despite Mumford's opinion, Great Neck hardly manifested the fractured spirit of the "aimless drift of human beings, spreading in every direction about our cities" or the "incapacity . . . to foster concrete ways and means of living well." Just the opposite: Great Neck formed an identity through its carefully constructed, pseudo-English setting. It reflected

the aspiring Great Neck Jews, the muted signs of prejudice could be comfortably ignored. Of course, some residential sections discouraged Jews from buying houses; and only two of the four golf clubs welcomed Jewish members. But Great Neck was proving to be an exception. It was a significant improvement on the harsh norm of America life in the 1920s: a Protestant-dominated society of pervasive social segregation and economic discrimination against Jewish arrivistes.

The new Great Neck was a place where Eddie Cantor and other Jews could safely remember the past and conquer the future. His Jewish benefactor, banker, and advisor Nathan S. Jonas and his wife were Cantor's models. "As I sit on the porch of the Jonas home," he wrote in his memoir, "inhaling new and rare species of roses and orchids that Mrs. Jonas cultivates in her hothouse, my thoughts fly across the dreary years when I wandered, homeless, hungry, and cold, through the lonely nights in the Ghetto." His parents came from Russia but barely survived the hardships of emigration. "I think of my poor grandmother who toiled in her dingy cellar, lugging the heavy trunks of servant girls to top-floor flats to earn the meager dollars that kept us alive." But in Great Neck, "all that misery and suffering [has] been transformed into something grand and symphonic, something so peaceful and majestic!"[70]

So marvelous and dynamic, for some; so disillusioning, for others. Great Neck in the 1920s was a bold experiment in social tensions and economic adventures: the ambitious mixed with the wary, entrepreneurs with artists, arrivistes with the old guard, the idealist with the cynic, old immigrants with the new, the Gentile with the Jew. Perceptions varied widely. Lanigan, the newspaperman, had glossed over the differences and worked at making the community sell. But Fitzgerald, the artist—with disenchantment and Jay Gatsby stirring in his mind—fled the expensive, highly charged social and economic pressures of Great Neck.

At the end of *The Great Gatsby*, Nick Carraway casts a penetrating, wistful, last look at the Sound from his rented home in West Egg. "And as the moon rose higher the inessential houses began to melt away until gradually I became aware of the old island here that flowered once for Dutch sailors' eyes—a fresh, green breast of the new world." With Gatsby dead, the romance of American purity and aspiration was gone. As was the landscape. "Its vanished trees, the trees that had made way for Gatsby's house, had once pandered in whispers to the last and greatest dreams; for a transitory enchanted moment man must have held his breath in the presence of this continent, compelled into an aesthetic contemplation he neither understood nor desired, face to face for the last time in history with something commensurate to his capacity for wonder."[71]

Residents—families and individuals—imbibed the community's mystique. Developers, real estate agents, businessmen, and publicists pushed unprecedented sales and profits. Swope set the style for his entourage of celebrities. But it was Fitzgerald, for whom the possibility of the place had already passed in 1925, who stretched Great Neck the farthest. He converted its geography, romance and risks into a metaphor for America. Great Neck and the North Shore provided the background for longings and aspirations. In the 1920s, Great Neck established its own small-scale presence in American life: to attract and repel, to raise hopes and destroy dreams.

2

Preparing the Ground

THE EMBODIMENT OF AMERICAN CULTURE

Before Black Friday, the stock market crash, and the Depressio Great Neck regarded itself as a suburban success par excelle country giddy with prosperity where white Americans sought havens between urban and small-town life, Great Neck's popu property values soared. By the late 1920s, Great Neck qualified ficant part of the suburban transformation. The presence of fam gave the community the vital edge of a marketable image an Great Neck was like a never-ending cocktail party—a subvers tion of the 1920s—in which unexpected guests, including Jews to amuse, divert, and shock the conventional social scene.

To do justice to Great Neck's particular history, it must in the broad context of regional and national developments. sociologists, psychologists, fiction writers, and other critics ha misjudged, and dissected suburbia's powerful impact on Am Some, such as Kenneth Jackson, have applied judicious but toug others, such as Lewis Mumford, expressed raw disdain. Ja leading historian of the suburban movement, regards the devel American suburban communities—reinforcing the demarcatio work, in the city, and family life, miles away—as "the qui physical achievement of the United States."[1] Jackson views the phenomena as the "embodiment" of American culture: "conspi sumption, a reliance upon the private automobile, upward m separation of the family into nuclear units, the widening di tween work and leisure, and a tendency towards racial and exclusiveness."[2]

the organizational responsibilities, needs, and tastes of its affluent residents, and, to be sure, the financial interests of its developers. In the 1920s, "living well" was what Great Neck was all about. A ride around the peninsula, with its golf, bath, and yacht clubs, would have revealed that playing was high up in the hierarchy of community values. In this respect Mumford, who viewed pleasure as an essential component of all suburbs, could have put Great Neck at the top of a long list of suburbs in the making. "As leisure generally increased, play became the serious business of life; and the golf course, the country club, the swimming pool, and the cocktail party became the frivolous counterfeits of a more varied and significant life. Thus in reacting against the disadvantages of the crowded city, the suburb itself became an over-specialized community, more and more committed to relaxation and play as ends in themselves. Compulsive play fast became the acceptable alternative to compulsive work: with small gain either in freedom or vital stimulus."[4] (The nationwide explosion of play was clear from the increase in golf courses between 1917 and 1930. In thirteen years, the number of clubs grew from 472 to 5,856 with all but 10 percent operated as private clubs.)[5]

The pull of play, however, took second place to another compulsive pursuit. Social mobility, always a powerful, determining force in American life, was even more fundamental to America's infatuation with suburban life in the 1920s. Great Neck's adventure in exclusivity and social mobility was part of a basic dynamic of American community building. Its sway went back to the eighteenth and nineteenth centuries, when the desire for social advancement moved the middle classes in large and small cities and towns to seek gentility and refinement. This process, described by social historian Richard Bushman, played out in the etiquette of social behavior; the design of homes, villages, and cities; and the importation of culture. The aspiration invoked contradictory impulses between republican and aristocratic values: hard work, modesty, and saving—in the Calvinist tradition—versus consumption and the cultivation of the arts and play.[6] "Emulation of the ranks," Bushman noted about the centuries he studied, "had become as much a middle-class trait as industry itself. How else was one to know how to live after industry and frugality had brought one wealth?"[7]

By the twentieth century, however, Calvinist modesty and restraint hardly constrained the pleasures of the upper classes. As they sought new diversions and associations, they invoked a second set of contradictions. The rich chased after another American trait that Bushman had identified

from an earlier period: "Gentility and capitalism collaborated in the formation of consumer culture, gentility creating demand and capitalism manufacturing supply. All the participants in the emerging industrial system had a vested interest, understood or not, in the promotion of gentility."[8] At the beginning of the twentieth century, Long Island's North Shore was just the right place to bring gentility to a high pitch in America's unrelenting, restless rearrangement of the social order. Estate owners reached new heights in elaborate residential construction, social ascendancy, and political domination in their local North Shore surroundings and village and country political institutions.

According to Dennis Sobin, there were over 600 estates, developed altogether at a cost of $500,000,000, encompassing between 50 and 2,000 acres.[9] There, the social elite and famous plutocrats built estates and clubs to satiate their hunger for luxurious living and display. In the landscape of great estates and private clubs, contrived and constructed to replicate English country life, the rich went hunting for fox and fowl; played polo; raced thoroughbreds; sailed in their yachts; played on their golf courses (on their own property or that of their private clubs); and entertained family, friends, business associates, and royalty, as was the case in 1924 when the young and stylish Prince of Wales was hosted by grandees of the North Shore.

Lavish spending was not the only key ingredient. To the architectural and social critic Brendan Gill, Long Island's estates were the products of "superlative feats of ego" and "superlative feats of artisanship." "Though Newport is probably the most famous gathering place of our American rich," Gill wrote, "it is Long Island that possesses by far the greatest and most interesting assortment of houses designed for the very rich, the rich, and the so-called well-fixed."[10] To meet these needs, most of the great, along with many of the less-than-great architects and landscape architects in America, built an immense inventory of residences, clubs, churches, casinos, libraries, and gardens.

The incessant pull of social mobility, gentility, and exclusivity formed multilayered aspirations that upset the rankings of society. Thus, there were those who regarded the Gold Coast as vulgar and unappealing from the moment it began its social ascent at the turn of the century. To one of New York's most acerbic and disillusioned social critics, the Gold Coast was nothing more than the sham display of mock-English pretensions— the money of the ill-bred and ill-born chasing and destroying the traditional class distinctions of a social hierarchy in decline. In the view of Mrs.

John King van Rensselaer, the Vanderbilts, Whitneys, Morgans, and Belmonts were new families, all with grandiose homes on the North Shore, who did not qualify for the inner circles of "blood and breeding" that formed the sacred social order of her youth.[11]

Bushman called these same arrivistes, the rich of the post–Civil War period, the "self-appointed aristocrats" for a society that was long fascinated by the wealth and power of English aristocracy.[12] "Buoyed by their fantastic success, Americans cast off all constraint and claimed . . . to be the complete equals of Europe's titled lords. They married their daughters to dukes and earls. They erected palaces to equal in grandeur Europe's great houses. They entertained in lavish style and patronized the arts in the best aristocratic tradition."[13] None of this pleased the van Rensselaer descendent of generations of Dutch families. Mrs. van Rensselaer bore the traditional Dutch enmity for English aristocratic life and utter contempt for its manifestations among America's nouveau riches. "Society once connoted," she wrote, in her 1924 book, *The Social Ladder*, "first of all, family; its primary meaning at present is fortune. Years ago, it also stood for breeding; now it represents, instead, self-advertisement."[14]

Her disdain for the new order, or, in her view, the new chaotic social alignments, was obvious on every page of her book. Society had dissolved into a cauldron of new wealth, social climbing, the ascendancy of reckless, dancing, drinking youth, and the passion for music and words written by immigrants and blacks.[15] "There are cliques and groups and circles and sets. There are the old families, and the not-so-old families, the big entertainers, and the circus set that loves the limelight, and the jazz set that haunts the cabarets and patronizes the bootleggers. You find them perched here and there on the ruins of the old social structure. Each of them claims to be New York Society. None of them is, and all of them together aren't."[16] It made no difference to her if the climbers had reputable standing in other cities, if their wealth came from the pre– or post–Civil War years, if they were part of Mrs. Astor's 400, immigrants or native born, Gentiles or Jews. "Steel barons, coal lords, dukes of wheat and beef, of mines and railways had sprung up from obscurity" and had collectively destroyed the power and dictates of her society.[17]

For van Renssalaer, Southampton, close to the eastern tip of Long Island, was the single place left intact for the diminished old order. This was the only spot where she felt comfortable. Southampton remained "a dignified, aristocratic community of wealthy men and women who live graciously in their pleasant homes, hold aloof from the noise and display of 'modern Society,' and turn austere and uncompromising backs on the 'jazz crowd' that now and again makes an unsuccessful attempt to gain a foothold in this last citadel of the old social order."[18]

SADDLE ROCK

No other place on the Gold Coast of the North Shore impressed van Renssalaer. Not Manhasset, Glen Cove, Locust Valley or any other towns that were the fiefdoms of the new rich, and certainly not Great Neck. But the North Shore, a bogus creation in the eyes of van Renssalaer, looked fabulous to just about everyone else who aspired to the sporting, good life of high society. The middle class watched the doings of the rich, especially New Yorkers, with their weekend jaunts to country homes near the city, and aspired for some of the same. One way to get there was to move close to the suburban edges of the North Shore. There was, however, another inherent conflict in this pursuit: on the one hand, promoting growth, the imperative of the capitalistic system; and on the other, acquiring the attributes of gentility through carefully chosen associations. In the suburban context the "supply" of gentility came from developers who produced a new consumer package of residential living for the middle and upper classes.

As the first community across the Queens/Nassau County border, Great Neck was the first in line to experience the tension of uncontrolled expansion in pursuit of exclusionary gentility on the North Shore. Rapid change blew through Great Neck with its burgeoning population, including a few hundred Jewish families, and multiple divisions of the landscape. Three figures—Roswell Eldridge, Louise Eldridge, and Eddie Cantor—exemplified the socially diverse strains of Great Neck's developing and transforming possibilities in the 1920s. The Eldridges represented Great Neck's old guard, drawing upon deep native roots, an Episcopal affiliation, and carefully developed financial assets. Cantor, at the opposite extreme, stood for the newly famous and seemingly rich drawn from industry and entertainment. The best known estates in Great Neck, although built on a minor scale compared to those on the Gold Coast to the east, belonged to men known on Wall Street and to the *New Yorker* crowd: the auto manufacturer Walter Chrysler; the lavish-living Wall Street investor Jessie Livermore; the oil magnate Harry Sinclair; the Graces, of shipping fame; the Brokaws, rich from clothing manufacturing; and the Barstows, whose fortune was made in association with Thomas Edison.

But the most significant estate in influence, size, and symbolism, and therefore in Great Neck's history, was Saddle Rock, owned by Roswell and Louise Eldridge. From the local perspective, the Eldridges reigned at the apex of Great Neck society, among 280 Great Neck people listed in the *Social Register*. The Eldridges' commanding position derived from economic and cultural sources that epitomized the values, and mores, even some of the mysterious intrigues, of the 1920s. In his lifelong, incisive critique of suburban life, Lewis Mumford, without knowing the Eldridges, captured the spirit of their lives: "To be your own unique self; to build your unique house, amid a unique landscape; to live . . . a self-centered life, in which private fantasy and caprice would have license to express themselves openly, in short to withdraw like a monk and live like a prince—this was the purpose of the original creators of the suburb. They proposed in effect to create an asylum, in which they could, as individuals, overcome the chronic defects of civilization while still commanding at will the privileges and benefits of urban society."[19]

All of it fits. The Eldridges were indeed unique. They lived in a distinctive home; in a self-centered existence of their own making; at times they withdrew like monks, but always lived like princes; and, finally, they lived apart from the New York metropolis but drew handsomely from its wealth and culture. From the beginning of the family's economic ascent in the eighteenth century, land and location were key: land on Little Neck Bay, good for farming and well-placed for trade with the metropolitan area.

The Eldridge family's holdings go back to one James Udall in the 1840s, founded upon the property of the Udall and Allen families. In the 1840 census James Udall is listed as a farmer; in the 1860 census, as a farmer and miller; and in 1870 as a wholesale merchant.[20] Udall sold hay and other farm produce in the city in return for manure for his land. In addition to being a wholesale merchant, Udall joined other entrepreneurs who saw that transportation to and from the metropolitan area was a potential source of wealth. Udall started a steamship line servicing New York City and the surrounding areas, including one linking Glenwood landing in Great Neck to the city. The assets accumulated handsomely. In the 1870 census, James Udall's assets were valued at $15,000 for real property and $9,000 for personal property. His wife's real property was listed at $4,000 and her personal property at $20,000. Udall had two children, a son, and a daughter Louisa. The son, who became a farmer and merchant, died before his sister. Thus, his daughter inherited the property intact. Louisa married William Skidmore, who identified his business as dealing in manure. He died at the age of thirty-three, leaving his wife and one daughter named Louise.

Growing up into a stout, small woman, it was Louise who, in 1894, at the age of thirty-four, married Roswell Eldridge. The somewhat uncertain history of that relationship is entwined in family lore. Eldridge was born in 1857 and grew up in Hempstead, close to Great Neck. His father was the treasurer of the town. Roswell got a job working on the Udall property as an office boy. He met Louise soon after. In one version of the family history, Roswell soon wanted to marry Louise but was rebuffed because of his lack of resources and possibly his undistinguished social standing.[21] It didn't take long, however, for him to prove his economic worth to the Udalls. After a few years, he took over management of the Great Neck property, then the Udall steamships and a treenail factory in Brooklyn that manufactured wooden nails used in boat construction. Although he remained a director of the treenail firm and a dealer in timber and posts, his entrepreneurial ambitions were realized in running ferryboats to and from Manhattan.

He succeeded in taking control of the Hoboken Ferry of the Delaware and Lackawanna and Western Railroad, the Astoria Ferry Company, and Union Ferry Company. With great prescience, he sold them at a huge profit before ferries became obsolete because of the new tunnels and bridges connecting Manhattan to New Jersey and Long Island. After selling the lines, he moved on to Wall Street as an investor in various enterprises such as the Hanover Bank. Eldridge worked under the aegis of the elusive Harry K. Knapp, who was referred to by the family and press as a well-known financier.[22]

Now possessed of sufficient means, Roswell Eldridge was able to present himself finally as an appropriate match for Louise. After the marriage, Roswell bought property contiguous to the Udall estate and more than doubled his wife's family holdings to 600 acres. The original Udall property remained in the possession of Louise Eldridge, including the large, Georgian, pink-painted brick house called Saddle Rock. The new acreage, however, was the property of Roswell Eldridge. Around 1910, he built a large, sprawling, columned mansion, appropriately named Udallia, which faced a large boulder called Saddle Rock. Large beech trees shaded the area; formal box hedges ornamented the grassy areas leading to the waters of Little Neck Bay with its sandy beach and beds of Saddle Rock oysters. Eldridge transformed the former farm into an elegant estate of gracious perennial and rose gardens, left in the care of a Scottish gardener, with handsome riding horses, recreation houses, gardens for vegetables, cows for milking and over twenty houses for the employees. Looking beyond his own embellished estate, Eldridge created opportunities to make money in the expanding community of estates. He speculated in some nearby property, which he sold for a golf course development. He started the Great Neck Bank in 1906 and also served as vice-president of the Great Neck Trust Company.

Eldridge refashioned himself as a genteel gentleman enjoying the fruits of financial plentitude and leisure. He sailed on his yacht, *Kehtoh*, staffed by a Japanese crew, which was moored in front of Udallia; joined the Racquet Club and New York Yacht Club in the city; rode his saddle horses on his estate and along quiet paths in Kings Point; went fox hunting and stag hunting every year in England; traveled to Europe with a handsome young woman, Mrs. Grace Vocario Merritt (who lived adjacent to Saddle Rock); and reintroduced the Cavalier King Charles spaniel to English breeders as well as to the American dog world through his active membership in the Westminster Kennel Club. The dogs may have been Eldridge's most original effort and enduring success as a gentleman of the North Shore. An article in *Town and Country* in 1981 credited Eldridge with making the Cavalier King Charles spaniel a favorite breed in the United States. "For hundreds of years the Cavalier King Charles spaniel has been a plaything of privilege—the favored pet, companion and comforter of kings and queens, dukes and dowagers, tycoon and celebrities. No breed of dog in history has achieved its equal in canine status or distinction."[23]

It was, however, his paternalistic interest in Great Neck, building institutions and assets that would complement his estate and devising strategies to preserve his holdings, that is of particular importance to Great Neck's history. Although drawn to Great Neck's commercial possibilities, Eldridge tried to freeze the English village-like atmosphere of the suburb. "It is said of him," the *Great Neck News* reported, "that upon completion of the new brick railroad station, Mr. Eldridge one Summer evening drew up before that spic and span structure and, with a sigh remarked: 'Good-bye old Great Neck! This is a symbol of the passing of your beauty.'" The *News* had little sympathy for his nostalgia. "This in spite of the fact that the old frame station, which had served for so long, was to most of the present-day commuters an eye-sore and a plague. In the antiquity and atmosphere of the old depot, Mr. Eldridge had seen the vision of his original Great Neck—his real Great Neck. Thus did he bid farewell to a fading landmark."[24]

While he couldn't stop change in the town, he could extend firm control over his realm of Great Neck holdings. In 1911, Eldridge moved boldly. He became the first estate owner on the North Shore to isolate his property from the effects of nearby development. The answer for him was to turn his estate into a separate village, protected from the reach of the town or county, which he could control and for which he would singularly bear the costs of providing roads, water, police, and fire protection. Cleverly, he assumed that the financial burden for his Saddle Rock estate would be far smaller than an assessment by an adjoining village or by the town of Great Neck, which needed costly improvements for the housing developments near Saddle Rock.

Incorporation by an act of the State Legislature was not hard to obtain, but the qualifying number of 250 residents for incorporation was beyond Eldridge's reach. According to Dennis Sobin, a chronicler of the North Shore, Eldridge had to arrange for the New York State legislature to change the incorporation laws so that his property, with its small population of only fifty family members and servants, could qualify. His solution was to give Saddle Rock property to some of the service people. As property owners they qualified as taxpayers, voters, and potential officers of their village government. A compliant governor and Republican bloc in the legislature changed the law to meet Eldridge's needs.[25] Saddle Rock became a village and Roswell Eldridge its first mayor.

His actions set a precedent for many other estate owners on the Gold Coast who wished to impede the development of roads near their properties and avoid the tax burdens of residential developments. Word spread as far as Kansas. The *Kansas City Star* was intrigued by the political phenomenon of estate villages: "Rich New Yorkers Turn Estates into Villages," was the headline for an article in 1931. It called the Eldridge village the most "unusual," since Louise Eldridge, who succeeded her husband upon his death, was the mayor, heading a government where "all of the village officials are her employees. . . . And so far as is known, none of Mrs. Eldridge's voting servant-citizens has ever even contested the idea that anyone but their mistress should be the mayor."[26]

Eldridge and his wife Louise made other significant contributions to Great Neck's life and history. They donated over $50,000 to acquire property and build the Great Neck Public Library, the effort of a trio that included Mrs. Merritt. The Eldridges gave generously to All Saints Episcopal Church, including donating its silver chimes. Louise was a strong financial supporter of the Great Neck Health League. Roswell and Louise Eldridge

were the force behind creating a safe public bathing beach at Elm Point
on Little Neck Bay, right next to their property. And they were the primary backers of the Great Neck Park District which included a village
green, a bathing area, and athletic fields. They did this despite the fact
that they never brought Saddle Rock into the Park District. In 1936, this
curious situation became a matter of public dispute. In the public campaign over election to the park board, one candidate campaigned against
the Eldridge "dynasty." The *Great Neck News* came to Louise Eldridge's
defense and castigated public "ingratitude" despite her benefactions to the
library and Park District, both of which she headed. "For a long time,"
an editorial stated, "there have been rumblings against the domination of
Mrs. Roswell Eldridge in the Park Board. Secure in her sense of right-
eousness, of doing what is best for Great Neck her actions are bound to
be called autocratic, and it is this, rather than anything she has done, with
one exception, which has provoked criticism."[27] That exception involved
a dispute with Walter Chrysler over the boundaries of a new public beach.
Despite the public controversy and Chrysler's wealth and influence, he
lost to Mrs. Eldridge. So did the candidate who attacked her so-called
imperious rule.

Louise Eldridge acquired her autocratic reputation after her husband
died in 1927 at the age of seventy. An obituary in the *New York Times* cited
his many business, philanthropic, and social achievements. In no way,
however, did it convey his disdain and distance from the encroachments
of suburban life in Great Neck. Since, however, he lived his later life in
the private style of gentlemanly self-containment—leisure, travel, control
over his own village-estate, and involvement in selected charities and
churches—his death provided the local papers with the rare opportunity
to describe Great Neck's leading figure. The *Great Neck News* referred to
him as Squire Eldridge, an "Old World Squire" who took care of the
people who worked for him and fought those who opposed him. After
duly noting his wealth and standing as the "most notable character in a
community of many notable figures in finance, letters and on the stage,"
and his support of the public schools, the editorial went to the heart of his
domineering stature. "His autocratic determination as to what the 'people' really wanted brought him into controversy with pretty much everybody in Nassau Country politics, regardless of party. . . . There was always
a visible cheerfulness among those whose civic, financial and administrative designs differed from his when it was announced that the Squire and
Mrs. Eldridge were about to take one of their long European trips. . . .

From the moment he boarded the steamer the political pot boiled: but he fought almost as well by cable as he did face to face. They seldom put over their designs before he was back and thundering at them again."[28]

Since they had no children, Roswell's death left Louise as the sole mistress and heir to the entire Saddle Rock estate. The income enabled Louise to be securely ensconced on a property that had been in her family for four generations. Her world remained predictably calm: circumscribed by her Saddle Rock gardens and literary and other cultural interests in New York and France. She was a less dramatic and dashing figure than her husband. In 1933 she was described by a local reporter as being "small in stature, with gray hair, sharp, intelligent eyes and restless hands that move constantly while she talks." She was reluctant to be photographed: "Like other people," the reporter noted, Mrs. Eldridge "has her idiosyncrasies. Chief among them is distaste for having her photograph taken. Not even for intimate friends will she be subjected to sitting before a camera."[29] Evidently, she succumbed from time to time, as is clear from a few pictures of her in which she is always shown in a sedentary state. Her tastes remained fixed throughout her life: a passion for raising and displaying roses, reading literature in foreign languages and traveling each summer to France. Her Great Neck charities remained focused on the library, Park District, and Health Association. Roswell left her most of his large estate of approximately $4,000,000. There were also bequests to a number of charities: $100,000 to St. George's Episcopal Church in Hempstead, $250,000 for the Friends Quaker meeting house in Manhasset, and $50,000 to the hospital in Mineola. Trusts were established for Roswell's brother Lewis and his family living on the estate. Lewis Roswell and his wife Elizabeth Huyck had four children, two of whom died in childhood. In 1930, Lewis and Elizabeth built a house, called Redcote, designed by Delano and Aldrich, the most prestigious architectural firm associated with Long Island.

From Broadway to Main Street

For the expanding Great Neck population, Louise Eldridge was the embodiment of Protestant wealth and social superiority, social inaccessibility, and firm political power. She reigned in Great Neck, seemingly oblivious to the quick tempo of arriving and departing families. Nothing disturbed the patterns of her life, not even the encroachment of numerous residential developments near Saddle Rock: 664 houses in Great Neck Estates; 122 houses in the Saddle Rock Estates, across from the Eldridge estate; 149 houses in Strathmore; 177 in Kennilworth; and 288 in Kensington, built for newly arrived escapees from the city. How different was Louise Eldridge's sense of financial security, social belonging, family rootedness, and community connection from the new residents, especially the Jewish families? She was born in Great Neck and stayed there throughout her life. Moving up and moving out played no part in her story.

Herbert Bayard Swope left for Sands Point, where he bought a multi-million-dollar estate. Ring Lardner took up residence in East Hampton. Fitzgerald was long gone. Nonetheless, through the ebb and flow of moving in and out, Great Neck in the 1920s remained a special outpost of Broadway, Tin Pan Alley, and Hollywood. Broadway came to Great Neck and Great Neck went to Broadway. The stars moved in but stayed close to the city's streets of excitement, success, and fame. Either by car, over the Fifty-ninth Street Bridge, or by train to Penn Station, Great Neck residents effortlessly went to the city to work or to see any of the 200-odd shows that made Broadway the entertainment heart of the country. "Lights turned Broadway into the 'Great White Way,' 'the Street of the Midnight Sun,' 'the Mid-town Coney Island,'" John Lahr wrote of those resplendent days in the 1920s when Broadway exploded in neon, opulence, riches, and fame. "Broadway held back the night just as it resuscitated high spirits." Broadway provided thousands upon thousands of songs, competing for fame, that "provided a backbeat of promise; in its happy endings, an escape from defeat; in the pratfalls of its clowns, the hope of resilient survival."[30] Promise, escape from defeat, survival—all were of piercing importance to Americans, especially the new immigrants in the city and particularly the Jews from Eastern Europe. Broadway drew them, spinning songs, out of the ghetto, on to fame. The best of the songs, Jesse Green observed, were written with wit, irony, and also touches of "haunting" sadness. "These were not softhearted men. And yet they did what few artists had ever done before: define love for one-hundred million people."[31] Love— as well as an endless supply of gossip for tabloids, radio, and magazines, that nourished fantasies about America's celebrity culture.

Among Broadway celebrities—the actors, singers, dancers and clowns— Eddie Cantor was one of the most conspicuous—and, certainly, the most conspicuously proud of living in Great Neck. He had made it out of New York, away from the Lower East Side and his sour memories of poverty, abandonment, and failure in the past. Cantor (born Itchik Kantrowitz) represented a new type of American symbol, particularly to America's Jewish immigrants: the man of misfortunes, and miracles. He was a figure of perpetual transformations who delighted and intrigued the American public. His parents were poor, befuddled, unfortunate immigrants. His mother died in childbirth, his father died two years later. Eddie's grandmother at age sixty-two started to care for him as best she could. "We were a couple of lonely creatures at the opposite poles of life," Cantor wrote in his 1928 autobiography, "one looking forward, the other backward, to the same welter of poverty, adversity, and toil."[32] In their impoverished surroundings the density was over 1,000 people per acre on streets such as Delancy, Broome, Allen, and Orchard.[33]

Cantor recalled the boy—he called himself a hooligan—who fought his way out of the Lower East Side and became an entertainer on the stage and in movies by clowning, acting, mimicking, singing, dancing, and desperately fighting for the lucky breaks. In the early stages of his career, he had perfected only one act, which he repeated in different ethnic guises. Finally, Joseph M. Schenck, the head of the vaudeville company that Cantor worked for, told him to create a new number. Cantor panicked and didn't know what to do.

> I sat in a blue gloom, toying with a piece of burnt cork that I picked out of a charcoal can on the make-up shelf. I tried a few dark lines around the mouth and they only made me look haggard. I tried to wipe off the marks, and they spread. My eyes fairly popped out of my head. I had it! Quickly I rubbed the cork over my cheeks, my brow, my neck, my ears, leaving an oblong of white skin around the lips to exaggerate their thickness. I was covered completely with burnt cork, as shiny as a lump of coal. Blackface! My eyes glistened, my teeth gleamed, and because I feared to get the cork dust into my eyes I amateurishly left large circles around them, but out of this blunder was born a new idea. I decided to cover the fault with a pair of white-rimmed spectacles. The spectacles gave me a look of intelligence without straining my face. Unwittingly I had added an intellectual touch to the old-fashioned darky of the minstrel shows. By putting on glasses the sooty spirit of the cotton fields was brought up to the twentieth century.[34]

From white to black—profiting from America's racial tensions and hatreds—Cantor discovered a route to success. White entertainers commonly resorted to blackface but Cantor's new character had a particularly ugly twist that pleased his audiences. From the typical white vaudeville comedian making low-class fun of blacks and immigrants, he transformed himself into a special kind of black character: part of "a sissy-bully team" in which he played the "cultured, pansylike Negro with spectacles." Whether teaming up with a white actor in blackface or a black actor, such as the great Bert Williams, Cantor invited ridicule for impersonating the black man who sought to be educated and cultured.[35]

In blackface, he finally joined the *Ziegfeld Follies* extravaganza. Making big money and a big name, he consorted with the great stars of the day: Will Rogers, W. C. Fields, Fannie Brice, Bert Williams, and Marilyn Miller. After a few years of delirious success, however, Cantor felt that he had once again exhausted his stage persona. He had to revert to his authentic self.

> I had made the resolve that old Black-face must die. In a moment of emergency I had put on his dark mask and he had helped me to success. Now the audience knew only this cork-smeared face, while I stood hidden behind it wondering what would happen if the blacking came off. I feared that in this lay the seed of a greater tragedy than any I had experienced, and I had made my mind up long ago to leave tragedy to the Booths and Mansfields. I was not going to be a slave to a piece of burnt cork for the rest of my acting days.[36]

He devised a new act, but Flo Ziegfeld was afraid to let Cantor switch and possibly flop. When Ziegfeld refused to let him do the act, Cantor threatened to leave the *Follies*. Ziegfeld relented. Cantor recalled: "This marked my first appearance on the musical-comedy stage in my own face, and, good or bad as that face might be, it was the first time that I felt revealed to the audience and in personal contact with it."[37] Out of blackface, Cantor transformed himself into a white weakling, an aviator in the first variation of the new persona, who got shoved around by a guy who gave Cantor a beating. With this debut, Cantor, the entertainer, was transformed again and for good. The new Eddie Cantor was the high-voiced, slightly frail innocent who sang, pranced, and danced to simple, jaunty, romantic songs. He was the lost, inept, young man, subject to pathetic and hilarious misunderstandings about American rituals, especially romantic ones. With Cantor on the stage there was no sign of the classy, smooth, romantic yearnings of a Fred Astaire or the clever wit of a Cole Porter. Cantor's voice was that of the befuddled, fumbling, young man trying to make money, and win a woman's interest: most often a woman who turned out to be dumb, dominating, ravenous, predatory, or ugly.

His repertoire of misogynist patter came from low-class vaudeville, the entertainment of pursuit, rejection, ethnic slurs, sexual machinations, social disasters, the fears of little men, marriage, and divorce: "I'm hungry, I'm hungry for beautiful girls," or "I go so far with Sophie and Sophie goes so far with me," "When My Ship Comes In," and, most famously "Making Whoopee." The style worked beautifully. Fame and money flowed to Cantor from performances in the *Ziegfeld Follies*; *Kidd Boots*, a long-running slapstick musical-romance, which started in 1923, about a crooked, clever golf caddie; and *Whoopee* in 1928. He made films in Hollywood and Astoria; sang; danced; made recordings; performed at private functions for the Whitneys, Astors, and Harrimans and others in high society and, as often as possible, performed at charity functions for Big Brothers, Surprise Camp, and numerous Catholic and Jewish charities.

Money had to be managed. For this, Cantor turned to his old friend Daniel Lipsky, who had gained Cantor's affection and confidence many years before. As they grew up in the Lower East Side, Dan, a sober and well-behaved young boy, had watched over his trouble-prone, beleaguered friend. As kids, they had performed together at weddings and went to the Educational Alliance's charity summer camp called Surprise Lake. Lipsky quit the stage of petty performances and turned to business. He married Cantor's cousin Annie; learned stenography; plotted his advancement; and drew the attention of Nathan S. Jonas, the chairman of the Board of Directors of the Brooklyn-based Manufacturers Trust. Slowly, Lipsky made his way up the ranks and became a vice-president of the bank. Jonas was a financial star and mentor for Lipsky.

Jonas, who was born in Alabama, had worked first as an insurance salesman and then organized his own Citizens Trust Company that gave loans mostly to immigrants. Jonas merged his bank with others until, finally, in 1924 the bank became the Manufacturers Trust. Jonas built his reputation as a major philanthropist in Brooklyn and Great Neck, a golf club and real estate developer in his new suburban community and a gentleman. Jonas was so successful in these efforts that he was included in the *Social Register* for 1930.

Lipsky and Jonas took control over Cantor's money. In the fabulous prosperity of the 1920s, Cantor accumulated investments and became a homeowner. With Lipsky managing his finances, Cantor moved out of a flat in the Bronx with his wife Ida and their girls, to a rented house in Westchester, and then to Great Neck after buying property from Jonas. Cantor hired the architect Archibald F. Gilbert to design a large, sprawling,

English-style, brick and half-timbered structure that meandered across a flat, open piece of land in University Gardens.[38]

In 1928, Cantor was entranced with what he had wrought. He and the rest of America were living with what Paul Johnson called, the "extraordinary exuberance in the delight of being alive and American."[39] With the creation of mass markets for consumer goods, Johnson wrote, "prosperity was more widely distributed in the America of the 1920s than had been possible in any community of this size before, and it involved the acquisition, by tens of millions of ordinary families, of the elements of economic security which had hitherto been denied them throughout history,"[40] including cars, houses, radio, stocks—and lots of credit to purchase them with. In ten years, Eddie Cantor, like so many of his fellow Americans, seemed well on his way to financial stability: from renter to house owner; from a man who spent all of his money to an investor in stocks, bonds, and real estate; from an uncontrollable spender to a saver. "A sense of growing security inspired me. I am building my house upon a rock rather than public whim. For the fortunes of my career might vary and the day might come when I'd walk out on the stage and the audience would say, 'Cantor, you're through. Go home.' And I'd answer, 'O.K. we owe each other nothing.' I'd go home, sit in the parlor, and read my clippings, not from newspapers, but from bonds."[41]

FROM RACING TO RESIGNATION

In 1928, the world looked secure to Cantor from his position of success on the Broadway stage and his quiet Great Neck property. He was oblivious to the drastic changes, occurring south and east of Great Neck in Nassau and Suffolk Counties, which put the Gold Coast under siege. In the mid-twenties and thirties, Robert Moses, the omnipotent head of the New York State Park Commission, went to battle against the baronies of the North Shore. The sparsely populated, parkless, rural island with inadequate roads perfectly suited the powerful estate owners. But not Moses. Appointed by Governor Al Smith in the early 1920s, Moses was determined to ensure that Long Island would become accessible to millions of people in the city.

Moses reigned over a public kingdom of his creation: open space and recreational parks, nature preserves, roads, tunnels, and bridges that radically transformed Long Island's accessibility, circulation, and character. For Moses, the automobile and road building were the weapons of conquest in assaulting the privacy and landed privileges of the Gold Coast estate owners. Ironically, it was one of their own, from his base in Great Neck, who had initially claimed Long Island for the automobile. Less than twenty years before Moses started his campaign, William Kissim Vanderbilt II had seized upon Long Island as the ideal terrain to build popular interest in the automobile, which, along with yachting, was one his passions. The young Vanderbilt, who became addicted to automobile racing in France, built a thirty-mile, sand-and-gravel, racing road, which went from his Deepdale estate in Lake Success to Mineola.

He loved racing, but, even more importantly, he wanted American entrepreneurs to make cars as fast and handsome as those made in Europe. Encouraged by the races, which started in 1904 and drew thousands of spectators, Vanderbilt organized the Long Island Motor Parkway enterprise. It financed the projected extension of the road from the city line to Lake Ronkonkoma, where automobile drivers could dine at the Petite Trianon Inn, built especially for them. The backers intended the road to be used for races, as well as pleasure drives.[42] The corporation built the extended motorway as a toll road. Vanderbilt's investors, who included August Belmont and Harry Payne Whitney, spent $10,000,000.[43] The investment may have paid off in pleasure, but never in monetary return. Vanderbilt's road-building example was deliberately ignored by many of the estate owners who didn't want to invite traffic near their preserves. In fact, public transportation on North Shore was abysmal—and deliberately so—in the service of preserving the privileged, quiet, recreational landscape.

By the 1920s, however, Vanderbilt had lost his taste for Lake Success, which did not provide him with enough privacy. He was also no longer interested in underwriting the motorway. He sold his estate, one part of which became the Glen Oaks Golf Club, and the other Deepdale Golf Club. In its place, Vanderbilt built an exotic and appropriately lavish estate in Centerport, Long Island. In one respect, his dreams had come true: American manufacturers were making and selling millions of cars for an enthralled public. In fact in the mid-twenties, Americans owned 23,000,000 cars. By the early 1930s, there were close to 800,000 cars in New York State alone.[44]

Vanderbilt was unsuccessful in disentangling himself from the motorway. He assumed that he could sell his motorway to Moses, who, on behalf of New York State, was cutting a toll-free, park-like, public road through the North Shore. Through acquisitions and confiscation and a ruthless will exercised in Albany and throughout the state, Moses was well on his way to fulfilling his stunning environmental and preservationist visions. He mapped his parkway on the North Shore across, next to, or near many of the Gold Coast families such as Morgan, Frick, Phipps, Carnegie, Kahn, Havemayer, and Whitney. Outraged, they used political pressure and lawsuits to fight the plan. Publicly, Moses accused them of arrogance, greed, and hostility to the needs of the public. With the solid support of the populist Governor Al Smith and brilliant political maneuvering in Albany and Nassau and Suffolk County, Moses could not be stopped from building the Northern State Parkway, proposed in the mid-1920s and started in 1932.

The estate owners could, however, negotiate over the parkway's course and contours to circumvent some of their special properties. William Vanderbilt, however, was not as lucky as some of his confreres. His motorway did not to fit into Moses's projected route designed for broad, divided, aesthetically pleasing roadways with limited access. Vanderbilt rejected the Moses proposal to buy just a small slice of Vanderbilt's enterprise close to Great Neck. Moses told him that the motorway would revert to the State sooner or later. He was right. Vanderbilt eventually gave it to New York State for nothing.

According to Robert Caro, the biographer par excellence of Robert Moses, other estate owners arranged with Moses for significant detours away from their properties as well as foreclosing any entrances to the parkway near their estates. Moses, according to Caro, "gave his solemn oath that state troopers patrolling the parkway would be under orders to keep automobiles from the city moving, not allowing their occupants to picnic, or even to stop, by the side of the parkway within their borders. Publicly, Moses never stopped excoriating the Long Island millionaires. But in private, many of them were coming to consider him quite a reasonable fellow to deal with."[45] But, Caro wrote, as part of his deals with the barons, he abandoned his pursuit of public parks on the North Shore. Moses, "had to promise the barons that there would not be a single state park anywhere along the parkway, or anywhere in the section of the North Shore that they controlled—and with a single exception . . . there are no state parks anywhere in that part of Nassau Country or western Suffolk that was known as the 'North Shore' or the 'Gold Coast.'"[46]

DESPERATION AND DECLINE

The invasive machinations of Robert Moses, wielding the power of the state in the name of the public good, challenged the baronial order of the

North Shore. It was, however, the stock market crash in 1929 and ensuing Depression that pitched the Gold Coast into decline. The suburbs around the city were struck even harder. Great Neck, along with most of the rest of America, gave up its fervid infatuation with the future. Beyond the few borders of privilege, such as the Eldridge estate, the Depression shattered the leisure-loving, money-loving, publicity-loving tenor of Great Neck life. Along with the rest of the country, Great Neck went into a grim financial decline. No longer could developers; journalist-publicists, such as the *Great Neck News* editor Hal Lanigan; Wall Street investors, such as Jesse Livermore; merchants; bankers; and Broadway entertainers assume that the town would keep growing; land and house values would zoom up; and the golf, tennis, boating, and hunting parties would play on. The fate of the Great Neck peninsula was fatally tied to Wall Street. From month to month and year to year, New York City plunged deeply into demoralization and hardships. Thousands upon thousands of business failed and went bankrupt, millions of workers were unemployed, and over a million people went on relief. Economic and social devastation plagued the once-proud, exuberant city.

A year before the Crash, Cantor had thought that he was building his house upon a rock. Daniel Lipsky and Nathan Jonas had managed Cantor's money in the favored method of the twenties: money by margin. Lipsky encouraged Cantor to invest heavily in stocks, including that of Jonas's own bank—buying big on margin. In 1928, Cantor boasted that the stock in the bank that he had bought for $172 a share was now selling for $900. That stock constituted "the bulwark of the modest little fortune that I gathered in less than ten years. Today I am one of the large stockholders in the Manufacturers Trust Company."[47] Cantor felt so secure with his holdings that he contemplated retiring, at the height of his career and earning power. "Any actor who is wise," he told the *Great Neck News* in 1929, "would do what I am doing, but most actors haven't got the sense to budget themselves and save their money. I've kept a budget just like a state or a city, preparing for the time when I might want to rest and take it easy, and that time has come now."[48]

Cantor feared the day when the crowds would no longer like his act and would tell him to go home. So he would go home, he thought, and clip bonds. But it was not the audience that told Cantor he was through, it was the stock market. Overnight, his stocks and bonds plummeted and Cantor's accounts were called. It didn't take long for Cantor to lose his "modest little fortune," investments, house, and his expectations of more income-producing, fame-producing Ziegfeld Broadway hits. His affection and adulation for Jonas, his recent idol, and Lipsky, his childhood friend, turned quickly to grief and bitterness. Suddenly, Great Neck became the symbol of raucous greed. He learned that his house was not built on a rock, but on the unstable stock market. The house became his albatross. In the latest of his transformations, Cantor went from feeling rich and secure to desperate and poor, along with the rest of America.

In desperation, he turned to his public—a mass public desperate to laugh. Like much of America, Cantor pictured himself as a financial innocent and bleeding victim of Wall Street. The little guy up against the wall. He told it all in two slim books: *Caught Short: A Saga of Wailing Wall Street,* published in the late fall of 1929, and *Between the Acts,* which appeared the following year. Ironically, the illustrations in the books showed Cantor back in blackface, providing an appearance that resonated with humiliation. "The night of the worst crash I was too frightened to go to my home in Great Neck. I went instead to one of the larger hotels in New York City and asked the clerk for a room on the nineteenth floor: The clerk looked up at me and asked. 'What for? Sleeping or jumping?'"[49] He imagined going to J. P. Morgan & Company, in blackface, to see how they are dealing with the Crash. "How did I get in? Leave it to Eddie Cantor. Being a blackface comedian, I put on the burnt cork and presented myself at the private door. . . ." He tells the secretary he is Kuhn, of Kuhn Loeb. And what do the senior bankers of the country discuss to solve the crisis in the in the middle of the panic? "We're facing a very serious situation, a situation fraught with danger and peril to all of us," one told the others. "Did you notice at the club of late that after a handball game you have to wait fifteen minutes before you can get a rubdown?"[50]

Cantor mocked the insouciance and indifference of Wall Street's titans to the suffering and disasters of little guys like him. His publisher, Simon and Schuster, proclaimed it was all satiric, hyperbolic fun. In the foreword, the editors described Cantor as a great entertainer, a genuine success moving from the East Side to the "dazzling heights of Ziegfeld stardom and Great Neck opulence."[51] Fortunately for Cantor and his publisher, the book sold 100,000 copies. *Caught Short* kept Cantor from going under financially, but he was forced to give up his house in Great Neck. He moved to Hollywood to act in movies, expecting a more promising place for work, since films required smaller investments than Broadway shows.

The saga made Cantor into a public hero of sorts, a symbol of the gullibility and powerlessness of the little guy. A year later he wrote *Between the Acts,* a sequel to *Caught Short,* which turned his bitter wit on Great Neck and the forsaken dreams of permanence in suburban bliss. Once again showing himself in blackface, Cantor told all about his catastrophic woes. First the architect proposed building a house that resembled the White House, Grand Central Station, and Madison Square Garden all in one: outlandish in size and cost. But Cantor went ahead anyway. Architect, builder, and "victims"—the Cantors—met and worked things out. On October 12, 1929, the Cantor family moved in to their new home. "We are happy. It is our home. No one can take it away—no one, except my banker, my broker and the builder who hasn't been paid yet."[52] Cantor advised readers who contemplated building their own homes: talk to an architect, talk to a builder, and then turn your back on the suburbs and rent an apartment in the city.

Cantor left Great Neck, his erstwhile suburban base of inflated expectations, as did many of the other entertainers who had given a glitzy cast to the town. In his Depression-induced retreat, Cantor gave Great Neck a new kind of fame: as a place of rapacious and extravagant bankers and builders. He couldn't sell his house, nor could he give it away. He never again praised Jonas and Lipsky; in fact, Cantor thought that his childhood friend had improperly profited from Cantor's demise. Lipsky stayed on Wall Street, but Cantor never invested in the market again. Within a few years, Jonas also failed and was forced out of the bank and his home in Great Neck. Only Lipsky remained in Great Neck as it felt the effects of the Depression.

With the departure of the stars during the bleak years of the Depression, Great Neck looked more like other Long Island suburbs, such as nearby Manhasset or Roslyn. Still, the habit of star-watching was hard to break. In February 1932, the *Great Neck News* featured "Why I Prefer to Live in Great Neck." Walter P. Chrysler; Joseph P. Grace, chairman of the Board of W. R. Grace & Co.; Thomas Craven, the writer; artist Max Weber; cartoonist Rube Goldberg; Nathan. P. Jonas, "Retired Capitalist, former Chairman of the Board of the Manufacturers Trust Company"; and Daniel Lipsky, president of the Pickbarth Holding Company, gave their reasons for living in Great Neck. Most were sober endorsements highlighting the beauty and convenience of the town. Whitney Bolton, drama critic of the *New York Morning Telegraph,* gave the most colorful views: "Great Neck has none of New Jersey's bleakness, none of Westchester's infuriating smugness, none of the South Shore's brash ambition to make itself the modern Coney Island. There is . . . only one flaw in the bright pattern of

Great Neck: the necessity of passing through the lush and awesome garbage fields of Queens to get here."[53] Mrs. Eldridge made no comment, although she lived through the Depression with little discomfort.

That bright pattern, however, wasn't shining all over Great Neck. Some people and businesses made it through the Depression with mild discomfort, but the nature of Great Neck's development drastically changed. Banks took over numerous homes and commercial properties. An auction in November 1933 sought to dispose of $1,000,000 of Great Neck real estate. Values dropped drastically, as was evident from the report of a member of the local real estate board. R. A. White wrote in one of the local papers that news of a house sale at a "ridiculously low price spread like fire through Great Neck," as homeowners felt they "had little equity left."[54] Hardly a new house was built. (Nation-wide, housing starts dropped 95 percent.) Local businesses suffered from lack of demand. I. G. Wolf cut back his real estate staff from seventy-five to ten.

Unemployment—9,000–10,000 people in Nassau alone—could not be ignored. A voluntary group, the Great Neck Employment and Relief Committee, set out to raise $10,000–$15,000 for support and to provide jobs for the unemployed. School salaries were cut 10 percent. Attempts were made to lower local property taxes. The publisher of the *Great Neck News* sold the paper in 1930. Its editor, Hal Lanigan, was fired and moved on to Florida. (The rival *North Hempstead Record* gloated over his departure: "We do not feel sorry for Hal W. Lanigan. For five years he has run wild in Great Neck with little regard for anyone except Hal Lanigan.")[55] Two of Great Neck's golf clubs went under.

BUILDING FOR THE FUTURE

Great Neck suffered, as did all of the surrounding suburban communities. But Great Neck differed from the others in one crucial respect: it was the only community on the North Shore that had a growing Jewish population. In such desperate financial times, any renters or buyers were welcome: including Jews. That is, anyone except blacks, who might add to the small number already there. From the early part of the nineteenth century, Great Neck had made a painless accommodation with a small black community that was concentrated on Steamboat Road in Kings Point, and the Valley—otherwise known as Spinney Hill. On the border between Great Neck and Manhasset, the Valley had served as a destination point on the Underground Railroad. By the 1920s, there were several hundred black families living there, directly across from Greentree, the Whitneys' estate. The small, cramped houses, often without plumbing, were crowded into a small hill with two modest churches and a public school that was part of the Manhasset school system.

From time to time, the local papers would report on the activities of a new minister, the construction of another church or efforts to find work for the unemployed. One story, in 1928, recounted that the "Rev. Mr. Walker, who is a practical man and a believer in the methods of the late Booker T. Washington, has visions of catering to the material as well as the spiritual needs of the 600 Negroes who have settled in this vicinity. Most of them are from the South living in a strange environment and in need of contacts which will improve their social status and raise their standard of living."[56] Paternalistic endorsement of Walker's initiatives came easily to the paper. So did swift condemnation of any actions by the black population that, in the view of the whites in Great Neck, impinged on their suburban security. Two years later, the paper lauded the decision of the Town Board of North Hempstead to reject the application for a dance hall in the Valley. "A precedent has been established. If any more promoters from Harlem or elsewhere in New York think they can do in Nassau what they do at home, they had better stop, look and listen. . . . Manhasset Valley, North Hempstead Township and Nassau Country are a far cry from Harlem."[57] As Harlem changed from a mixed population of middle-class whites and blacks to a mostly black population, dominated by lower-class blacks, the suburban and racial borders of the 1920s and 1930s around the city became more rigid. For the white suburb, just a train ride and subway ride away from the densely populated Harlem, the affirmation of geographic, racial, and cultural separation was critical.

The growing Jewish presence in Great Neck fundamentally differed from that of the black community. Blacks represented a dire threat, Jews just an undesirable intrusion—a challenge to the town's social makeup and economy, based upon homes, clubs, and developments. Great Neck's acceptance of Jews occurred during a period of virulent anti-Semitic sentiment in America. Antiforeign sentiment, which had exploded after the First World War, resulted in the imposition of immigration quotas in the 1920s. Congress effectively stopped the entry of foreigners from so-called "undesirable" eastern and southern European countries. As to those immigrants already in America, social and economic barriers were thrown up—particularly against Jews, immigrants and native-born alike—in major industries, businesses, associations, educational institutions, clubs, and residential areas. The Depression exacerbated the suspicions and differences between Gentiles and Jews.

It was one thing for Great Neck in the 1920s to have accepted Jewish Broadway stars and theatrical personalities. The Eddie Cantors were the cutting edge, making their mark on the social configuration of an ambitious community. They brought fame, money, and the benefits of public recognition to the suburban community that hungered for distinction and commercial success. Cantor and company had been useful to many local causes, such as the Great Neck Association, organized to enact zoning restrictions. And, in return, Great Neck was useful to the Broadway contingent, mostly Jewish immigrants or first-generation Americans, by conferring an aura of domestic respectability and neighborly well being on people from lower-class backgrounds.

But what about the other Jews in Great Neck who tried to make the same kind of social transformation and transition as did Cantor? When Cantor fled Great Neck during the Depression, he left behind a growing Jewish community with far fewer luminaries that Great Neck could boast about. Those who remained were mostly businessmen and their families leading prosaic lives. They had heard, during the late twenties, that Great Neck, almost alone among the communities on the North Shore, accepted Jews. Their presence, after the shock of the Crash and ensuing Depression, represented the real test of acceptance.

From the perspective of Great Neck's Jewish population, the community was a test in progress, one that was working reasonably well for them, especially in respect to anti-Semitism nationwide. Their presence in the community followed the traditional American pattern of settling in and organizing some tentative form of religious observance. But the efforts of Great Neck's Jews departed from the usual Jewish pattern in America of first establishing Orthodox synagogues and schools that most faithfully replicated those of their Eastern European backgrounds. Instead, the Jews in Great Neck turned to the liberal Reform movement, the most socially conscious and inclusive branch of Judaism.

As the number of Jews in Great Neck grew, several men and women started the process of building Jewish educational programs and even a temple. It took four years—from September 1928, when four men on the 9:15 commuter train to New York discussed holding services for the High Holy Days, for the Jewish community to move into its own permanent religious establishment. Hints in the notes of the first organizing efforts reveal the many complexities that needed to be worked out. On the second day of discussions, one of the organizers "called for a report on obtaining the Rabbi and other paraphernalia" for the High Holy Days. That so-called paraphernalia consisted of one hundred prayer books and a Torah scroll, which was loaned to the congregation in Great Neck by Central Synagogue in New York City. They also hired Rabbi David Goodis to officiate at the holidays at a cost of $150. (At the same time they engaged an organist and quartet for $300.)[58] These efforts followed earlier discussions by a number of women who formed a Jewish Sisterhood in 1927. They wanted a Sunday school for their children so that they would not have to travel to Brooklyn or Flushing for religious instruction. The group favored establishing the school but was strongly divided about the nature of Jewish education. One cryptic remark was highly revealing: "Mrs. Kaplan— Thinks it very vital to have a Sunday school near home. Wants her child to learn Hebrew."[59]

After the high holidays in the fall of 1928, the group continued to organize and plan for a permanent home. Rabbi Goodis, at the age of thirty-two, became the permanent rabbi of Temple Beth-El. The first president of the new congregation, David Adler, took primary responsibility for raising the necessary funds to build the temple. At a "glistening get-together" at the Community Church in April 1929, Adler announced that $20,000 had been raised already. He thanked All Saints Church for housing the new congregation in the Episcopal chapel, but, he added, "we must not forget that we are guests; and I am assured that you feel as I do that we don't want to remain permanent guests, a privilege heretofore monopolized by mothers-in-law."[60]

Eighteen months later, the Jewish community succeeded in constructing their Reform temple on Udall Mill Road, despite the Depression, the sudden death of Rabbi Goodis, and the need to raise over $75,000. In September 1930, Temple Beth-El hired Rabbi Jacob Philip Rudin to succeed Rabbi Goodis. Rudin's background, presence, and goals suited the new congregation perfectly. He came from an Orthodox family in Massachusetts, was educated at Harvard and spoke with a powerful voice in a fine New England cadence. He had been the assistant to Rabbi Stephen Wise and the director of placement at the Jewish Institute of Religion in New York. At Rudin's installation, attended by Rev. Donovan of St. Aloysius and Rev. McKechnic of All Saints, Wise guided his protégé. According to one report, "Dr. Weiss [*sic*] spoke of the need for Great Neck Jewry to make themselves felt in the life of the community after the finest principles of Judaism and American life."[61] In the same year, Daniel Lipsky, Eddie Cantor's erst-while financial adviser, became the third president of the congregation.

The formal and joyous dedication dinner celebrated the completion of the building in October 1932. The proud congregation enjoyed an eight-course dinner including sweetbreads en roulette, among other fancy edi-bles; speeches; and a musicale performed by four operatic stars, including one artist from the Metropolitan Opera Company. The building's style, tone, and setting reflected Rudin's objective to make the Great Neck Jew-ish community "part of the fabric of our country's life." The first plan, featured in the *North Hempstead Record,* had shown a building in the "Nor-mandy type architecture" with Romanesque arches and a tower or turret-like structure at one end.[62] Over the next few months, the design was toned down to English Episcopal. The fieldstone building, designed by the New York architects Black and Hess, blended perfectly with the tone of much of Great Neck's public architecture. Inside and out, from the intimate and beautifully proportioned chapel, dominated by proliferating dark wood beams, to the handsome stone facade, Temple Beth-El sought to show its character as an "American synagogue." Its design, which sought to enhance, but not challenge, the dominant Protestant and English-flavored tenor of the town, was consistent with the instincts of the congre-gation, the Reform movement, and the traditional method of architectural accommodation practiced by Jews all over the world. In this defining moment, the young congregation proclaimed its Jewish purpose but fol-lowed the aesthetic tastes of the surrounding Christian population.

A few years before Beth-El was organized, Lewis Mumford, in the Jewish journal *The Menorah,* had posed a series of questions about the challenges of building synagogues in a country with a relatively new and rapidly growing population. "With old structures wearing out and with new congregations needing a new home, the quest for an appropriate form for synagogs [*sic*] and temples has become an urgent one; and the problem cannot be put aside until the general relation of Jewish culture to West-ern civilization has been adequately examined and threshed out. The architectural needs of the Jew in fact give a concrete basis for working out the problem. What are the resources of traditional Jewish culture? How far can they be utilized today? Should a synagogue be in harmony with the buildings around it, or should it stand out and proclaim the cul-tural individuality of the Jewish community?"[63]

The answer, in Great Neck, at least, was harmony over "cultural in-dividuality." And yet, to Jews and Gentiles alike, that individuality was

obvious through the growing Jewish presence itself. The Jewish community sought acknowledgment of its social and religious events as well as
the assertion of its political voice. No longer were marriages only held in
the town's churches. On the front page of the *Great Neck News* in December 1933 readers saw a prominent picture of a Jewish wedding party with
the headline: "Miss Beulah Brandt Married in First Temple Wedding."
More surprising was the news that local politics carried a particular edge
of ethnic challenge and conflict. "There was an indignation meeting," the
Great Neck News reported, "following Mr. Kehoe's defeat in the Great Neck
Sewer District election by Jerome Harris by forty-nine votes . . . resenting
what they described as the introduction of race and religious prejudice in
the campaign." A letter that Rabbi Rudin had sent to his congregations—
all 360 families according to the account—incensed Kehoe and his allies.
Rudin's letter asked for support for Harris: "Not only because he is the
only Jew running for office on the Sewer Commission . . . but he has shown
himself worthy of confidence." Kehoe told the paper that he objected to
the appeal based on "race and religious prejudice" which seems "not only
highly improper but going out of his way to arouse the antagonism about
which his people complain so bitterly. As a matter of fact it has aroused
bitter resentment." Kehoe stated that he never would have asked his priest
at St. Aloysius, the leader of 1,500 parishioners, to influence the vote on
religious grounds.[64]

The flare-up over the election was part of the process of integrating a
middle-class Jewish community—no longer the irresistible Jewish celebrities—into a predominately Protestant town with a significant Catholic
minority. In contemplating a move to the suburb, the lure for Jews was
no longer the presence of stars, but the growth of a Jewish community
consolidating around Temple Beth-El. Josselyn M. Shore, a businessman,
but not a business *star*, as Jonas had aspired to be, exemplified the interests of the new Jewish resident. "Word started to spread," he recalled,
"about a beautiful temple of Reform Judaism, with a vibrant congregation
and an outstanding young rabbi, way out in Great Neck."[65] In the late
1930s, he and his wife Irene considered other communities in Westchester
and Long Island, but "Temple Beth-El was the magnet that drew families
. . . in increasing numbers from Brooklyn and New York. . . . It represented all we wanted in our lives as our families grew up."[66] For the Shores,
the temple and the growing Jewish community were the new foundations
for their social, religious, and civic life—foundations that would bring

them both to prominence in Great Neck organizations and in the 1940s and 1950s on behalf of Zionism.

The presence of the growing Jewish population—which was exactly what attracted more Jews—was not what many non-Jews in Great Neck wanted in their lives as part of their quest for upward mobility. The community was no longer a place where Gentiles confidently expended their social capital. Shore thought that "most of those NOT of our faith resented the large influx of 'foreigners' as they call us. The only newspaper in town printed all the scurrilous letters it received—one, I remember vividly, had to do with moving vans from Brooklyn and the Bronx cluttering up our streets." Shore complained to the editor of the paper, pointing out that if he continued, he would be committing economic suicide. "We became friends and played tennis together." After their encounter, those kinds of letters did not appear anymore.[67]

Shore was particularly sensitive to anti-Semitic slights and insinuations. Before his move to Great Neck, he had come up against the force of prejudice in two ways: as a runner and in his work. In 1923, soon after his family settled in New York, Josh Shore fortuitously found himself racing on a beach in the Bronx against three citywide one-hundred-yard champions. The twenty-one-year-old Jewish kid from Providence beat them easily, although he had never run a race and had no racing shoes, training, or affiliation with a racing club. Astounded by his speed, they suggested that he join the New York Athletic Club. Calls to the NYAC brought Shore in contact with coaches and other runners. Shore started to run competitively, won many races, and attracted the attention of the popular press. Most of his competitors belonged to or were sponsored by well-known athletic or running clubs. Shore ran without either. It wasn't long before the NYAC invited him to join but on the condition that he not reveal that he was Jewish. The athletic director was eager to have him join, Shore was told, "but can't send you an application if you state you are Jewish. . . . You have a great potential and the fellows like you. You have proved your ability and there is no telling how far you can go with the proper training."[68]

Shore decided that he would not lie to get into the club. The decision was particularly painful since it came at the same time that he lost his job because he was Jewish. When he interviewed for the job he had known that the company did not want Jewish employees. The question of his religion, however, never came up in the interview. When it became known that Shore was Jewish, after two years of working for the firm, his employer told him to leave since he would have no future in the company. Challenged as a Jew in two areas, Shore faced up to the prejudice around him. "It was one thing to hide my identity in order to bring home a paycheck each week, but it was unthinkable to lie about my religion as a prerequisite for admission into an anti-Semitic athletic club. . . . It is understandable that I was devastated."[69] He knew that he was giving up the training that would have made him into a great runner. Despite the setback, he continued to race, came under the sponsorship of the Melrose Athletic Association and nearly won the 300 National Junior indoor Championship at Madison Square Garden in 1925. Two years later, he decided to give up racing. He married, worked as a manufacturer's representative for ladies lingerie, started a family, and moved to Great Neck in 1939.

His serious disappointments and confrontations with prejudice quickly gave way to happiness in Great Neck. Although Temple Beth-El and Rabbi Rudin had drawn the Shores to Great Neck, they thrived on being part of a suburban community that was developing appropriate educational, religious, and governing institutions. These organizations depended upon the voluntary participation and initiative of community members. As several Great Neck Jews, such as Shore, sought involvement in local affairs, they confronted Great Neck's Gentile hierarchy. It was headed by leaders such as Louise Eldridge, the private and remote president of the Park District and mayor of Saddle Rock, and William H. Zinsser, the activist founder of the Great Neck Association and mayor of Kings Point.

Zinsser's long-time activities and interests exemplify the best ideals of the renowned sociologist E. Digby Baltzell. Baltzell both honored and castigated the Protestant establishment: he honored WASPs for their tradition of exercising authority responsibly on behalf of American society; he castigated them for rigidity and for abandoning their obligations through the mid-to-late twentieth century.[70] Zinsser, however, was not among those in Great Neck who retreated from community responsibilities or subscribed to anti-Semitic beliefs. When he built his house on four acres in Kings Point in 1920, he quickly discovered that he lived on a peninsula that was a developer's paradise, with its intense demand for housing; inconsistent, ineffective, and incoherent zoning laws; public apathy; multiple villages jurisdictions; "inadequate schools;" and local public officials with poor qualifications for meeting the town's burgeoning needs. "There was no force of unified public opinion and no understanding leadership," Zinsser wrote in his family memoir in 1962. "One or two real estate developments had seceded from the township and set up incorporated villages, drawing boundaries around what they wanted, leaving eyesores, unkempt districts and popular dumps outside of their restricted areas. There was no thought of a master plan for the entire peninsula."[71]

Zinsser simply went to work. He founded the Great Neck Association, attracted one hundred dues-paying members ($2.00 per year), and cleverly used Great Neck's celebrity culture for his civic purposes. "Fortunately Great Neck at that time had a large actors' colony which I also enlisted in the cause of civic pride and betterment. Each monthly meeting was attractively announced by mail as a fun gathering. Men like Ed Wynn, Eddie Cantor . . . and Donald Brian, the first 'Merry Widow' leading man, would alternately be featured as the main attraction. It was in the intermission periods that I harangued our citizens on modern garbage incineration, adequate sanitation, underground grade crossings, a better curriculum in our schools, etc., etc."[72] Zinsser, aided by Hal Lanigan at the *Great Neck News,* sought to build broad community support for writing and implementing a Master Plan for Great Neck. "Zinsser Flays Selfish Real Estate Developments: 'Menaces to beauty of Great Neck growing Like Weeds at Thresholds of Incorporated Areas'—Lauds Master Plan and Nathan S. Jonas's Liberality," was one of numerous articles that Lanigan ran about Zinsser's work.[73] Nathan Jonas donated $1,000 and raised another $6,000 to hire Warren Manning, the well-known landscape architect, to write the Master Plan.

The community failed to adopt the plan, which was perceived as too bold in pursuit of rationalizing development and reorganizing village jurisdictions in Great Neck. Zinsser's efforts, however, were more successful in the village of Kings Point. Under his leadership, the area incorporated in 1924 and took control of its own police, garbage collection, and road maintenance. A minimum of one-acre zoning was implemented, although Zinsser believed it too small: "This size parcel we felt was the most that could be legally defended, as even in those days big holdings were no longer considered democratic." He served Kings Point as a trustee for thirteen years and then as its mayor for another seven.

Zinsser ran William Zinsser & Company, a family shellac business, started in the mid-nineteenth century and located on Fifty-ninth Street and Tenth Avenue in the city. Compared to the rich stockbrokers, bankers, and industrialists down the roads in Kings Point—the Walter Chryslers or Jesse Livermores—the Zinssers lived quiet, modest lives. Fortunately, the business allowed the family to pass through the Depression years with little economic injury. Throughout the 1920s and 1930s, Zinsser and his wife and children moved easily between their pastoral home, looking out on both Manhasset Bay and the Long Island Sound, and the city. He commuted to work every day; the family shopped at Best & Co. and De Pinna in New York; they used doctors in the city as well; and, at least once a week, Zinsser returned to Kings Point to dress before returning to the city for an evening with his wife at the opera or symphony. He belonged to Piping Rock Club in Westbury and the Manhasset Bay Yacht Club.

Yet, his active leadership in Great Neck civic affairs notwithstanding, Zinsser and his family lived a detached social existence in the community. They related most memorably to the bay in front of their home—the peaceful panorama of wildlife and sailing vessels—the small village establishments such as Gilliar's Drug Store, the Great Neck Playhouse, and the railroad station a few miles away. Zinsser's son, William K. Zinsser, who became a well-known writer and editor, felt that the family was different from others in the community. They were not connected to the heartbeat of the suburb they lived in. The remoteness may have had something to do with the location of their house, oriented to the water at the tip of Kings Point, miles away from commercial Great Neck. But their social world was distant as well. According to the younger William Zinsser, he grew up in a family "living in a vale of prosperous WASPs."[74] While beautiful and serene, "it was nowhere near as posh," Zinsser wrote, "as the villages farther out on that gilded coast, like Locust Valley and Oyster Bay, but it did have a prosperous Republican look."[75] There were no Catholics or Jews in their social world, especially since he and his sisters went to private schools in Great Neck and then to boarding school. Their opportunities for advancement and social associations extended easily beyond Great Neck. Boarding schools and clubs made Great Neck less central to the realization of their social and educational ambitions. Beyond their enclave in Kings Point, the Zinssers could reach out to a large, well-connected, receptive WASP world.

For the Zinssers, turning away from Great Neck was not a snobbish or prejudiced flight from the "foreigners" from the Bronx and Brooklyn but recourse to immediately accessible paths of opportunities. The discriminatory obstacles that Jews faced were, in part, the invention of people who automatically took their privileged positions from religion, breeding, and lineage, but not personal accomplishment. E. Digby Baltzell bristled at what he thought were false pretensions and excessive interest in the "ancestry and bloodlines" of the Protestant establishment. Baltzell, his eulogist Art Carney wrote in the *Philadelphia Inquirer*, "knew . . . that for all the so-called 'right people' in the Social Register there were also plenty of bounders, rascals, poseurs, ciphers, phonies . . . and ne'er-do-wells who, deluded by their own mystique, looked down on the vulgar hustlers and strivers who outstripped them in talent, ability and accomplishment, and sought relief from the rage of irrelevance by obsessing over the feats of dead forebears and retreating to their clubs, their hounds, their horses, their racquets or the bottle."[76]

Much of the anti-Semitic animus in Great Neck and throughout America in the 1920s and 1930s came precisely from those who resented the Jewish "vulgar hustlers" and "strivers" with their "talent, ability and accomplishment." This was not true of the Zinssers. Nonetheless, Jews and Gentiles in Great Neck—the Eldridges, Zinssers, and Shores—lived in separate worlds formed by different backgrounds and possibilities. Jews and Gentiles could share common expectations and community accomplishment, but not the same opportunities. None of the Jews in Great Neck could easily enter the Zinssers' world. Jewish students could not be assured that they would be accepted by Ivy League schools; Jewish lawyers and architects could not belong to well-known professional associations; nor could Jewish doctors practice in the medical institutions of their choice. The lines were firm, as Baltzell made clear in *The Protestant Establishment*. So was the damage to American society. The claim to continued leadership by the WASP elite was undermined, he wrote, by its "unwillingness, or inability, to share and improve upper-class traditions by continuously absorbing talented and distinguished members of minority groups into its privileged ranks."[77]

Despite these severe social and economic impediments, the Jewish community in Great Neck believed Great Neck was their entry point into the mainstream of American life. Having built Temple Beth-El and staked their claim to a permanent presence in the community, they turned to local civic life, especially to improving the schools. In moving away from the New York ghettos, they made Great Neck the focus of their dynamic ambitions and aspirations. Their continued mobility and, more importantly, that of their children, depended upon a strong educational system. Detachment from local educational issues and politics—and the two were inextricably intertwined—was not an option for them as it was for Protestants and Catholics.

There was no place, as well, for detachment from the larger realm of national and international events. As America struggled through the Depression, the hopes of Great Neck's Jews were focused on the New Deal; their fears centered on the aggressive anti-Semitic campaigns in Nazi Germany; and their hearts reached out to the impoverished and threatened Jewish families in Eastern Europe. "Spurred by the need for speeding assistance to refugees and other victims of intolerance and oppression in Europe," the *Great Neck Record* stated in June, 1939, "both men and woman in the Great Neck area have organized committees to conduct intensive drives on behalf of the emergency campaign of the United Jewish Appeal for Refugees and Overseas Needs."[78]

This was not the first instance when Great Neck Jews committed to help other Jews in need. But in 1939, their apprehension was different from before. "With the plight of thousands of homeless refugees and the millions of others who are suffering discrimination overseas representing one of the greatest tragedies of modern history," Martin Nadelman, the president of the committee said, "we are prepared to conduct the most intensive relief campaign that Great Neck has ever seen." From their suburban base of relative security, the Jews in Great Neck looked urgently to the west— to their businesses in the city and the sources of their charitable aid—and to the east— to ominous events in Europe, far beyond the enticing play and social privileges of the North Shore.

3

War and Renewal

An American Synagogue

On Rosh Hashanah evening, October 2, 1940, Rabbi Jacob Rudin cast out words of fury and faith to his Temple Beth-El congregation. "No generation of rabbis ever faced a more difficult task than does the one of which I am a part. We see about us a world in disintegration. Jewish life is tortured and hard pressed. Melancholy and despair ride the heavens, glowering birds of prey feeding on the broken hearts of a people well-nigh bereft of hope and faith."[1] He was speaking of Europe, Hitler's power, the unrelenting persecution of European Jewry, and the failure to comprehend what was at stake for democratic nations and humanity. He was telling his congregants that international and national concerns were overtaking their lives. It was the beginning of the decade when Great Neck, his suburb, was impelled to respond to national demands and responsibilities.

Rudin's words presented a disquieting and far-reaching challenge to his small congregation: look beyond the small, white, American community to Europe in conflict and Jews under siege. His members were still recovering from the Depression, thankful just to survive in business, pay taxes, and complete their temple. Gone was the spirit of the 1920s that gave Great Neck its dazzling identity. The retreat to modest needs and ambitions was the order of the day. The interests and predilections of Rudin's congregants (and, in many respects, those of the entire Great Neck population) were conventional, mundane, and locally circumscribed: sustaining business and professional careers in the damaged Depression-ridden economy; meeting mortgage payments and, in a few fortunate instances, enjoying country club memberships; providing a suitable setting for children at home and at the local schools; gaining acceptance and recognition from Protestant and Catholic neighbors; and keeping connections to the city through work, their immigrant families, and friends.

Rudin simultaneously relied upon—and contested—this limited vision of individual and community well being. He confronted the unresolved tension between the spiritual, moral thrust of his leadership and the financial and materialistic fixations of his congregants. In this respect, Rudin's task was similar to that faced by every member of the Great Neck clergy. But, for Rudin, there was a special intensity to the conflict. Since the Reform movement placed little emphasis on ritual, the external and internal signs of religious involvement were primarily focused on activities with broad social, political, and moral issues. As spiritual leader, Rudin had a passionate obligation to share and disseminate his moral and religious beliefs. He sought to imbue his congregants with spiritual caring and responsibility for Jewish learning, traditions, and fellow Jews in Europe and Palestine. To Rudin, Great Neck was a seemingly secure base from which to take on the additional burden of concern for national and international religious and secular issues. Rudin's efforts to bring his moral concerns to his congregation, to turn its attention away from business needs and material pleasures, would strongly mark his long tenure as spiritual leader of Beth-El. The process of reconciling or mediating between his vision and his congregants' way of life would become more intense as postwar prosperity increased the wealth of his members. He wanted and needed strong financial support from the hard-working businessmen and professional members of his young congregation to sustain and expand Beth-El's membership and his position as rabbi.

On that particular Rosh Hashanah eve in October 1940, Rudin combined morality and spirituality with a new emotion—fear. For many in America, both Gentiles and Jews, events in Europe were ominous. But what they meant and how to respond was a matter of raging dispute. How long would Europe cower before German aggression? Who would resist? How far would Germany's internal anti-Semitic war spread across the Continent? How would Europe's turmoil, pitting Fascist states against democratic ones, affect America? For the moment, in the early fall of 1940, President Roosevelt and his administration were executing delicate strategic maneuvers to support Great Britain and, at the same time, maintain America's distance from the conflict.

Rudin quoted the renowned liberal Rev. Harry Emerson Fosdick, pastor of the Riverside Church in New York, who had stated that the war in

Europe was "not primarily about humanitarianism or democracy." Fosdick spoke indignantly of the Nazis extreme and unforgivable "cruelty" towards the Jews as well as the abysmal current state of Polish Jews. But, in Fosdick's view, persecution of the Jews was not a cause of the war. In fact the minister observed that the "the persecution of the Jews could have gone on, as it has gone on for centuries, with no war started about it." "This conflict," he concluded, "does involve issues that will affect the democratic cause, but at bottom it is a fight for the balance of political power in Europe."[2]

Rudin dissented from this traditional nineteenth-century international doctrine: "Harry Emerson Fosdick is wrong! This war *is* about the Jews!" Rudin exclaimed. "It's about those very Polish Jews whose persecution, he says, could have gone on for centuries into the future. This war is about the indifference of the world that let that persecution go on. This war is about the German Jews who were hounded and torn and crushed into the Nazi mire. This war is about injustice concerning which men kept silent, about unrighteousness that men accepted, about savagery that men said was an internal affair of Germany."[3] On this point, Rudin was emphatic.

But what role did Europe's Jews play in terms of the causes of the war? Rudin was equally assertive and bold. Despite the isolationists and anti-Semites, such as Charles Lindbergh and Father Coughlin, who led one side of the vitriolic American debate, Rudin refused to allow the onus to fall on the Jews. "Then is this war because of the Jews?" Rudin asked. "No, not because of the Jews. But Jews are the microcosm. They reflect within themselves the larger humanity. It is not because mankind was indifferent to Jews, as Jews, that the war came. It was because mankind was indifferent to mankind. . . . This war is because men let hate loose in the world and did nothing to stop it."[4]

How, Rudin asked, must his congregants face the threats, despair, and uncertainty confronting Europe and America? "What shall Israel say in this dark hour? Do you seek an easy, comfortable answer? There is none. These are evil days, when men must be giants. Out of every abyss of despair and from every lonely mountaintop, Israel's voice of fortitude and of patience, of rock enduring faith has echoed. 'Even though He slay me, yet will I trust in Him.' And Israel on this New Year's Day is not afraid. Israel knows, Israel knows that God, Israel's Redeemer, liveth."[5]

These thunderous, portentous words of fury and faith were delivered to a small group of Jews, joined together in the only temple on the North Shore, surrounded by Gentile neighbors in a peaceful community, sixteen miles from New York City. Despite the seeming normalcy of life—

business, children, and an array of leisure distractions—their rabbi was raging on monumental matters. Rudin took on the role, as a Reform rabbi, of moral authority and conscience.

The congregation expected nothing less from Rudin, a protégé of Rabbi Stephen Wise, founder and leader of the Free Synagogue and Jewish Institute of Religion in the 1920s in New York. Wise sent Rudin as his emissary of social concern to the burgeoning Jewish community in Great Neck. Wise, the radical rabbi, took on the world from his pulpit as an eloquent and irrepressible activist for social justice: founder of the American Jewish Congress, the Zionist Organization of America, and the World Jewish Congress. His campaigns on domestic and foreign issues, especially after Hitler gained power in Germany in 1932, transformed him into a national Jewish figure with access to President Roosevelt and members of Congress and the Supreme Court.

Rudin first encountered Wise as a junior at Harvard. The young student planned after graduation to study for the rabbinate at Hebrew Union College in Cincinnati, the established rabbinic teaching institute of the Reform movement. Wise's "voice shook us as a wind shakes the reeds," Rudin wrote many years later about the rabbi's visit to Harvard. He "talked about Jews and Jewish identity. He talked of a homeland for the Jews. He talked about justice in an unjust world."[6] Wise completely captivated the aspiring rabbi-to-be who switched his sights from the traditional training ground for Reform rabbis in Cincinnati and joined Wise at his small, experimental school in New York. Wise's style and many of his concerns became the hallmark of Rudin's rabbinic career: a strong emphasis on social issues; lesser stress on rituals; services in English; little communal study of Torah; a fervent belief in Zionism; and a use of spirited oratory, on behalf of social issues, that magnified the centrality, personality, and authority of the rabbi. The two men became close; Rudin became Wise's assistant in the synagogue and Institute—despite the fact that when Rudin gave his first sermon in class, Wise remarked that it "set new standards in ineffectiveness."[7]

Wise officiated at the wedding of Jack Rudin and Elsie Katz, a teacher from Brooklyn, in 1926. The next year, with Wise's blessing, the Rudins moved from the city to lead Temple Beth-El. Wise remained the dominant influence on Rudin. (Elsie and Jack Rudin named their son after Stephen Wise. When Steve Rudin was a bar mitzvah, it was Wise who officiated since Rudin was serving in the Pacific as a Navy chaplain.) Beyond the discrepancy in their ages, however, there were marked differences between the idol and acolyte. For many years, the young Rudin's

sphere of influence did not extend beyond his suburb and local constitu-
ency, compared to Wise's broad connections to state and national political
leaders. One might observe that Wise had fire in his belly in his role as
national activist, while Rudin, the rabbi of a fledgling suburban Reform
temple, tempered his passion and eloquence in the service of a suburban
congregation. Within the Reform movement itself, of approximately 60,000
people affiliated in 285 temples, Wise was a rebel who went so far as to
lead services at Carnegie Hall for Jews and Christians.[8] Rudin, on the other
hand, never established any radical theological or liturgical views throughout his career in Great Neck or later when he gained national leadership
in the Reform movement.

But building an appealing, successful Jewish community was a gamble
and a feat in the suburbs. There were challenges a-plenty for Rudin in
leading the way to Jewish institutional and individual acceptance in Great
Neck. His job was to build a permanent place for Jews among Great Neck's
Gentiles and to gain for Temple Beth-El the allegiance of Jews who were
venturing beyond the ghettoes of the immigrant city. That migratory tide
was running strong as Jews abandoned the Lower East Side. The Jewish
population fell by half between 1916 and 1930, to 121,000 people.[9]

Beyond his youthful years, ever appropriate to the young temple, Rudin
brought the image and experiences of a transitional figure who had been
raised in a modest Orthodox family in Roxbury, Massachusetts but had
successfully adopted the precepts of the most assimilating and assimilated
branch of Judaism. Harvard educated, Reform-trained, eloquent in English, impressive in appearance with a broad, handsome face and a sono-
rous, powerful voice, Rudin presented the image and reality of American
Jewish religious success.

Amazingly, Rudin and his congregation had built their temple during
the Depression, when membership dramatically declined among the 3,700
American synagogues. Beth-El gained its members in a period, according
to historian Michael A. Meyer, of prevailing "lassitude with regard to
observance and education." Religion among both Gentiles and Jews, he
wrote, was seen "as an ornament of bourgeois culture."[10] According to the
sociologist Nathan Glazer, there were 50,000 affiliated Reform Jews, 57,000
affiliated Conservative Jews and 200,000 Orthodox Jews who altogether
constituted only one-quarter to one-third of all Jews in America.[11]

And yet, there was something compelling about Reform Judaism, especially for many in the younger generation who sought to escape Orthodoxy
but still maintain Jewish religious connections as part of their suburban

lives. In the 1930s Reform Judaism was successful at attracting Jews who
were on the rise financially and socially, particularly Eastern European
immigrant Jews. The value of assimilation, especially in the early suburban Gentile model, worked in Rudin's favor. Beth-El had no competition
in terms of other types of local Jewish affiliations. His temple was the
single focus of institutional Jewish life. There were no indigenous Jewish
social welfare or cultural organizations that made financial demands on
its members; nor were there any observant Conservative or Orthodox institutions that might have visibly highlighted a self-imposed separation of
Jews and Gentiles.

Rudin called Beth-El an "American synagogue . . . part of the fabric of
our country's life."[12] It was a religious institution that sought to establish
a foothold while creating no offense or challenge to Great Neck's Protestant and Catholic churches and Gentile population, which included many
who still barred Jews from buying homes in certain areas and discouraged Jewish membership in its most prestigious clubs. Rudin had a considerable challenge in reaching out to Catholic St. Aloysius, with 2,500
members; the Episcopal St. Paul's Church and the Grace Church, which,
together, had over 1,100 members; and the Community Church, with its
263 members. In befriending the Christian clergy and parishioners, according to an official Beth-El history, Rudin "leveled the ground for Jews in
Great Neck, making this a community where Jewish life could flourish."[13]
Rudin's association with the Christian clergy and access to the churches
through the friendly etiquette of suburban mixing served as the symbol
of acceptance. It was, in fact, the substitute for any real socializing and
interaction between Gentiles and Jews in the community.

THE GREAT NECK JEWISH PROFILE

Numbers, satisfaction, and dedication were crucial in building a Jewish
temple and making Jewish life "flourish." The existence of the temple was
an essential sign that Jews could live in Great Neck and that there were
enough of them, committed to religious participation through the Reform
movement, to make it safe and desirable for others to try it out. But what
really attracted Jews to Great Neck, and what kept them there? Pauline
Boorstein's 1937 master's thesis for Teachers College at Columbia University provides some answers. Boorstein, a graduate of Smith, took the
town that she had recently moved into as her sociological subject.[14]

Unquestionably, a sample of residents has limited value in representing the community as a whole. The quantification of answers to Boorstein's written questionnaire and personal interviews gives few insights into the dynamics of leadership and individual contributions to community life. Nonetheless, her compilation of attitudes and expectations indicate prevalent views. Boorstein's field of inquiry was a community of approximately 17,000 people, mostly between twenty-five and forty-five years of age, situated in fast-growing Nassau County with its population of 303,000. Her fifty subjects were equally divided between Gentiles (both Protestants and Catholics) and Jews (overwhelmingly Reform). Almost all of the people in the study were between thirty-five and forty-five years old. Most had been married at least five years. The Jewish interviewees were people with whom Boorstein was friendly. The Gentile interviewees were parents of her children's friends; people recommended by her friends; and referees from Margaret Johnson, the principal of Kensington School, one of Great Neck's two elementary schools. Boorstein collated statistical information and drew conclusions from questionnaires that she distributed to each of the participants and from personal interviews she held with each of her fifty participants.

A major, but hardly surprising, conclusion weaves through her study: the differences between Gentiles and Jews in terms of background, interests and objectives were deep. "After several families had been questioned," she wrote, "there were to be found decided differences between the Gentile and Jewish groups as regarded their adaptability to suburban living."[15] The differences began with basic histories: one quarter of Jews were foreign-born, the rest were born in New York; none came from New England, the Middle West, or the South, where most of the Gentiles had grown up.[16] One-tenth of the Gentiles were foreign-born. According to the Fifteenth Census, among the city's suburbs, Great Neck had the highest percentage of foreign-born inhabitants, with 48.9 percent; Cedarhurst was the next, Garden City and Bronxville last.[17]

Gentiles had grown up in houses in small towns or the country; Jews in apartments in the city.[18] All of the Jewish families had lived in New York City before moving to Great Neck. Three-fifths of the Gentiles had not lived in the city.[19] Gentile families were generally larger than the Jewish ones.[20] Jewish women and Gentile women generally had similar educations, whereas Gentile men were more likely than Jewish men to have completed college.[21] More Jews rented their homes than owned, but the Jewish owners had more expensive houses.[22] Gentiles were more likely to buy when they moved to Great Neck, whereas the Jews started off by rent-ing.[23] The medium length of residence in the suburbs was eight years for the Gentiles and four for the Jews. Three-quarters of the Gentile men were in professions or executives in large corporations; three-quarters of the Jewish men owned their own businesses, with a fifth of them in the clothing business.[24]

The differences continued: most of the Gentiles moved to Great Neck for business reasons whereas most of the Jews said they wanted to live in a better neighborhood and convenient location. A second group of Jews said that they moved to be near friends or relatives while the third rea-son given was to get more room.[25] Only eight of the Jewish subjects said that they were interested in being "near good schools."[26] In fact, most be-lieved that the schools in Westchester were better than Great Neck's. While Manhasset schools were also regarded as better, Boorstein noted "there is a decided racial exclusion of the Jews in that community or many of the Jewish families living in Great Neck might have preferred Manhasset for that reason."[27] There were other sundry reasons that made Great Neck desirable for Jews. It developed the reputation that it had a "nice" Jewish community with a temple.[28] Rentals were lower than in Westchester, as were taxes for schools. Socializing with friends was more informal than in the city. Commuting was better on the railroad than the subways. Boor-stein posited that Jews moved to be near friends or families, because of "the gregarious characteristic of Jews as a whole."[29]

Boorstein was particularly interested in examining a basic conclusion of the President's Conference on Home Building and Ownership. The 1936 report stated that half of the people who moved to the suburbs did so to "benefit" children and family life.[30] Boorstein's interviews did not confirm this conclusion as far as the Jewish families were concerned. The Jews moved to Great Neck after having had children and in time for them to go to school. Gentiles moved there mostly before having children.[31] Boorstein stated that "the husbands are not better fathers [than city peers] nor are they fonder of the home than city men. The general outside opinion is that sub-urban husbands are even less devoted to their families than city husbands."[32]

Many of the female interviewees mentioned the indifference of their husbands toward the children and only in ten of the Jewish families was companionship of husband and children emphasized.[33] Some reasons were given for the lack of companionship, such as getting home late from work in the city, the diverting activities that the community provided, and the increased time that children spent with their friends. "Many times at social gatherings when the husbands are discussing their golf scores, the wives are registering complaints on the lack of companionship between the husbands and the children and wives are often heard admonishing their husbands for this."[34] And yet there was a striking and surprising response when the interviewees were asked why they thought their friends moved to Great Neck. Fifteen Jewish respondents and an equal number of Gentiles said that their friends had moved for the children's sake. Thus the general perception, which may have been erroneous according to Boorstein's respondents, was that other people moved to Great Neck to benefit children and their families as a whole.

Jews participated in community activities less than Gentiles.[35] The Jewish residents were most active in the temple and raising money for Jewish causes in the city as well as aiding refugees. Jewish families tended to go to the city much more than Gentile families, during the day as well as for evening events. Friendships among Jews and Gentiles did not develop frequently or with ease: "while the Jewish and Gentile children play together, very few Gentile and Jewish families 'mix' socially in Great Neck. One Jewish woman tried to mingle with the parents of her children's friends, and to introduce her friends to them. She found that the Gentiles who were willing to become friendly were undesirable and she dropped the matter, admitting that she was much happier with her Jewish friends."[36] Among some Jewish interviewees, there was the impression that Gentile daughters had a better social life in Great Neck than Jewish ones.[37] One Jewish mother commented: "My eldest daughter is dissatisfied in Great Neck and we object to her going out with the garage man's son or the gardener's son, who are popular boys at the high school. These people are not on her social level and in the New York progressive schools she will meet suitable companions."[38]

Nearly half of the Jewish families said they would have preferred to live in the city, while only five of the Gentile families expressed that preference.[39] Many Jews said they would move back to the city if they had the financial means.[40] Thirteen Jewish families said they wanted to stay in Great Neck, as did fourteen of the Gentile interviewees. Jews also thought that none of their friends would stay in the suburbs, while Gentiles thought most of their friends would stay.[41]

In summary, the statistical profiles that Boorstein gathered, as well as her conclusion, confirmed many generally recognized patterns of social and family life in the 1930s. The Gentiles were used to living in the country or suburbs, whereas the Jews were used to city life. Jews and Gentiles did not mix socially. Jews tended to spend more time in the city working for Jewish charities and seeing their families. Both Gentiles and Jews chose Great Neck over more expensive towns in Westchester—such as New Rochelle for the Jews or Bronxville or Scarsdale for the Gentiles. Gentile families expected to stay in Great Neck or another suburb. The Jews looked forward to moving back to the city at some point.

There were, however, some surprising conclusions. While people thought that others moved to the suburb for the children, a significant number of interviewees denied this intention. And once in the suburbs, the benefits for family life proved to be something of a myth as well. In her final conclusion about suburban Great Neck and the family, Boorstein stated bleakly: "It seems therefore that suburban living is not an agency for keeping the family intact."[42]

In this period, almost ten years into the Depression and a decade beyond the fun years of the 1920s, Great Neck encouraged few inflated expectations nor, for the Jewish interviewees, a sense of permanence of place. It was simply convenient and a step up. For many Jewish families who had close ties to their immigrant families in Brooklyn or the Lower East Side, living in far-off places such as California, or even Westchester, which was hard to reach from Brooklyn, was not acceptable. Great Neck was relatively inexpensive, pleasant, and well-situated within a network of trains and highways connecting to the city. There was easy access to the city for work since Penn Station was just a few blocks south of factories and showrooms in the garment district. Great Neck allowed people to escape the confinements of Jewish city neighborhoods while still fulfilling family rituals and responsibilities: on Friday nights, Sabbath dinner at their parents' apartments or homes in the city; on Sundays, the visit, in reverse, when parents took the train to Great Neck to see their children and grandchildren at play. The visits, however, were not necessarily filled with joy and satisfaction. One young non-Jew who grew up in the 1940s recollected: "It seemed like my Jewish friends had relatives visiting them almost every weekend. And most of the relatives were what I subsequently learned were called 'kvetches.' Complainers. The grandmother on the father's side was always complaining about the children being too skinny, and on the mother's side that the garden didn't look as nice as last year, or that the food was too salty or too cold or too hot. They were all there on the Bar Mitzvah day too but nobody ever complained on that very special day."[43]

Although there had been some expansion in its population in the previous decade, in 1940 Great Neck was basically static in character and spirit.

The contours of the Gentile community seemed simple and enduring: two Episcopal churches; one Catholic Church; one Methodist and the Community Church—totaling over 4,000 members; one Reform temple with 200 members; a few banks and stores on Middle Neck Road, a railroad station, a high school and two elementary schools; and a small number of locally employed doctors, service people, and real estate agents. For many women, there was a sense of emptiness that permeated the weekdays when husbands went to work in the city and women filled their days taking care of their children and participating in local organizations. But the compensations were compelling: modest property costs and taxes that were less demanding than the city's or Westchester's; a plentitude of homes to buy or rent; an attractive residential landscape, with clean streets and nice lawns, which reinforced the all-important differences between city and country life; the insignia of social and economic mobility; for Jewish residents, assimilation into a Gentile community; and, for all those living in Great Neck, distance from America's racial issues.

The Pressures of War

These were the assets of normalcy—the essence of peacetime concerns—in the minds of Great Neck residents until dire European events intruded into their suburban world in the fall of 1939. When Germany invaded Poland, neither the Atlantic Ocean nor the mental grip of isolationism could shield America from the European conflict. America's well-being was at risk. From that moment on, Great Neck's fate was inextricably tied to Washington, D.C. and decisions taken by President Roosevelt, his administration, and Congress. On all fronts—politically, militarily, economically, socially, and racially—American life and expectations began to depart from ordinary, prosaic domestic concerns. For American Jews the importance of European events transcended America's vulnerability: anti-Semitism was a lethal weapon of German power and conquest.

National and international issues engulfed Great Neck's perspective and orbit. Impersonal forces, national and international in scope, assumed deeply personal consequences. In Great Neck and throughout the country, everyone looked to Washington as the president forced the country to take account of its weaknesses. The most pressing related to military weakness, raw materials and industrial production: the American army ranked eighteenth in the world; Germany had 6.8 million men trained for war, the

United States had 504,000; the arms industry was moribund; and there was only a six-month supply of tin and rubber, 90 percent of which originated in the Dutch colony of Indonesia.[44]

In June 1940, after Germany had conquered most of Western Europe, the President told Congress that within twelve months, the United States would start to produce 50,000 airplanes a year to exceed Germany's capacity. Roosevelt placed the country on the offensive in terms of industrial production. Privately owned American manufacturers in concert with the government had to convert to a war economy to supply America and Great Britain as well. America was to be prepared in case it went to war, but Great Britain was fighting for America which at the time had no intention of declaring war against Germany.

The introduction of conscription accelerated industrial production for armaments and manufactured goods, especially clothing for the military. These developments deeply affected life in Great Neck. Fathers, husbands, and sons were drafted into the armed service; those who couldn't serve produced essential goods. Many women, although few from middle-class Great Neck, went to work to replace men who had gone into the service. Production took precedence. All other economic and social demands and issues were secondary. This meant that the development of industrial and military strength, as Roosevelt demanded, would accommodate to America's racial patterns and ethnic prejudices. Intolerant American attitudes made the issue of European Jewish refugees intractable and tragic—and particularly poignant for the few refugee families that settled in Great Neck. Despite the pleading of Jewish leaders such as Rabbi Stephen Wise, America restricted the entry of Jewish refugees from Germany and other countries threatened by the Nazis. Between 1933 and 1940, the United States had taken in only 105,000 refugees. Anti-immigrant legislation passed in the 1920s and anti-Semitism in the 1930s—at its strongest in American history—pressed upon Roosevelt's policies. FDR, in the words of historian Doris Kearns Goodwin, was sympathetic to Jews and concerned about the refugee situation, but he would not openly fight the national mood or repudiate the State Department's unfriendly policies to Jewish refugees. It was clear in 1940, as would be the case throughout the war years, that Jewish issues were not regarded as vital or compelling in the framework of American needs and priorities.

In the realm of America's conflicted social and economic order, American anti-Semitism, fueled in the 1930s by deep suspicions of Jews in general and Jewish immigrants in particular, took second place to the potentially explosive issue of segregation. Racial intolerance against America's black population permeated every American institution, organization, and workplace. It affected the whole country, even white suburbs such as Great Neck, which, for the moment, lay far from the front lines of Jim Crow laws. The administration's need for manpower in the armed forces and industry came into conflict with the desire to maintain blacks in positions of servitude and separation. Blacks were consigned, by pernicious law in the South, and habit in the North, Middle West and West, to the lowest jobs and opportunities. The Armed Forces were no different. There were a few thousand blacks in the Army and Navy, but none in the Marines, Air Corps, Signal Corps, or Tank Corps.

In 1940 and 1941, as the country prepared for the possibility of war, England, despite American aid, grew weaker. Some relief was gained when Germany opened its eastern front and invaded Russia. For Roosevelt, events in the Pacific were equally troubling. He feared that America would be first drawn into a war in the Pacific. The President's apprehensions were fully justified. The Japanese stunned America with a surprise attack at Pearl Harbor on December 7 in addition to air assaults on the Philippines, Hong Kong, and several other Pacific Islands. Unprotected and unprepared—not even on alert—the navy lost 3,500 men, eight destroyers, and half of the airplanes in the Pacific.

On December 8, FDR informed Congress and the American people that the country was at war and that it would triumph. American isolationism was dead. The country went on a full-time war basis. On December 11, Hitler declared war on the United States. From that moment on, the country fought on two fronts across two immense oceans in what Kearns characterized as "history's greatest armed conflict." American industry, FDR told the American public, would produce equipment at a staggering rate: by 1943, the United States would be turning out "a plane every four minutes . . . ; a tank every seven minutes; two seagoing ships a day."[45] This wasn't all. Clothing, ammunition, rations, housing, trucks, airplanes and tanks and thousands of essential materials to outfit the armed forces for war would be manufactured. A faltering consumer economy, still burdened by the Depression, stopped in its tracks and became a full-fledged war economy that would find new resources; make new materials, equipment, and medicines; and produce new armaments and weapons, including the atomic bomb.

In Great Neck, the personal consequences were immediate and profound as thousands of men in the community went into service, including

159 members of Temple Beth-El. Rabbi Jack Rudin was one of them. The day after the attack on Pearl Harbor, he enlisted in the Navy as part of the Chaplain's Corp. The need to serve and minister to men who would fight America's enemies turned Rudin into an activist in the clergy. His absence from Great Neck over the next three years would leave a spiritual hole in the congregation that he had led for the past thirteen years. For his congregation, the rabbi's commitment to the war effort reinforced the reality and importance of the war, the departures from normal life, the sacrifices and dangers.

Rudin joined the Navy, the branch of the armed forces that attracted a disproportionate number of privileged Gentiles, while strongly discouraging the inclusion of blacks and Jews. Rudin, having honed the skills of gaining respect from Gentile Great Neck, may have felt capable of making a mark where Jews were not welcome. The experience of giving spiritual guidance to men away from home and close to combat affected Rudin deeply. One of the highpoints of that ministry occurred in 1943 during his four-week visit to Alaska and the Aleutian Islands. He was dispatched to conduct Sabbath and Passover services to Jewish soldiers in the Navy and Army who were stationed at the farthest outposts on the North American continent. To reach the men, Rudin flew over 4,000 miles by plane to Anchorage and the Aleutian Islands.

He reported on the trip to his superior officers in Washington: "Everywhere that I went," he wrote, "I was greeted with the deepest kind of satisfaction by the men. The presence of a Jewish Chaplain for the Passover made the holiday meaningful to them. Services, naturally enough, had to be conducted in some places where the physical surroundings left much to be desired." That was no impediment to the rabbi's mission. "Yet," he continued, "everywhere a sense of humble reverence and of quiet worshipfulness created their own atmosphere and transformed drabness and dullness into shining beauty. My own spiritual life has been quickened and enriched by this contact with men who, in the midst of war, and far from all that is dear and precious to them, are yet able to keep the fires of faith burning bright and clear."[46]

Rudin, the Reform rabbi, brought bibles, hagaddahs, tallitim, matzos and 225 mezzuahs for the men who attended services at the many stops that he made. When he couldn't find wine for the Seders, he borrowed some from the Christian chaplains who used it for communion. In Dutch Harbor, the Seder was held in an Army mess hall, with food prepared by a kitchen crew of non-Jews. Rudin called it a "gala" event for 200 men.

"It was absolutely traditional," he wrote proudly, "down to the last raisin and chopped nut." And, "it was really a thrilling sight. The packed mess hall echoed with the obviously happy voices of the men. Many were at their first service in years. Others rejoiced because they had been afraid that their military service would render a Seder impossible."[47]

When he returned from the trip a month later, he wrote letters to the families of the men that he met to report on their welfare. At the end of his eighty-three page, handwritten report, Rudin concluded: "I suppose the trip might be described as being hazardous, at times at least. Frankly, I never considered it in that light at all. There was always a sense of deepest satisfaction and of accomplishment." In a veiled reference to his suburban experience, he observed: "Rabbis are not always sure that what they are doing has meaning for others. I *knew* that this work was rich and good. Men needed something that I was privileged to bring them. The ancient Jewish tradition of sharing faith and fellowship and Torah was mine to fulfill. It was a joy to serve in this tradition. It was a source of pride to wear our country's uniform and wearing it, to speak of Israel's deathless loyalty to God."[48]

While Rudin was in the Pacific, the war changed the lives of his congregants who remained at home. Everyone knew someone in the armed forces; everyone feared casualties and deaths. Many Great Neck men who could not serve due to age or physical handicaps became rich in industries making goods, such as clothing, that were critical for the war effort. In nearby New Hyde Park, the Sperry Gyroscope Corporation built a large plant to fulfill defense contracts. Close to the plant, developers built hundreds of modest houses, distinctly different in size and price from the rest of Great Neck, for its workers. Beth-El members planted a victory garden at the temple. It was also considered for use as a potential bomb shelter.

The physical changes in the community were modest in comparison to many other parts of the country, but Great Neck families were affected by new social, religious, and economic conditions. From America's heartland, Protestants and Catholics came into contact with Jewish men for the first time. For Jews from immigrant families, assimilation intensified at unprecedented rates. Soldiers traveled to parts of the country they had never seen before. City men trained for the service in rural America. Suddenly, the prevalence of overt anti-Semitism began to recede under the gargantuan needs of the war machine.

White America started to accept white ethnic and religious groups as part of their own community: white, not black. Although FDR committed the United States to defeat the Germans and the Japanese and uphold the dignity of all men, the rhetoric and goals glossed over the ugly realities of American racial prejudice against blacks and Japanese Americans. Despite the moralistic war goals and the need for manpower, white America was not prepared to grant blacks parity in the military or substantial opportunities in industry through improved wages and working conditions. Blacks left farms in the South to work in plants in Northern cities but they had to endure segregated housing, inferior employment, discrimination in housing and transportation, racial attacks, and riots.

On April 12, 1945, Roosevelt died of a cerebral hemorrhage. His successor, former Vice-President Harry Truman, fulfilled FDR's goals: Germany's defeat; Japan's capitulation, after America dropped the atom bomb; and the birth of the United Nations. When the war ended, the Allies assessed the dimensions of destruction in Europe and the Pacific. Russia, rapidly turning into the America's newest foe, lost twenty million soldiers and civilians; Germany and Japan, ruined and occupied, lost 6.8 million and three million people respectively; and Britain, proud but weak, lost almost 500,000 at home and in the Commonwealth.

European Jewry was diminished by the deaths of nearly six million people. Their deaths transcended the common expectations of western countries in regard to warfare: combat, conquest, spoils, retreat, defeat, and victory. German-inspired anti-Semitism obliterated Jewish life in Eastern Europe and devastated survivors and their families throughout the world. Rudin's words, spoken in October 1940, were prophetic: "No generation of rabbis ever faced a more difficult task than does the one of which I am a part. We see about us a world in disintegration. Jewish life is tortured and hard pressed. Melancholy and despair ride the heavens, glowering birds of prey feeding on the broken hearts of a people well-nigh bereft of hope and faith." In 1945, American Jews, Great Neck Jews among them, began the long, slow task of coming to terms with their devastating losses. The suffering, for all Americans, Gentiles and Jews, from the horrific traumas of war were buried under stoic efforts of quietly and privately forgetting. America celebrated victory and tried to put aside the fears, sacrifice and psychological wounds of combat.

Great Neck Jews, like the rest of America, rushed back to the concerns of family, friends, and work. Victorious America emerged as a different country with particular significance for American Jews. The changes brought about by the war were staggering. Twelve million men and woman had served in the military; fifteen million men and women had moved to new jobs; families moved from one part of the country to the other—all forging a new national identity. America was no longer a nation where xenophobia and anti-Semitism were as rampant as they had been in the 1930s. In the postwar accounting of victories and losses, American anti-Semitism lost much of its previous force under the pressure of democracy's wartime goals. American Jews were the beneficiaries, but not American blacks.

PROSPERITY AND THE FORCES OF CHANGE

America's new position as undisputed economic and military leader of the democratic world helped ease the trauma of the war years. Unheard-of levels of income and wealth reached vast numbers of white Americans. Generous government benefit programs for GIs, including mortgages and schooling, continued the transformation of American life. There was a new assertiveness and confidence in possibilities of meeting pressing demands. Industrial growth and restricted consumer spending during the Depression and war years gave way to a spending spree on housing, appliances, clothes, and entertainment. In Great Neck there was an explosion of expectations, needs, demands for educational improvements for children and adults, expansion of religious institutions, services, goods, housing, shopping centers. Great Neck came alive with realizable ambitions for families to return to normal life, for men to succeed at their jobs, for children to work hard at school, and families once again to have fun.

Men, if they had been in the services, went back to making money for their families and children. Those who had not served, but stayed in business during the war years, benefited as never before from the wealth that flowed out of the city's commercial life. An entrepreneur's wildest dreams of selling consumer goods to the mass market came true. Great Neck cashed in. The new economy favored large numbers of Great Neck Jews who owned their own businesses, especially in the manufacture of expensive or cheap clothing; well-made or "schlock"; high-end or low-end; fancy or casual; for men, women, and children. Shirts, dresses, coats, furs, sweaters, lingerie, zippers, pants, and suits—all designed and largely produced in New York on Seventh Avenue for America's national market. Wilfred Cohen, one of the most successful of the clothing manufacturers who lived in Great Neck, promoted his line of Arthur Allen Clothes.

But clothing didn't make up the whole story: Great Neck's entrepreneurs owned small-scale operations in real estate, jewelry, shopping centers, construction companies, cemeteries, parking lots, the production of corrugated boxes, furniture, paper bags, plastics, magazines, and hair-dressing equipment. An array of insurance brokers, accountants, and advertisers, as well as stockbrokers who invested the profits and lawyers who implemented the deals, serviced these entrepreneurs.

Once again, fortunes were made in suburban land as developers converted estates, farms, and woods into sites for houses. More homes meant more people, roads, shops, and parks. Among individuals and the community as a whole, a renewed spirit of competitive dynamic change took hold. With the strong economy and high demand, men worked hard and women, who didn't need to or were not expected to work inside or outside the home, gained more free time. With zeal, they joined community and religious organizations, shopped, pursued cultural interests, and played sports. A fever of consuming and community building set in that went hand-in-hand with a sober set of actions and aspirations. Great Neck needed to meet the increasingly ambitious educational demands of its residents and, with success, attract people—all kinds of people—on the move to the suburbs.

This spirit of purpose was decidedly different from the frenzied 1920s as well as the late 1930s when Pauline Boorstein had concluded that a majority of her Jewish interviewees were destined to return to the city after their children had grown up: "As for racial differences," she wrote, "the suburb is more likely to exist as a more permanent institution for Gentiles than for Jews."[49] The war changed this predisposition and trend. As the numbers increased, Jews in Great Neck felt a more permanent sense that the suburb, and Great Neck in particular, was the place to be.

Transforming Public Education

Great Neck residents, new and long-established, turned to activism as the pace of suburban living sped up. They embarked on crusades of civic participation in neighborhood, educational, religious, political, social welfare, and recreational organizations. Not limited to the perimeters of the peninsula, residents also looked to similar efforts in the city, state, and nation. Talented leaders, both men and women, emerged to seek community-wide influence and power in education, philanthropy, religious institutions, and politics: John L. Miller, Jack Hausman and his wife Ethel, Wilford P. Cohen, David and Norma Levitt, Joe and Hilda Liff, Max Rubin, Josselyn Shore, and Bernard Thomson. These people put Great Neck back on the competitive map. They relished growth, prosperity, success, and emerging regional, state, and national recognition.

In the postwar period, the attraction of suburban excellence began with education. It was both a need and passion that grew along with Great Neck's expanding, impatient, and demanding Jewish population. Education in Great Neck meant Americanization, the critical integration of the second generation into Protestant America's ethos and manners. As the historian Paul Johnson observed, American public schools were nonsectarian, but "not nonreligious." America's separation of church and state in its public educational structures was of a particular kind. "In the American system," Johnson wrote, "the schools supplied Christian 'character-building' and the parent at home topped it off with sectarian trimmings."[50]

This was fine with the Jewish population in Great Neck after the war, a population that mainly belonged to the Reform Temple or was nonaffiliated, that eagerly sought dialogue with its Christian counterparts; Gentile teachers; Gentile administrators; and traditional neighborhood schools built of red brick, guarded by white columns, and graced by ascending steps to their entrance doors. All of these reinforced the image of American assimilation. The underlying principles were republican but the spirit was Christian. The combination, Johnson wrote, worked "because in effect republicanism was itself based upon the old Protestant moral and ethical consensus . . . the American way of life began to function as the operative creed of the public schools and it was gradually accepted as the official philosophy of American state education." Jews and Catholics, who opted for the public school system, "became to some extent Protestantized, thereby aligning the political ideals and practices of the United States with a broad-based Christianity."[51]

Finding the Christian-American spirit in the public schools was desirable as long as the Jewish population could push the system to the extreme of academic excellence. Superior standards were indispensable to ensure access to America's colleges and universities. Great Neck fathers, many with no more than a high school degree, were making big money on Seventh Avenue or in real estate ventures. But their children had to aim for Harvard, Yale, Princeton and other schools that were seen as the gateways to American status and success. Real mobility, from the Jewish perspective, related to educational and professional achievement. Restrictive quotas in the Ivy League and other prominent American academic institutions placed Great Neck's Jewish students at a disadvantage for a limited number of places at colleges and universities. Great Neck students had to have a strong shot at the few places available to Jews within the quota system. To make this possible, the Great Neck public schools had to equal or exceed the quality of private schools that traditionally fed students into the best of American colleges and universities. At the very least, Great Neck schools had to match the quality of high schools in Brooklyn or the Bronx.

While the country as a whole faced a postwar crisis in its school systems because of too few teachers, poor pay, segregated schools, deferred maintenance of buildings, and controversies over the vocational or academic nature of high school education, Great Neck asserted its educational priorities. Education came first. The taxpayers would pay. College preparation was the goal. The school administration accommodated the leadership of its most demanding and ambitious parents. Teachers were respected. Discipline was maintained. Even the suburban landscape contrived to fix the focus. There were no visual or structural competitors to challenge the supremacy of the schools or draw attention away from them. There were no commercial centers that dominated the town, as they did in great urban areas, no grand buildings and no monuments to the past. The Great Neck landscape was a pleasing blend of churches, a temple, a few farms, new homes that supplemented the older stock from the turn of the century and the boom years of the 1920s, new roads, and a few modest-sized commercial buildings. Everything in the postwar period conspired to pay homage to the centrality of school structures and encouraged the process of elevating the stature of teachers and incorporating parental resources.

An increased population of school-minded people meant a larger tax base to draw from. The school board, teachers, administrators, parent-teacher associations, all the players in the educational field, became the focus of scrutiny and community-wide associations after the end of the war. The drive affected the character of the community and not just the schools themselves. With the exception of the Catholic population that supported an elementary parochial school, the Great Neck schools became the unifying mission and force among Great Neck's many villages. There were different police, fire, sewer, and park departments, but the school district encompassed the whole peninsula. In 1945 the educational stock consisted of three elementary schools, Kensington, Arrandale, and Lakeville (originally there had been two Lakeville schools, one for whites and one for blacks), and the high school, completed in 1929.

Before the late 1940s when Great Neck reinvented itself through its schools, the Depression had put it through hard times. School taxes were kept low. Fights over expenditures often led to hotly contested school board elections. Teachers were forced to take a 10 percent pay cut in a system that did not pay well, compared to Manhasset and other communities. The system was viewed as rigid and nonprogressive. The problems were compounded in 1938, when high school students rebelled to protest the firing of four popular teachers. The headline in the *Great Neck News* told it all: "Students Strike at High School: 400 Refuse to Attend Classes Yesterday After Dismissal of Four Teachers." The principal and superintendent tried to address the students but they wouldn't listen. In the evening, 1,500 parents met to confront the crisis. Within a short time, the principal, superintendent, and several teachers lost their jobs.[52]

In 1942, the system stabilized when Dr. John Lewis Miller became the new superintendent. He was a committed teacher and educator, trained as an undergraduate at Bates College, in Maine, and at Harvard, where he received his Ph.D. in literature. He started as an English teacher on Cape Cod and worked his way up in the Massachusetts system to become superintendent of the Brockton schools. It was a big job but one with little future in a shoe manufacturing city in decline. Miller was a natural fit for Great Neck, which had always attracted teachers from New England, and from Maine in particular. For Miller, Great Neck felt like rural country, a beautiful, friendly low-key place, with the added attraction of being close to New York.

His arrival marked the beginning of a period of school improvement during which he gave firm direction to a community increasingly committed to educational excellence. The demographic figures propelled much of the change. The population, which had expanded by 35 percent through the 1930s, reached 19,000 residents in 1940. Four thousand students were enrolled in three elementary schools and a combined junior and senior high school with a staff of 211 teachers and administrators.[53] In 1946, the population jumped to 25,000 with more than 95 percent of the children enrolled in the schools. Seventy-nine percent of them attended the same four public schools. In 1950, there were 30,000 people in the school district and by the end of the 1950s there were fifteen schools for a population of 48,000 residents.

Miller was ambitious, diplomatic, receptive to strong public involvement, adroit at public relations, skilled at straddling flexibility and his inherent conservatism, and welcoming of Jews. His familiarity with immigrant Jews went back to his childhood in Quincy, Massachusetts. In his later years, Miller fondly remembered that his grandfather rented part of his barn to the bottling business of a Jewish immigrant who affectionately called the young boy "mine little chonniey." When he moved to Great Neck, Miller became aware of suburban anti-Semitism. He was shocked by attitudes towards Jews: a woman from whom he rented his home advised him not to buy goods from a "Jew merchant in town;" and when Mrs. Eldridge sold a piece of her property to Bob Knolls, a sign appeared reading "Hebrew Knolls."[54]

Miller confidently walked a middle line between Gentiles and Jews, befriending all who would support his cause of educational improvement. He held the power to resist or accept change in educational policy and the ethnic and religious dynamics of the community. He took the latter course. Soon after assuming the job in 1942, Miller gave the Board of Education a memorandum of aims: to reduce class sizes to twenty-five students and to employ counselors, school psychologists, and psychiatrists. One shocked school board member wrote on the memorandum: "sounds like Teacher's College, sounds like socialism, sounds like Manhasset." Miller was not to be discouraged. Under his direction, the system was disciplined with an emphasis on basics. Great Neck was open to innovation, but never radical experimentation, while committed to traditional forms of education, especially in secondary schools.

It was an expensive operation. To support and pay for the improvement and achieve his goals, Miller needed new blood on the Board of Education. The expanding population also wanted structural changes to involve them in the system, a focus on educational content, and support for increased taxes. Funds were needed for new school buildings as well as higher salaries for the teaching staff, which increased from 193 in 1947 to 313 in 1952. Within three years of his arrival in Great Neck, Miller acted upon his concern about teachers' salaries: he increased the pay for teachers with doctorates from $3,900 to $10,000.[55]

Teachers and parents developed new organizations to meet their needs: the teachers formed the Great Neck Teachers Association; in 1943 the parents supported the new Great Neck Education Association, consisting of professionals and parents, to make the Board of Education accountable to the changing community. This was necessary for many reasons. In Miller's view, the former nominating committee and Board of Education had one major purpose: "to keep Jews off of the Board of Education." To diversify the ossified Board of Education, where some members had served for over twenty years, the Non-Partisan Citizens' Nominating Committee was started, with representatives of nonpolitical and nonsectarian organizations. The mayors of the villages lost their hold over the educational system when the public was invited to meet the candidates for the Board of Education from which the nominating committee made its selection.

But all of these changes were not enough for the grass-roots educational activists. Better-paid teachers, an able and responsive superintendent, and new community-wide parents and teachers associations did not satisfy all the concerns of many Great Neck parents. They wanted to improve and diversify the staff and the limited curriculum. They were dissatisfied with the large numbers of older teachers who might not understand the needs of students whose parents had been educated in some of New York's best public schools. Hilda Liff said that she knew something was wrong since her children were not reading Shakespeare, as she had done in the New York schools.[56] The absence of any Jewish teachers was a conspicuous concern. An inflated reputation did not satisfy these parents.

Acting upon their dissatisfaction, the parents hired a team of consultants from the Institute of Field Studies of Teachers College at Columbia University beginning in the fall of 1946. The Great Neck Education Association raised $20,000 to implement a two-year survey of the Great Neck school system. Cadres of parents solicited the funds by going door-to-door to ask for support. Miller was on board. The parents were engaged. The teachers, however, were less convinced of the need. Many believed that the schools were already of high quality. But they supported the survey anyway to insure that the system would maintain and improve its standards as it expanded in the future.

It was an innovative, cooperative effort. Its purpose was clear: Great Neck parents insisted on a credible evaluation from outside the system that would recognize them as an integral part of Great Neck's educational structure. Therefore, the survey involved educational professionals from Teachers College, Great Neck teachers and administrators, members of the community, and students. Representatives from all of these groups except the students organized a Joint Steering Committee. They prepared questionnaires and evaluations to obtain information on Great Neck's educational attitudes, conditions, and expectations. It was a major grass-roots effort that involved hundreds of people going to street after street to make inquiries on a monthly basis. Block captains got the reports and sent them to Columbia. The consultants collated the information and brought it back to the Education Association members. Naturally, there were many in the community who were uninterested or opposed to changing the operations of the schools. But for those who pressed on, the survey proved to be a productive adventure in the democratic process.

The result of this effort was a dense, two-volume report, published in 1948, dealing with the organization of the system and its curriculum, teaching, administrative staffs, and student life. Its aim was to help develop in Great Neck "one of the nation's finest school systems."[57] The physical conditions, according to the study, were adequate for the time. The relationships among teachers, many of whom had been teaching in Great Neck for over fifteen years, and the administration were more problematic since, according to the report, there was "undoubtedly the tradition and continuing practice of autocratic relationships, especially between administration and teachers."[58] This practice, however, was similar to conditions in other parts of the country. The teachers were well trained. Approximately 85 percent of elementary teachers had bachelor's degrees and half had obtained their master's degrees; all the secondary school teachers had bachelor's degrees and two-thirds of them had master's degrees.

The report cited a lack of initiative and democratic engagement in running the schools. It called for a more diversified staff. It also recognized a rather rigid approach in training for college. The system was lacking initiative. The consultants directed their strongest criticism against the stultifying relationship between the administration and teachers who felt that their job was simply to "carry out orders" given by the administration.[59] Close supervision by the administration was seen as a means of "checking on the behavior of the teachers." The report concluded: "the whole atmosphere of the schools was permeated with this autocratic tradition. Halls and cafeteria were under constant supervision by teachers; a teacher had to watch the loading of the buses at the close of the school day; some of the teachers in the elementary school felt that they had to obtain permission from the principal to deviate from the daily schedule of studies. In general, there was an atmosphere of having to obtain permission when one wanted to do anything different from the usual practice." One teacher observed: "By and large, teachers are not treated as adults. They seem to be part of a matriarchal system. Principals treat them like children who need constant guidance."[60]

The system was good, but not good enough. The teachers were competent but needed a more cooperative approach. But this was already beginning to change. With some satisfaction, the report stated that the methods used in the survey itself had fostered more flexibility and involvement of teachers as well as the initial objective of improving the curriculum. "Perhaps the most significant achievement was the apparent transfer of the methods used in the Study itself to the classroom, and to some degree to school policy. Teacher participants reported that administrative practices had become increasingly flexible and were including greater opportunity for teacher participation. In addition, many participants stated that they were more aware of the necessity of following cooperative problem-solving procedures in their own classrooms. If this trend should continue, it may emerge as the greatest contribution of the Study."[61] The client, the Great Neck Education Association, got what it wanted: recognition of the value of the cooperative approach to education. The parents had worked their way into the educational system as restrained activists. And the community, neighbor to neighbor, had dug itself out of indifference. The experts had done their work, but with a particular spin: the administration was put on notice that it would be held up to outside professional standards.

THE CONSERVATIVE PRESENCE

The ferment over educational policy, the activism of parents, and the increasing acceptance of Jews as partners in improving the system enhanced Great Neck's reputation and desirability for Jewish residents. Great Neck's reputation, hospitable to Jews and focused on its educational system, encouraged more and more Jews to move there. Most, but not all, were disposed to join Temple Beth El under Rabbi Jacob Rudin's strong leadership. It still reigned supreme in the community, although in somewhat modified form. After the war, Rudin, like other Reform rabbis in the chaplaincy during the war, incorporated more traditional rituals and departed from Protestant influences. Conservative and Orthodox practices, not Reform, had been the common denominators among servicemen. Rudin returned from the war with increased stature and was well on his way to becoming an institution in himself. He was the respected, ecumenical, forward-looking temple incarnate: the prophetic-like figure of conscience with a strong, clear voice and expressive hands that reinforced the import of his words. A man capable of intense kindness as well as stern admonitions, who was loved, admired, feared, and sometimes ignored—or just tolerated—because of his torrential words of angry rebuke. (One congregant threatened to raise a white flag if Rudin didn't stop shouting during his sermons. The flag never went up and Rudin never stopped shouting.)

Rudin was the leader of intelligent, hard-working, fiercely competitive, successful, fun-loving businessmen and professionals and their wives (who rarely were in business or had careers) who were long on wealth and local status but short on spirituality, observance, and knowledge of Jewish tradition and meaning. Wilfred Cohen, who grew up in an Orthodox family and came to Great Neck in 1929, exemplified the unique cast of characters: wealthy, charitable, and ambitious—an officer and eventually president of the temple. Each year he held the Passover seders in the conference room of his showroom in the garment district in the city. As the only place large enough to hold forty family members for a sit-down dinner, it was a marriage of the family fortune and religion.

A larger Jewish population inevitably meant a more diverse religious community. By 1947, Temple Israel, a fledgling Conservative synagogue of one hundred members, organized six years earlier, brought Rabbi Mordecai Waxman and his wife Ruth to Great Neck. (The synagogue needed a new rabbi to lead the membership away from divisive battles over Zionism.) Both Waxmans came out of the learned, observant, Zionist world of Chicago Jewry. Both had attended the University of Chicago. The rabbi had received his undergraduate training in political science and Ruth her Ph.D. in comparative literature in 1941. Instead of becoming a lawyer, as his mother wished, Waxman studied at the Conservative movement's rabbinic school, the Jewish Theological Seminary in New York, from 1937 to 1941. Although the employment prospects for a rabbi were not promising, his reason for choosing this course was clear and simple. As he wrote many years later, he "wanted to serve the Jewish people."[62]

After training at the seminary, the young rabbi led a small congregation in Niagara Falls, New York, and then returned to Chicago. The war intervened. Waxman joined the Army's chaplain service and spent three years at the reception center at Fort Dix in New Jersey. When the calling to Great Neck was extended to the young rabbi in 1946, the goals and interests of the Conservative rabbi and his wife meshed closely with those of the new congregation: dedication to Jewish learning, building a vibrant, observant community, and gaining community recognition and acceptance. When they arrived, with two suitcases holding all of their possessions, they were not prepared for the informality of suburban living. Whenever Ruth Waxman had gone downtown in Chicago, she had worn a hat and gloves. She wouldn't think of doing without. The day after her arrival in Great Neck in August 1946, she was invited to a garden party given by the sisterhood. Dressed properly, she wore a big beige hat, beige gloves and a lovely dress. The hostess greeted her in a "green play suit." Waxman looked aghast. "I am overdressed," she said and took off hat and gloves and left Chicago behind.[63]

That was the beginning of their suburban adjustment where, as a team, they brilliantly fulfilled their calling. The rabbi himself defined his calling as "a combination of service to the Jewish people and intellectual activity in the study and the communication of Jewish tradition."[64] With Great Neck as his base, he would become a deeply respected and influential interpreter of Jewish thought, tradition, and ritual as well as an astute, vigilant, and articulate observer of American political, social, and cultural forces. Through his teaching and writing, he imparted this to his congregation as a leader in Jewish education, a national figure in the Conservative movement, a dedicated Zionist and, finally, a key negotiator of differences among Jewish, Protestant, and Catholic ecumenical forces in the 1970s, 1980s, and 1990s.

Ruth and Mordecai Waxman were summoned to Great Neck by men and women from Orthodox backgrounds who wanted more ritual in the service, intense study of Torah and Hebrew for themselves and their children than the Reform movement provided. They adopted Conservative Judaism, which had developed in reaction to the mass abandonment of Orthodoxy in the United States by immigrants from Eastern Europe. The Conservative movement, which established the Jewish Theological Seminary in 1901, sought to find a viable middle way among competing religious and nonreligious movements and beliefs: Orthodoxy dominated by European-trained rabbis and teachers; America's secular temptations; the Reform movement, which incorporated ritual aspects of the Protestant tradition; Jewish movements born in Eastern Europe, such as Zionism and Socialism. In addition to the seminary, in 1913, the Conservative movement started its own national organization, the United Synagogue of America.

Great Neck's two rabbis, Mordecai Waxman and Jack Rudin, shared many of the same challenges: enlarging, educating, uplifting, and serving suburban congregations in formation in a community in transition. Their members were from similar Eastern European immigrant backgrounds; most had grown up in New York; worked in the same types of businesses, especially in the clothing industry and professions; nurtured the same ambitions for their families and children; and experienced the same challenges and temptations of assimilation. But Rudin and Temple Beth-El were there first: the founding, established, assimilating fathers of Jewish life in Great Neck. The newcomers, considered the observant Jews, adhering to kosher laws, walking to synagogue on Friday evenings, Saturdays, and holidays—were regarded with some unease by other Great Neck Jews who had perfected the style of blending into inconspicuous religious participation in Protestant Great Neck. A new and unusual pattern was in the making. In almost every other American community, Jewish life had proceeded from Orthodox observance to more liberal forms and interaction with the grass-roots Gentile world. In Great Neck, the process moved in reverse—from Reform to Conservative and eventually to Orthodox adherents and institutions.

By the end of the 1940s, Great Neck seemed to have everything that could be wanted. Its residents were not isolated in small town America or small city America—places like Watertown, New York; Bangor, Maine; Des Moines, Iowa; or Kalamazoo, Michigan—which were distant from the hubs of Jewish life in New York, Chicago, Boston, or Philadelphia. Although, in many cases, families lived with the expectation of moving back to the city after the children had gone to college, the Great Neck families could feel that they were passing time in a superior suburb. They lived in comfortable homes with the latest appliances, large lawns, cars, and garages. Great Neck was no Levittown—no instant Long Island community development of 17,000 prefabricated, low-cost, single-family homes built for veterans on thousands of acres of flat land bought from potato farmers. (For some in Great Neck, however, it was a source of pride that the famous real estate kings of mass residential housing, William J. Levitt and his brother Alfred, actually lived in Kings Point.)

In 1947, Great Neck was further distinguished and differentiated from other suburban communities by serving as a temporary home for the United Nations. Lake Success, one of the Great Neck villages, became a world-famous byline as reporters covered the United Nations. The new organization was a cauldron of Cold War tensions and regional crises in the Middle East and Africa. Thousands of newly gathered international employees formed the United Nations bureaucracy. They came to Lake Success to work in the Sperry Rand facility that had been used as a defense plant during the war. And many of them, such as the sociologist Gunnar Myrdal and diplomat Joseph Korbel, father of the future Secretary of State Madeleine Albright, found Great Neck an attractive place to rent or buy homes, send their children to good schools, and maintain easy access to the city. Ralph Bunche, however, encountered the racial divide. It was rumored in Great Neck that he wanted to buy a house but one real estate agent was told that if she sold to Bunche, she would never sell another house in Great Neck. He didn't buy.

In the postwar years, Great Neck developed its own unique spirit of high-keyed suburban life. While its population fostered positive connections to the city, its strongly residential character demarcated the suburb. Great Neck's cosmopolitan population was active and ambitious in educational matters, politics, and culture. It was less insular than ever. Its Jewish population was deeply committed to the birth of a Jewish state in Palestine. With local pride, Lake Success was the byline for the historic vote to create the state of Israel in November 1947. Writing in 2003, the famous Israeli author Amos Oz recalled the excitement in Jerusalem as his family and neighbors received the news from the United States. "The bars opened up all over the city and handed out soft drinks and snacks and even alcoholic drinks until the first light of dawn, bottles of fruit drink, beer and wine passed from hand to hand and from mouth to mouth, strangers hugged each other in the streets and kissed each other with tears . . . and frenzied revelers climbed up on British armored cars and waved the flag of the state that had not been established yet, but tonight, over there in Lake Success, it had been decided that it had the right to be established."[65]

As a result of wartime service, there was a new familiarity with America's diverse regions and groups. Narrow regional, ethnic, and religious identifications and divisions grew less pronounced as men in the armed forces mixed with non-Jews and Jews drawn from the vast country. The racial divide remained the greatest exception to a more integrated and equitable society in Great Neck and all over the country. Black men had migrated to the north for industrial work; black women for domestic employment as maids in middle class homes. They broke away from the South only to enter the growing black ghettoes such as Harlem and others in the urban north. The residential market, one of the key indicators of social and economic acceptance, openly and boldly discriminated against them. While Jews confronted restrictive clauses or "gentlemen's agreements" that prevented them from purchasing homes in certain Long Island communities and areas, Jewish buyers could always turn to alternative communities. Blacks, however, were unwelcome in all northern suburban areas, including Great Neck. The market remained closed to them by habit, tradition or, in some cases, blatant contractual language. Levittown may have been the most flagrant example of intolerance since it started a new type of community seemingly free of rooted social or economic precedents. Each lease stated: "The tenant agrees not to permit the premises to be used or occupied by any person other than members of the Caucasian race. But the employment and maintenance of other than Caucasian domestic servants shall be permitted."[66]

Domestic work was the exception. Black southern women freed the prosperous postwar suburban white women from labor in her home. While men were at work in the city earning for their families, their children were at well-funded, well-supported schools and their wives were spending their daytime hours on community, educational, and religious organizations; culture; fun, and sports. Black women took care of the homes. Black maids did the housework, cared for the children, and anchored many families—women such as Florine Brown, Chassie Burr, Della Rose, Lucy Andersen, and Ruth Helen Palmer. Most lived with the families for whom they worked six days a week with a day off every Thursday and another every other Sunday. A few lived in the centuries-old black section of Spinney Hill in Manhasset or Steamboat Road. Others commuted on a daily basis in a pattern that was the reverse of white men going to work in the city. A graduate student who wrote a thesis about the Great Neck school system in 1947, remarked "one of the most striking observations of the economic status of the community can be made by one who arrives at Great Neck from New York in the morning. He rides on a train carrying many domestics to work in Great Neck. As he steps from the train the visitor can watch for the train to New York, which stops at Great Neck and receives its heavy load of men and women on their way to offices in Manhattan. In late afternoon the emigration is reversed."[67]

In Great Neck, black women introduced their traditions, religious beliefs, southern dialects, and hopes for a better life. At first hand, and for the first time, Great Neck Jews, these new Americans themselves, connected to the complex, tragic reality of America's discriminatory and racist mentality in the South and urban north. Blacks and Jews were two groups at opposite ends of America's economic spectrum: the highly educated middle class or wealthy Jews and the uneducated, poor blacks. Great Neck and other white suburbs not only reinforced the disparity between the two groups but also increased it. Furthermore, the desire for residential racial separation was crucially supported by government policies. The federal government favored and blessed the white suburbs through the Homeowner Loan Corporation policy, which, beginning in 1933, directed mortgage subsidies in places that were deemed safe for investments. Safe meant white. Safe dominated by single-family homes, as suburban zoning laws favored residential building over industrial and commercial development. Safe meant local control. And safe meant separation from cities through "invisible fences" or "walls of wealth," in the words of historian Kenneth Jackson.[68]

Yet, at some basic level, American blacks and Jews were joined by a religious spirit and mythology drawn from extreme experiences of hatred, discrimination, and persecution. Their situations were vastly different: Jews profited from America's postwar prosperity and enlarged democratic vision; blacks remained in conditions of poverty and inferior status, enforced by unjust, discriminatory laws. But both groups remained American outsiders, waiting for full acceptance and trying to understand depths of cruelty and injustice. One black myth, in particular, poignantly drew them together. Zora Neale Hurston, the anthropology student at Columbia University and gifted writer of the Harlem Renaissance, retold the story. In the middle of the Depression, Franz Boas, the famous Columbia University anthropologist, had enlisted her to research black lore and myths. Hurston headed for Eatonville, Florida, her hometown, the only all-black community in the state. As she approached the town, after years of living in the north, she remembered a story from her childhood about God, man, and the soul. God, she wrote, wanted to share the soul but:

folks went round thousand of years without no souls. All de time de soul-piece, it was setting 'round covered up wid God's loose raiment. Every now and then de wind would blow and hist up de cover and then de elements would be full of lightning and de winds would talk. So people told on' another that God was talking in de mountains.

De white man passed by it way off and he looked but he wouldn't go close enough to touch. De Indian and de Negro, they tipped by cautious too, and all of 'em seen de light of diamonds when de winds shook de cover, and de wind dat passed over it sung songs. De Jew come past and heard de song from de soul-piece then he kep on passin' and all of a sudden he grabbed up de soul-piece and hid it under his clothes and run off down de road. It burnt him and tore him and throwed him down and lifted him up and toted him across de mountain and he tried to break loose but he couldn't do it. He kep on hollerin' for help but de rest of 'em run hid'way from him. Way after while they come out of holes and corners and picked up little chips and pieces that fell back on de ground. So God mixed it up wid feelings and give it out to 'em. 'Way after while when He ketch dat Jew, He's goin' to 'vide things up more ekal.[69]

Things, however, were hardly "ekal" for Blacks or Jews after the War. Blacks gained little from service in the armed forces or employment in war industries. Jews had to face the facts of genocide, a term that would slowly gain currency in the shocking vocabulary of the postwar world. Rudin had asked in 1940 if the war was because of the Jews? "No, not because of the Jews. But Jews are the microcosm," he answered. "They reflect within themselves the larger humanity. It is not because mankind was indifferent to Jews, as Jews, that the war came. It was because mankind was indifferent to mankind. . . . This war is because men let hate loose in the world and did nothing to stop it." In 1939, hate was let loose in Europe and the Pacific. It took six years of warfare for the Allies to triumph through the monumental mobilization of men and materials. International and national forces brought to the fore in World War II ended America's Depression, created the country's mighty financial and industrial machine, thrust it into global leadership, moved and mixed the American population, laid the foundation for the postwar consumer binge, restored American confidence in creating dynamic communities, started the process of mass black migration from the South to other parts of the country, and revitalized educational and religious institutions.

With the end of the war, attention turned back to the local world. Work, wives, children, schools, hospitals, churches, synagogues, and suburban growth were what people in Great Neck cared about. As the complexion of Great Neck changed, as more and more Jews were attracted to the community, as parents pushed the school system to expand and excel, ethnic tipping occurred. Many Gentile residents moved to less-mixed communities on the North Shore where restrictive practices effectively discouraged the emergence of a significant Jewish population. For Great Neck, the postwar 1940s were a transition period when its expanding population of demanding residents took count of what was needed to improve the schools, develop its public landscape, enlarge and diversify its Jewish religious institutions, and establish adequate medical facilities close by—facilities that would not discriminate against Jewish doctors and their patients as was the case at the nearest hospital in Nassau County.

In 1947 the last vestiges of the old order were dying out. Mrs. Roswell Eldridge passed away. Her heirs sold what remained of the large Great Neck estate to developers. The fiefdom, long inhabited by Eldridge family, friends, and retainers, was transformed into a plethora of split-level homes. Only the name Saddle Rock was left of the old order. Even before her death, it was clear that large-scale residential development was inevitable. Mrs. Eldridge herself had sold off some of her property for housing in what became Harbor Hills. She then split off another piece that the Board of Education purchased to build Saddle Rock elementary school. Mrs. Eldridge also negotiated to sell a portion of her estate for a hospital. But the needs of the community, and the ambitions of many of its residents, exceeded the boundaries of her diminished estate.

Instead, Great Neck's leaders turned to America's real landed gentry, the nationally recognized millionaires, the John Hay Whitneys and their friends in Manhasset, who were the social leaders of the North Shore Gold Coast. The meeting of wealthy Great Neck Jews and the crème de la crème of Gentile society would send Great Neck spinning for the next few years. Great Neck still looked to the city for family, culture, and entertainment, but for the first time in its modern incarnation, the community made significant connections east of the Peninsula.

By the 1950s, Great Neck was unmistakably on its way to becoming a Jewish suburb and the most talked-about Jewish suburb in the country, bringing down upon itself a mixed reputation as cultured, ambitious, successful, rich, dynamic, brutally competitive, materialist, shallow, and spoiled. The community was back to showing off, but not through its show-business celebrities. This time, Great Neck sought to gain recognition through its smart, ambitious, and cultured children who excelled at excellent schools. This, the highest priority, would become the source of family pressure; the route to community superiority; the means of gaining regional, state, and national recognition; and, for its Jewish residents, the favored road to integration and assimilation in America. At the time of Paula Boorstein's survey, Jews were heading back to the city as soon as they could. By the 1950s, however, they were in Great Neck to stay or to break through the seemingly impenetrable Gentile wall of the communities to the east.

4

The Quintessential
Jewish Suburb

STEPCHILD OF NEW YORK

Great Neck of the 1940s and 1950s belonged to multiple realms: a prosperous and powerful postwar American nation; a vibrant, aggressive New York City; and the new, enlarged and enriched suburbs linked by road and rail to the city. First and foremost, Great Neck was the creation and wealthy stepchild of New York's immense expansion and achievements. "A new kind of city," Peter Hall, the British author and professor of planning, called New York: "the quintessence of the early twentieth-century metropolis, based on massive economies of central agglomeration and equally massive potential for suburban deconcentration."[1]

Hall's tome *Cities in Civilization*, published in 1998, is a guide to the dynamics of urban growth and achievement. He included sixteen great cities over two millennia, from Athens to Los Angeles, probing for their cultural, political, technological, and managerial achievements. New York, in Hall's view, did not belong to the section on "The City as Cultural Crucible," with Berlin and other cities; or "The City as Innovative Milieu," which focuses on Manchester and Detroit; or "The Marriage of Art and Technology" highlighting Los Angeles and Memphis. Instead, Hall placed New York in his section on "The Establishment of Urban Order." For Hall, engineers, architects, entrepreneurs, and regional planners made New York "the apotheosis of innovation," not New York's celebrated artists, intellectuals, financiers, and manufacturers.

For sixty years, until New York's population reached 3.4 million in 1940, the city was a pioneer in meeting multiple tasks, including running its vast ports, providing housing on a small dense island for its commercial

life and, moving its massive population between work and home. New
York covered itself in this period of growth and unprecedented innovation with bridges, subways, tunnels, skyscrapers, roads, and housing in
newly acquired boroughs such as Brooklyn and the Bronx. By 1940, when,
according to Hall, New York's innovation and expansion were coming to
an end, the city was the center of a vast population stretching out to new
and old middle-class suburbs in Westchester, Long Island, and New Jersey.

In the 1950s and 1960s, Great Neck was in the right place at the right
time with the right needs, resources, spirit, and ambitions. It drew from
a young, restless population on the move, funded by federally subsidized
housing and educational programs. By all appearances, Great Neck had
a balanced mix of established and new residents; Protestants, Catholics
and Jews; and old and young families. Energized by its newest (and mainly
Jewish) residents, Great Neck set out to be a leader and apotheosis of
the suburb transformed. According to a report for the Nassau County
Christian Council in December 1948, "Probably the process of social evo-
lution . . . has gone farther in the Great Neck region than elsewhere along
the north shore. Here, with the exception of a few sections occupied by
relatively large residential properties, the land is for the most part solidly
built up, and the suburban quality of the communities is now clearly
established."[2]

The community surged ahead in its own special way: a small-sized mix
of New York's spirit, drives, values, and first- and second-generation immigrant population. Intellectuals may have sneered at the bland conformity
of the suburbs—at the "little boxes, on the hillside . . . all made out of
ticky tacky."[3] But Great Neck refused to see itself that way. No one thought
that living in Great Neck was living in Nowhere, USA. In truth, Great
Neck was a vibrant home base for reaching beyond suburban isolation,
self-containment, and self-satisfaction. What couldn't be brought to Great
Neck itself could be found few a miles away in the city's museums, music
conservatories, symphonic halls, opera houses, colleges, universities, religious seminaries, kosher restaurants, department stores, and bohemian
culture of Greenwich Village. The community was a staging area for its
aspiring children and families. From Great Neck, the children sought
entry into America's colleges and universities; from Great Neck, parents
prepared to enter national religious, educational, and political organizations. Looking beyond itself came easily since the community housed an
array of regional and cosmopolitan influences: international representatives at work at the United Nations in Lake Success; New England-born

teachers; European refugees from World War II; and needy artists—painters, dancers, and musicians such as Robert Rauschenberg and Anna Sakolow—who commuted to Great Neck to teach culturally aspiring Great Neck children and adults.

Great Neck's good fortune in the 1950s depended on three mega forces: the country's prosperity, fueled by consumer spending with easy credit; the wealth and dynamism of the triumphant city; and the commercial possibilities of the ascending suburbs. According to Lizabeth Cohen, the end of the Second World War started an "historical reign of prosperity, longer lasting and more universally enjoyed than ever before in American history."[4] Incomes doubled. Developers built millions of homes. From the end of the war through the 1960s, a temporary balance of prosperity between the city and the suburb gave Great Neck the best of all worlds. In the past, Great Neck had been a gilded shadow of the city. Now, for the first time, Great Neck's growth and influence were tied to economic developments beyond the city. Suburbia became a force, the premier target of America's consumer economy, as the cities began to lose population. "It was an article of faith," Thomas Hine wrote, "that the style of America was being set in the suburbs. What was true and measurable was that people in suburbs were buying more than their share of what America was producing. . . . In 1953, suburbanites accounted for about 20 percent of the population, but more than 30 percent of those of middle income or higher were in the suburbs."[5] The suburbs, he concluded, were getting richer, the cities poorer.

What assets and opportunities awaited ambitious, mobile, aspiring, hardworking suburban white families. For those in their twenties and thirties, people born during the Depression, there were new openings at colleges and universities and plentiful jobs providing the means to enter the middle class. Spending on housing, goods, and services from 1945 through the early 1950s buried the consumer constraints of the Depression and war years. The times were so good that the postwar period only served as the foundation for what Hine called one great shopping sprees.[6] With such prosperity, style and desire trumped need and practicality. Hine, an architecture and design critic, focused on the tastes of the period from 1954 to 1965. "Populuxe" was the way he characterized the period in which Americans went mad for TVs; cars with tailfins; picture-windowed, air-conditioned, ranch style or split level homes—the "little Versailles along a cul-de-sac."[7]

The suburban populations, Hine wrote, were "physically separated, out on their own in a new muddy and unfinished landscape, but," he continued, "they were also joined as never before through advertising, television and magazines."[8] They were linked, as well, by adherence to America's prevailing values. Suburban family life was arranged in accepted patterns of individual and collective obligations: men worked at jobs in the city; women ran the houses and tended the children; children, in or out of school, accepted the goals and constraints set by their parents. In the postwar years, the American suburban reality fulfilled American dreams: more and more families lived in single homes; more and more parents and children attended churches and temples; people spent more and more time and money at stores and shopping centers.

The 1950s are viewed as the complaisant watershed between the years of want and service—the Depression and the war years—and the changes in the 1960s brought about by the Civil Rights movement and youth culture. To be sure, there were national and international conflicts and tensions generated by the Cold War, Korean War, and the McCarthyite red scare—tensions and conflict that generated suspicions and fears in the cities and suburbs alike. Several Great Neck families found themselves in the vise of anti-Communist suspicions and accusations through their real or alleged associations with socialists and communists, especially during the Depression and the Spanish Civil War. The community, with its considerable Jewish population, felt the chill of vulnerability. In the less-menacing sphere of partisan politics, passions ran high in the presidential campaigns in 1952 and 1956. A tiny cadre of fervent Democrats challenged Republican-led Great Neck when Dwight Eisenhower and Adlai Stevenson fought for the Presidency.

But in Great Neck's white, suburban world, the 1950s were not principally a time of fomenting social challenge or facing the harsh realities that infused the lives of some of its residents. Some dreams of success and family contentment unavoidably met up with family turmoil and economic and social failure. The consuming aspiration to achieve, economically and socially, took its toll. When the ideals of harmony and stability fell apart, through the impact of physical illness, family strife, divorce, abuse of children, and mental illness, they were hidden from the views of neighbors and the community. Suburban women, the benighted organizers and custodians of the home, expended their ambitions and economic and intellectual capital in the service of their children; city-working husbands; and community educational, religious, and social organizations. Women had few opportunities to develop careers and thereby absent themselves from their homes and children day after day.

There were tensions between the middle- and upper-class Jewish children and those from working class Irish, Italian, and Ukrainian families. Not all children could keep up with Great Neck's unrelenting challenge to be smart, sophisticated, athletic, attractive, and popular. Great Neck was, however, more ambitious than most of its suburban counterparts. The community's needs and tastes extended far beyond the heady consumer cultures: it demanded and was willing to pay for costly, new, family-centered community institutions, organizations, and programs. With more certitude than most communities, Great Neck measured its resources and importance through the dynamic success of family life and the achievements of its children. In Great Neck, outstanding schools populated by healthy children were the expensive and carefully crafted engines needed for educational and professional accomplishments and upward social mobility.

In the late 1940s and 1950s, Great Neck was willing to pay to realize its goals that were child-oriented, but not child-dominated, as in contemporary culture. The communal drive for improving the schools and building hospitals and religious institutions and organizations served a dual purpose: it was, indeed, for the benefit of the children, in the name of the children, but it also satisfied the social, educational, and religious aspirations of the parents. The deep involvement in community organizations—an involvement that consumed the energies, intellectual gifts, and social passions of parents—meant that the parents, especially the women, focused their energies in the same places as those of their children. Women devoted themselves to the child-centered schools, churches, and temples. For many of the men, businessmen used to asserting themselves at work, community issues provided a way to be leaders in the civic realm and not just the familiar Jewish philanthropic world. Locally, they turned their skills in making deals and massaging numbers—their practiced arts of tough persuasion and cajoling—from their day-to-day business affairs in real estate, the garment industry, and manufacturing, to fundraising.

Great Neck's expanding and ambitious population developed a consensus about the three types of institutions that the community needed to maintain and expand on behalf of its population, especially its growing Jewish population. Having left urban centers for a different style of life, residents wanted assets that were the products of urban concentration, wealth, and expertise. Good hospitals in or close to the community—and ones that would incorporate Jewish doctors—were essential. Secondly, the community wanted the requisite number of excellent schools to prepare students to compete for college admissions. Finally, Jewish residents sought more Jewish organizations to accommodate traditional ways of religious observance and service to Jewish social, economic, and cultural needs.

The pressure to expand on these three fronts called for changes in the leadership and social and physical profile of the community. A sense of excitement emanating from a growing, affluent population attended the community in transition. Ultimately, however, the dynamic for change modified and ultimately undermined Great Neck's traditional social and physical façade—precisely those characteristics that had made it appealing in the first place. While Great Neck basked in the aura of small town, white, Protestant-dominated life, developers tore up farms and estates to house the growing population of new Jewish residents. The pressure for change did not wait upon the approval of old names and old money. Although there was still evidence of Gentile leadership in the schools, local governing boards, and newspapers, through attrition and the incessant demands of the Jewish population, Great Neck's old guard, or traditional leaders, lost ground. They could not ignore the insistent aspirations of Jewish residents. Significant growth and change took place within a new social frontier as new people seized new positions of leadership.

Two Hospitals

An accident in 1945 suddenly made clear to some people in Great Neck that they lacked an essential service: they had no adequate and quickly accessible hospital. The young son of one of Great Neck's well-connected, wealthy, Jewish residents fell through the grate over a cellar window and incurred serious injury. The closest hospitals were mediocre centers in Mineola and Flushing; the next closest, the fine medical institutions in New York City. Neither one would do in an emergency such as befell Danny Udall's son. The accident prompted a meeting of Udall's friends, including David Levitt, the young president of the Doughnut Corporation of America, who told his friends that medicine was a "disaster" in Great Neck. A hospital was needed: "you can't," Levitt said, "have good medicine without a hospital."[9]

A committee was formed with the goal of establishing a hospital of over one hundred beds in Great Neck. From the beginning, it was clear to the organizing group of Jewish residents that the effort had to be launched by a mixed group of ten founders. Superintendent of Schools John L.

Eddie Cantor's Home at Great Neck, Long Island, N. Y.

Eddie Cantor's house. Great Neck Library Local History Collection.

Eddie Cantor.
Great Neck Library
Local History Collection.

House rented by F. Scott Fitzgerald. Great Neck Library.

Louise Eldridge.
Great Neck Library
Local History Collection.

Roswell Eldridge. Great Neck Library Local History Collection.

Chassie Lee Burr.
Courtesy of Judy Goldstein.

LOOKING NORTH ON MIDDLE NECK ROAD, GREAT NECK, LONG ISLAND, N. Y.

Middle Neck Road in the 1930s. Great Neck Library Local History Collection.

At the Great Neck Train Station, 1943.
Courtesy of Judy Goldstein.

John Hay Whitney.
Courtesy of the Greentree Foundation.

Tex McCrary, Betsey Whitney, Jinx Falkenburg, Joan Payson, and Saul Epstein at the groundbreaking ceremonies for North Shore Hospital, May 6, 1951. Courtesy of the David Taylor Archives, North Shore-LIJ Health System, All rights reserved.

Great Neck Stone Church. Great Neck Library Local History Collection.

Temple Israel. Great Neck Library Local History Collection.

Temple Beth-El. Great Neck Library Local History Collection.

Rabbi Mordecai Waxman.
Courtesy of Hillel Waxman.

Confirmation class, 1967, Temple Beth-El, with Rabbi Jacob Rudin and Rabbi Jerome Davidson. Courtesy of Temple Beth-El.

Great Neck High School. Great Neck Library Local History Collection.

Jack Fields teaching a high school class, 1960s. Courtesy of Jack Fields.

Miller, one of the Gentiles, recalled being part of that carefully contrived group: "a committee of ten including five Gentiles, nicely matched—Jews, Gentiles."[10] They made a firm commitment that Jewish doctors, who were not accepted on the staffs at the Mineola or Flushing hospital, would be welcomed on the proposed hospital staff.

Mrs. Eldridge carved a piece of property out of her Saddle Rock estate and donated it for the hospital. An ambitious funding goal of $2,000,000 was set. Raising money became a way of life for the small group of founders, including David Levitt's father, know as Pop Levitt. For some, such as Miller, the fundraising was on an unusual scale. "The ten of us," he recalled, "had several meetings, and I remember too vividly one. We sat around a table at the—well, at a golf club—I think it was Fresh Meadows, and the question was raised by Tom Fitzgerald, the Chairman, 'How much will *you* give?' and I thought 'Oh, boy. I can't cope with these other people. Maybe a thousand dollars.' They got around to Pop Levitt. He said something like this: 'Becky and I have talked it over, and we've decided that the most we could do was to give a hundred thousand dollars,' at which point I shrank."[11]

The committee stalled despite having raised $600,000 in pledges. The group realized that the Eldridge site was too small and that their leadership was inadequate to the task. It was clear that Great Neck's Gentile leaders lacked the resources, as did its driving Jewish population, exemplified by men such as Wilfred Cohen. He had graduated from high school at sixteen, gone to City College of New York, taken business courses at night, and, despite dreams of becoming a surgeon, worked in the family garment business. Immensely successful, ambitious, and exuberant, Cohen took on community building in Great Neck when he moved there in the 1930s. He was small, standing only five feet, but handsome, self-confident, and sharp. He was also a realist. "That's a great gift," Miller recalled Cohen said about the Eldridge gift, "but we don't want the Hospital to be known as the Great Neck Jewish Hospital. We want to get out of Great Neck if we can. Maybe we should get Jock to give us some land.'"[12]

And who was Jock? None other than John Hay Whitney, chairman of the board of the New York Hospital, grandee of Greentree, the 600-acre estate in Manhasset, and one of America's richest and most socially prominent men. While the Gentile establishment was dying out in Great Neck, it was thriving on the town's eastern border, in Manhasset and into the further stretches of the North Shore. Jock Whitney's immediate and extended family was a key part of it: his wife, Betsey; his sister, Joan Payson;

and his sister-in-law Babe Paley, whose husband, William Paley, had purchased an estate next to Greentree in 1935. A vast social and economic world separated the Willie Cohens, the newly and moderately rich Jewish population of clothing, small manufacturing, and real estate entrepreneurs from people such as the Whitneys, Graces, Vanderbilts, and Phippses, those blessed with inherited mega-wealth from steel, railroads, securities, and the media.

Geography enforced and emphasized the separation between the expanding Great Neck suburb and the many great estates to the east. Spinney Hill formed the first line of separation through topography and race. From the top of Spinney Hill, bisected by Northern Boulevard—the major east/west artery running from Queens through the North Shore—an immense, pastoral panorama spread out to the east. The lush vista provided the first sign of the hilly, variegated terrain of small towns and large landholdings. Within that expansive wooded landscape, weekend royalty lived on fabulous estates, often with the legal status of incorporated villages, linked together by verdant chains of golf courses, beach clubs, polo fields, and hunt clubs. That was the bucolic view from Spinney Hill: beautiful, unfamiliar, but off limits to the Great Neck population.

The other view was totally different. That was the Spinney Hill of shacks and a few small seedy bars and hotels for blacks that lined Northern Boulevard from Great Neck into Manhasset and continued down to the bottom of the hill. On Valley Drive, Greentree shared the two-lane dirt road with black residents, some of whom lived in modest, well-kept homes, but many in shacks without running water and electricity, They were the heirs to the long-established black community with its houses, small shops, Zion Church and segregated school. From the top of the hill to the bottom, the racial divide separated white residents from the forbidden and neglected black territory. White people knew nothing about the bars and hotels that hosted some of the best rhythm and blues players in the country. White people, caring little about the dire conditions of the residents on Spinney Hill, turned away and looked past its people and buildings to the lush shallow valley, the Greentree estate, between Great Neck and Manhasset.

In need of land and financial support in 1948 for their venture, Willie Cohen thought wistfully about Greentree and their august neighbor Jock Whitney. Whitney was the grandson of John Hay—secretary to Abraham Lincoln—and son of great sportsman Payne Whitney and Helen Whitney—poet and collector of prized racehorses, horticultural collections, and literary publications. He spent his youth living at Greentree, a Fifth Avenue townhouse, a Georgia plantation, and estates in the Adirondacks. After attending Groton, he distinguished himself in the Yale class of 1926 on varsity crew and as a horseman, polo player, and tennis player.

The younger Whitney inherited $30,000,000 when his father died in 1927. A few years later, after his mother's death, he inherited Greentree, which his father Payne Whitney had bought in 1904 and transformed into one of the greatest estates in America. A staff of 200 cared for the main residence and guest houses, the horse stables, dog kennels, a nine-hole golf course, polo field, three grass tennis courts, an indoor tennis court, an indoor swimming pool, a Turkish bath, a facility for playing court tennis, and a gymnasium. Whitney's model was the English country house. And what a model it was. According to an English social historian, from 1890 to 1914 the owners of English country houses reached their height of lavishness and leisure—spending much of their time at sports and the "sheer act of living elegantly."[13]

After returning from wartime service, Jock Whitney emerged as a vigorous and enlightened philanthropist, astute businessman, and innovative venture capitalist with a particular penchant for investing in movies and theater. A sportsman and figure in café society, he had married and divorced, and then been married again in 1942 to Betsey Cushing, daughter of a famous Boston surgeon and former wife of James Roosevelt, the eldest of Franklin and Eleanor Roosevelt's children. As a generous donor and fervent collector of great Impressionist art, he became the chair of the board of the Museum of Modern Art. Maintaining the family's traditional connection to New York Hospital, with gifts totaling $40,000,000, he became vice president of its board.

A leader of society, Whitney nonetheless refused to confine himself to the social safety of the WASP establishment. His love of the theater and movies in particular led to a close friendship with the Hollywood mogul David Selznick. Whitney immersed himself in the film business and its particular world of finance, distribution, and beautiful women.[14] In fact, Whitney pushed Selznick to pay $50,000 for the movie rights to *Gone With the Wind*. After the opening in 1939, the movie proved to be one of the greatest financial and publicity investments that Whitney ever made. According to E. J. Kahn, Whitney's biographer, Whitney and Selznick were an unusual pair: the tall, dark-haired patrician and the homely son of an immigrant Jewish peddler.[15] The mix of cultures took hold: "David taught Jock half a dozen Yiddish words and phrases, and when

Jock parroted them back east his polo-playing and horse-racing friends would kid him, nervously, about being part Jewish." Whitney also sought to establish new directions in the philanthropic world. According to Kahn, he insisted that New York Hospital appoint its first Jewish member of the board.[16] In 1946, Whitney declined to be named in the Social Register, as he no longer wanted to be associated with its restrictive society listings.

No stranger to Jews, he was disposed to deal with Great Neck. And Great Neck was more than eager to work with him. When Willie Cohen suggested turning to Whitney to establish a hospital, Tom Fitzgerald, the country clerk in North Hempstead and one of the ten founders of the Great Neck hospital effort, said he thought he could get Whitney "and some of the real goyim to do it."[17] Fitzgerald offered one route to Whitney, but there was another, even more promising way to go: enlist John Reagan "Tex" McCrary, the public relations impresario and media and public personality, and his wife Jinx Falkenburg, the couple who lived on the Whitney estate. Two Yale men, Whitney and McCrary shared adventurous war years in London and an array of social, sporting, and theatrical friends. Born in Texas, educated at Exeter and Yale, McCrary became a newspaperman and, for a short time, the son-in-law of Arthur Brisbane, a major figure in the Hearst media empire. McCrary moved easily in the world of big money and big names such as Swope, Annenberg, and Whitney. Whitney had introduced McCrary to Jinx Falkenburg, the Spanish-born beauty, actress, and athlete. They married and went into business together. From their home at Greentree they discussed current events and interviewed celebrities on "Tex and Jinx," the first of the radio "talk shows."

The Great Neck appeal for help with a hospital could not have been directed to a more willing, better-situated, or more effective person than McCrary. Idealistic, inventive, smart, energetic, imaginative, and ambitious, McCrary devoted himself to mixing (to mutual advantage) his multiple interests: supporting his public relations business, editorial work on the *American Mercury*, appearances on his own radio and TV programs, aiding charitable endeavors and, in efforts closest to his heart, supporting the Republican Party. Historian Richard Kluger referred to McCrary as "shrewd, melancholy, aggressively well-connected."[18] Based at Greentree, McCrary was well-situated to gain clients for his business and influence in pursuit of his many projects. He had a feel for bringing people together, drawing the crowds, getting publicity, and reaching out to the public by putting stars together. "In all these things," he once remarked on his career, "you can call me a catalyst on a hot tin roof. But the catalyst does not always go along for the action; in fact, he mostly gets lost. He just makes it happen."[19]

In the campaign to build a hospital, McCrary hardly got lost. He took stock of the business success of his Great Neck neighbors such as Willie Cohen, Jack Hausman, Sol Atlas, and William Levitt, who were making mini fortunes in the postwar boom in the clothing, textile, and real estate businesses; they, in turn, were drawn to McCrary for his savvy under-standing of WASP society and public relations. Working together on the hospital would serve their common business and philanthropic purposes. McCrary always got the big picture of new trends and needs. With the explosion of suburban populations, especially around Greentree, he rec-ognized opportunities born of necessity. Replicate urban assets: shopping centers with first-class urban stores and hospitals with first-class care. Already, Manhasset profited from the Miracle Mile, the work of Great Neck developer Sol Atlas. If Manhasset could have a Lord & Taylor, why not a hospital that set standards similar to Whitney's New York Hospital? The land was at Greentree; the money was in Great Neck and the other communities on the North Shore. The key person was Jock Whitney, who could immediately draw upon the support of his wife Betsey, his sister Joan Payson, and his sister-in-law Babe Paley. McCrary was sure that the two sisters Betsey Whitney and Babe Paley, daughters of a famous Boston sur-geon, would be immensely supportive of a hospital drive.

One critical deal had to be made concerning the composition of the hospital board and staff. From the initial meetings in Great Neck in 1945, it was recognized that the effort had to result in a hospital that would not discriminate against Jewish doctors. The requirement was openly dis-cussed as Great Neck's leaders turned to Whitney and others in Manhas-set for support. David Levitt recalled meetings with the Whitneys, Paleys, McCrary, Jack Hausman, and Pat Whelan during which large sums were pledged. Levitt and Whelan, a Great Neck resident in the photography business, renewed their original offers of $100,000 each. They were set to move ahead but only on the condition that Jews would share equally in the governance of the hospital. David Levitt remembered the "feeling on the part of the Jews that it had to be 50–50 or the Jews wouldn't go along. . . . we were afraid it would be like in all the other hospitals where doctors couldn't practice."[20] As part of the understanding, McCrary in-sisted that a Jew and Gentile would alternate in the position of president of the hospital.

The project, newly named the North Shore Hospital Fund, came alive. McCrary took Whitney up in a helicopter to show him the area around Greentree and the expanding population that would use the hospital. Pointing to the polo field that Whitney could donate for the hospital building, McCrary made the pitch quite personal: "Some day if you have a hospital here that can deliver the same medicine that New York Hospital does in New York, the way Lord & Taylor delivers the same clothes that Lord & Taylor Fifth Avenue does, this may save your life."[21] McCrary used the same line with Great Neck's Seventh Avenue supporters through a slight twist by reversing the order of references: "If you can sell quality-clothes on Miracle Mile, you can have the same quality care as in Manhasset as in New York."[22] McCrary later speculated that the ride gave Whitney his first opportunity to see on Long Island, beyond Greentree, the Links and Meadowbrook Clubs.

Whitney followed McCrary's suggestion and took on the hospital project. In 1949 he and his sister Mrs. Charles S. Payson donated ten acres on Valley Road. Joan Payson became president of a thirty-member board with a balanced combination of Gentiles and Jews. A campaign was launched to appeal to the family-centered suburbs. The rationale was clear: Nassau had 1.8 hospital beds per thousand versus Westchester with five beds per thousand. "The significance of a first class hospital to a first class community is obvious," the board maintained. "The dignity and desirability of the community are that much more enhanced. It more soundly becomes a place where one may live and bring up children."[23] The funding goal of $3,000,000 was within reach since $847,000 had already been raised, with pledges of $776,000 from Great Neck alone. Broad support was evident from the fact that 3,000 people in Great Neck and 1,200 from Manhasset had contributed average gifts of $173.

In addition to the gift of land, Whitney and Payson each gave $500,000. Over the years, their gifts multiplied. Jack Hausman and Willie Cohen, who each gave a million dollars, devoted themselves to the hospital in an unrelenting campaign to raise money. They worked on the weekends and during the weekdays when they invited potential donors to lunch at the famous "21" restaurant on Fifty-second Street. They were called "the Golddust twins," David Levitt said. "Before you finished the lunch, the lunch cost you 50,000 bucks."[24] For Hausman, North Shore Hospital was not the only charitable need on his charitable agenda. The father of a child with cerebral palsy, in 1948 Jack and his wife Ethel joined with Leonard and Isabel Goldenson and Jane Hoving to establish the United Cerebral

Palsy Association. The Hausmans raised millions of dollars for the fund along with their prodigious efforts for North Shore.

Of course it was costly, but the effort provided unexpected fun and excitement. Who in Great Neck had ever attended public events and private dinners hosted by the Whitneys, Vanderbilts, Paysons, and Paleys? These were some of the icons of the Stork Club, the featured grand dames of *Harper's Bazaar*, the brilliantly dressed, coiffed, and traveled elite of the New York social scene. For the trustees there were special gatherings at Greentree and at Joan Payson's home. In April 1950, the Whitneys hosted a dinner for 200 people. For the Great Neck Jews it was as if they had entered the Promised Land: "I wasn't so interested in social climbing," David Levitt remarked many years later. "But I must say that I loved being with Jock, and Bill and Betsy and Babe. And we were invited to their homes and you know, when we walked into Jock's home the first time, I mean holy smokes, the art that you studied in art school, you know the great paintings on the wall, the nineteenth century Impressionists . . . millions and millions." The art was dazzling but he thought the beautiful furniture was "rundown," and "a little threadbare." It didn't matter. For David and the other Great Neck invitees, it was a ball: "We all loved this business of being with them. And then we used to have these balls that we all attended. It was more fun. It gave the Jews of Great Neck 'yichus', you understand. That's what you call yichus!"[25] (In Yiddish, an impressive background.)

In 1950, Tex and Jinx (as they were always known) became the official heads of Public Relations and Publicity, with Paul Townsend as their director. Their strategy was clear; "through Mr. and Mrs. McCrary's radio and newspaper associations, especially advantageous publicity can be developed. Publicity media will include news releases, photos, reprints of magazine articles in the local press, talks on modern medical care and symposiums." Three public relations pros, McCrary, Falkenberg, and their friend Paul Townsend started a blitz of public campaigns that descended on Nassau County and targeted local doctors, businessmen, clergy, teachers, students, political leaders, and residents. Fundraising dances were held at the Sands Point Bath Club, Fresh Meadows, North Hills, and Glen Oaks Country Club. There was a Miss Hospitals competition and a childrens' penny parade that gathered 250,000 pennies.

Show biz came out to Nassau when the trio organized Star Nights at Roosevelt and Belmont Raceways, at one time drawing an audience of 81,000. McCrary brought out the big names such as Frank Sinatra, Sam

Levinson, Ezio Pinza, Perry Como, Jackie Robinson, Ethel Waters, and Ginger Rogers. There were Thanksgiving balls at the United States Merchant Marine Academy, the former Walter Chrysler estate, co-chaired by Babe Paley and Betsey Whitney; hunt balls; dog shows; art shows; and film benefits. Committees multiplied. An architect was chosen as well as a hospital administrator. By the end of 1951, the thirty trustees had raised $2,619,000. In 1951, Bernard Baruch, Paulette Goddard, Perry Como, and others participated in a televised ground breaking. The next year, in 1952, North Shore got three federal grants totaling $442,000.

Two years later, North Shore Hospital opened its 150-bed facility, including maternity and pediatric facilities, with 253 doctors, 108 nurses, and hundreds of volunteers. Clinics for the nonprivate patients opened soon after. Valley Road, newly paved and modernized, was now called Community Drive to symbolize the community effort and the unifying aspect of the hospital. New housing was built for some residents of Spinney Hill. The hospital had raised over $4,000,000. Another million was raised over the next two years. Altogether, by 1955, Great Neck had contributed $1,497,403, Manhasset $1,776,916, and Port Washington $338,654, with $1,075,972 from governmental and other sources. The thirty trustees gave $1,917, 000. The McCrary-inspired benefits raised $310,000. The grassroots support was obvious as well: 21,145 people gave $100 or less; 2,719 gave between $100 and $499; and 228 people gave between $500 and $999.

North Shore Hospital's great success was due to a fervent, ambitious suburban community spirit, the prosperity of the late 1940s and early 1950s, and the participation and visionary leadership in a unique gathering of old and new wealth: the Whitney clan and their friends, especially Tex McCrary and Jinx Falkenburg; and the Willie Cohens; Levitts; and Hausmans. They sold the hospital story because they wanted New York City medical care close to their suburban homes, whether they were on magnificent estates or those already broken apart for residential and commercial developments. John L. Miller, an acute observer of the Great Neck community, lauded the spirit of community contribution. What made the campaign succeed? "Vision," Miller said, "on the part of a number of people including doctors, trustees, but also a deep sense on the part of the people of the fact that this was *their* hospital serving *their* community." He linked the hospital drive to the fervor for outstanding schools. "One of the things," he remarked, "that made the Great Neck public schools what they were was that the people of the community had a deep-rooted conviction that they wanted the best, and they were willing to pay for the best. We had great success in getting budgets passed, bond issues approved and so on. Well, it was those people added to the people in the rest of the service area who supported the idea of a community hospital of high standards." Leadership, as Miller so well knew, was crucial. "And of course people like Joan Payson and Jock Whitney tended to lift the sights of the people here because they *knew* what a good hospital was."[26]

And yet, the sense of community was more complex than Miller let on. In fact, when it came to building a hospital, there were several community interests and identities that reflected the different social and religious strands of the community. The North Shore Hospital campaign, representing one set of aspirations, stressed the need for a balanced effort of Jews and Gentiles to work together to insure equality of professional service and care. At the same time, there was another strand, promoted by people from the same Jewish social circles in Great Neck that focused on the primacy of the Jewish community and the need to insure opportunities for Jewish medical professionals and their patients. In this view, only a Jewish hospital would satisfy the educational, medical, and dietary needs of the Jewish community. Many people, such as Willie Cohen and Jack Hausman, served both causes and communities.

The campaign for a Jewish hospital took shape in 1949, at the same time that Cohen, Levitt, Whelan, and the others in the Great Neck contingent made their alliance with McCrary and the Whitneys. The supporters of a Jewish hospital, a Long Island Jewish Hospital (LIJ), based their needs on the population explosion in Nassau and Queens. According to their surveys, Queens was "30 percent short of minimum hospital needs" and Nassau had only 53 percent of needed hospital beds. In addition to beds, the areas lacked adequate medical services, care for the indigent, and facilities for research and medical education. There was another clearly stated need that referred to discrimination and exclusion in places such as New York Hospital: "It was recognized," according to an internal LIJ memo, "that a teaching hospital was not only essential to the practice of good medicine, but such a hospital would provide sorely needed training opportunities for young Jewish doctors who found doors difficult to open elsewhere."[27] The existence of a Jewish hospital would make certain that Jewish doctors would have the full range of medical opportunities offered at other medical centers.

The two Great Neck leaders of the Long Island Jewish Hospital were Saul Epstein, a manufacturer of corrugated boxes, and Gustave Berne, a lawyer turned real estate developer. At first they formed a 120-member board to achieve strong grass roots support. Epstein and Berne obtained a $500,000 grant from the Federation of Jewish Philanthropies. The social welfare organization, with leaders such as the two men, recognized the fundraising potential and importance of the growing Jewish suburban communities. With frenetic intensity, the businessmen educated themselves about the complex range of hospital requirements involving staff appointments, standards, building requirements, and nursing needs. They met with medical, architectural, and administrative experts on a weekly basis and sometimes several times a week for over ten months. When they were finished, they knew what they wanted to build: a medical center with specialized services for premature infants, research laboratories, educational programs, and residences for staff.

The Jewish roots of the enterprise can be read in its mission as well as the brief institutional history that the board acquired through the purchase of a seventeen-acre site next to Hillside Hospital, an eighty-eight-bed mental hospital newly associated with the Federation of Jewish Philanthropies. Hillside Hospital traced its history back to the Committee for Mental Health among Jews established in 1919 by a small number of Jewish neurologists and psychiatrists.

Attributing mental illness among Jews to their existence as immigrants crowded in urban areas, the group established a hospital in Hastings-on-Hudson in 1927 "for the study and treatment of nervous and mental disease among Jews."[28] The Hastings Hillside Hospital, as it was then called, claimed to be the "first voluntary mental hospital in the country to use psychoanalytic method in treatment."[29] Litigation ensued when the hospital sought to expand. The courts upheld a local ordinance that prohibited any "pest house or institution for the insane."[30] Driven out of Westchester, the facility relocated in Queens in 1942 after purchasing a fifty-four-acre farm site on the Queens/Nassau border.

Hillside and LIJ agreed to form an associated mental and medical establishment. The new hospital, designed to handle 13,000 patients a year, deliver 1,500 babies, and have clinics for lower-middle- and low-income families, would be located near major highways on the Nassau County–Queens border. The cost was $7,500,000. Board members and volunteers began their fund drive in 1949 through appeals to sectarian and nonsectarian pride and ambition. One theme was that LIJ would be "the beginning of a great medical center in the great tradition of Jewish sponsored hospitals in the US."[31] "A living symbol of democracy at work!" Excellence was another: "Beyond treatment and care," the Jewish hospital would seek "to extend the frontiers of medicine and science through research, teaching and opportunities for specialized training." And finally, the founders appealed to the pride of Jewish communities in Queens and Nassau counties: "Completion of the Hospital is a test of the unity and mettle of the Long Island Jewish community—rapidly becoming one of the most important on the Eastern seaboard. No hospital contributed by Jews to the general community is adequate if it embodies anything short of the highest standards of design, equipment, and service."[32]

It took five years of planning and fundraising to bring LIJ into existence. In 1954, a year after North Shore started its service to the community, LIJ opened its six-story building with 214 beds (including sixty for nonpaying patients) forty bassinets, kosher and nonkosher food, and outpatient departments for those who could not afford private medical service. It was the first federation-sponsored hospital, from start to finish, and the first voluntary hospital on Long Island with research and education programs. "It is the first contribution of the entire Jewish community to the health and welfare of the Island. The Hospital marks the 'coming of age' of the Long Island Jewish community. The Hospital has already shown evidence that it will continue in the great traditions set by Jewish hospitals in the United States."[33] Government funding through the Hill-Burton Hospital Construction Act provided $1,500,000. Twenty-six thousand families contributed $4,800,000 with board members contributing $1,600,000 of that amount.[34]

The building of two Great Neck–inspired hospitals, one in Manhasset and one in Queens, was a staggering achievement for a community of 35,000 people. The founders had raised over $11,000,000 in ten years from private and government sources for the two institutions. The vision, commitment, energy—the near obsession—of the founders of both institutions reached deep into the population of Great Neck and its surrounding communities. The success was a testimony to the regional grassroots support involving thousands of contributors and volunteers. The efforts reflected not only the challenge of meeting medical needs—quality hospital care, adequate facilities for the expanding population, and appropriate services for general practitioners and specialists—but also the social, cultural, and religious needs of the changing communities.

Hospital building in Great Neck represented a medical as well as a religious, economic, and sociological engagement of forces. The two hospitals represented two different and sometimes conflicting tendencies in Great Neck and in American life in general: on the one hand, in the

American democratic tradition, breaking down discrimination along social and religious lines; and, on the other hand, also in the American democratic tradition, building institutions to serve particular ethnic and religious groups. Rich and confident in the euphoria of community expansion and innovation, Great Neck in the late 1940s and 1950s successfully balanced the two traditions when it built two hospitals. North Shore Hospital challenged the tradition of excluding Jewish doctors from practicing in hospitals. It deliberately designed parity between Gentiles and Jews in the organization of its board and staff. Long Island Jewish continued the tradition of specifically designated Jewish institutions providing opportunities to Jews that were foreclosed in other places. LIJ continued the tradition of Jews taking care of Jews, while the North Shore Hospital brought Jews and Gentiles together and broke the traditional segregated and discriminatory patterns of medical service.

Hospital building caused the Great Neck community to reach out beyond its immediate borders to other populations in Queens, the North Shore, and the South Shore. The cooperative efforts thrived, ironically, precisely at the time that the strong threads of ethnic and religious cohesion—with their concomitant strands of exclusion—were gaining strength in the ever-changing composition of each of the individual suburbs. Who moved to which suburb was most often based on the religious and ethnic nature of the population. While Nassau County, east of Great Neck, was still off limits to most Jews in the early 1950s, Great Neck became increasingly confident in its Jewish identity. That balance of ethnic and religious interests manifested so successfully in the building of North Shore Hospital was an exception. But balance failed to hold firm in other critical areas of Great Neck's development.

RELIGIOUS INSTITUTIONS

A growing, assertive Jewish population, strong on the grass-roots level as well as in its leadership, led to the diminution of the Gentile population and a weakening of its religious institutions. The Protestant and Catholic clergy recognized that they lagged behind in the competition to gain adherents in the religious ranks of Great Neck's expanding population. The Community Church had 1,000 members; the Catholic Church maintained its elementary school as well as well-attended masses for its Irish, Italian, and Ukrainian congregants; and All Saints and Saint Paul's

Episcopal Churches retained their high social status, although shrinking in size and wealth. Although Great Neck in the 1940s might have appeared—to both Gentiles and Jews—to have more Jewish than Gentile residents, this was not the case. Most people misperceived the nature of the community's composition in the social mist of a tilting, transitional population. Dynamic growth was in the Jewish community and not in the Gentile one. By the end of the 1950s and early 1960s, Great Neck finally lived up to its hitherto misleading reputation: the long-awaited Jewish majority finally materialized.

Although many Jewish families who moved to Great Neck did not become involved in Jewish affairs, the demographic transformation was immediately evident in sectarian institutional weight: the expansion of Temple Beth-El and Temple Israel; the founding of Reform Temple Emanuel, the second Reform congregation; and the founding of Great Neck Synagogue as the first Orthodox one. The signs of success were evident in the proliferation of religious buildings, schools, and educational publications; the numerous Jewish philanthropic organizations; the high status of established Jewish leaders, such as Rabbi Jacob Rudin and Mordecai Waxman; and the emergence of new ones such as Rabbi Walter Plaut. Local leadership formed the base for national leadership; local ambitions became the testing ground for national ambitions. Religious education for children and parents, support for Israel, responsibility for Jewish social welfare—these were consuming interests that brought forth a frenzy of activities within the community and on a national level. The Great Neck Jewish community connected itself to Jewish organizations that addressed every obvious Jewish interest and need: support for the newly created State of Israel, recovery from the Holocaust, and building Jewish social services for the growing population in Nassau County.

Recognition on the local level was key to measuring influence and accomplishments for both the Gentile and Jewish residents. The weekly *Great Neck News* tracked the striving of Great Neck's multiple religious and philanthropic ambitions. In the 1950s, however, the news tilted towards Jewish activities. Week after week, articles and photos heralded synagogue building campaigns, committee meetings, lectures, and holiday observances that reflected the outpouring of fervid organizational endeavors and creative fundraising. The paper, a pale reflection of its ambitious, 1920s version, now found its audience in narrowly tracking local events for specific groups. In contrast to its earlier mission, the paper made no attempt to analyze news, shape events or build a community in some preconceived image. The *News* simply reported on a succession of local events—taxes, ordinances, meetings, marriages and deaths—among the many religious groups, but particularly in the energized Jewish community.

In fact, the *News* was also used to address political issues along religious lines as a means for sending messages to the Jewish community from its leaders on behalf of their favorite local politicians. Saul Epstein, head of the Long Island Jewish Hospital board, placed a full-page advertisement in the *News* in favor of his non-Jewish candidate running for town supervisor of North Hempstead. Embedded in his appeal for votes was a manifesto on the good Great Neck life: "As you know, most of my friends and I are 'naturalized' Great Neck-ers. We left the city with our families to find a healthier soil on which to put down roots. We wanted good schools, a house and a bit of ground for elbow room, a community in which our children could play safely in the open air, and tree-lined streets to help us relax when we return from the City each evening. Most of all we wanted to live in a community small enough and neighborly enough to enable us to share in its development and large enough to provide all the facilities for comfortable living." The political directive finally followed the manifesto: "I'm proud to tell my friends I'm for you and because I know the kind of community they want to continue to live in, I know they'll be for you, too."[35]

Epstein's name carried weight since he was part of the Jewish leadership in the 1940s and 1950s, along with Willie Cohen, Gus Berne, Josselyn Shore, and Jack Hausman, the leaders who organized and raised funds for Jewish religious, social, medical, and Zionist institutions and organizations. In 1953, Epstein and Hausman were founders of the National Bank of Great Neck. As the head of the LIG board and a leader of Federation, it was hardly surprising that Epstein would be a member of Beth-El, which retained its premier position in Jewish Great Neck. It was the leading Jewish institution in terms of membership, wealth, and influence. In fact, in the New York area, Beth-El ranked second in 1958, with a membership of 1,100 families, behind Temple Emanu-El on Fifth Avenue in the city. Throughout the 1950s, Beth-El epitomized the suburban adaptation of strong congregational assets. Within and without the community, Rabbi Jacob Rudin was recognized as a man of impressive status leading a congregation that set high educational and philanthropic standards. In the 1950s, Rudin remained, to some of his congregation, a performer with great personal charisma, although to some of his more astute and learned critics, his scholarship was secondary. Nonetheless, Beth-El's active educational programs constituted a critical aspect of shaping Jewish identity in Great Neck.

Rudin enhanced his authority and stature in part because he was the incarnation of a strong transitional figure. Since his arrival in Great Neck in 1932, he had led the way for a reconciliation with Jewish identity, according to one who knew him well, for "certain disaffected, alienated, marginal, upwardly mobile Jews."[36] Rudin's congregation consisted of many successful businessmen who were becoming more worldly and less interested in traditional Judaism. Nonetheless, Great Neck Jews still responded to the lingering strains of urban-based patterns. The sounds, learning, and habits of the Yiddish, socialist, and Orthodox backgrounds— implanted in the Lower East Side, Brooklyn, and the Bronx—filtered through the emerging suburban experience. Rudin, a congregant observed, had "his foot in both worlds"—the modern secular ways and those of traditional observance and knowledge. Rudin was "the bridge," presenting himself "as a really comfortable American and Jew"[37] and the model to which many Great Neck people aspired.

Beth-El, the epitome of suburban Jewish ambition, confidence, and success, attracted numerous new members and young clergymen as well. Assisting Rudin became one of the best jobs for a young Reform rabbi. One of the fortunate ones was Jack Stern, who was drawn to the spirited Jewish community that had sufficient resources and will to finance congregational needs, including a staff to assist Rudin. An inspiring young man, especially to the children in the congregation, he stayed for a few years, just long enough to marry Rudin's daughter. Rabbi Jerome Davidson, a native of Kansas City, Missouri, followed Stern. Having immersed himself in Reform Jewish youth programs, inspired by the social concerns of Rabbi Samuel Mayerberg in Kansas City, and trained at Hebrew Union College, Davidson was ready to enter the Great Neck Jewish world. "Rudin had a sterling reputation as a great speaker," Davidson observed, "a warm, devoted rabbi, generous to people who worked with him, and the congregation had the reputation of being fine and active."[38] In his quiet manner, Davidson would prove to be a worthy successor to Rudin.

It was an exciting world, different from the modest circumstances of his Kansas City background. There was, he recalled a "lot of comfort and wealth, not displayed in an ostentatious way,"[39] and a lot of big personalities, including the Levitts; the Shores; and the "living dynamo," Willie Cohen. Despite the wealth, the challenges seemed conventional to the young rabbi. Great Neck presented itself as a quiet community with a homogeneous life style: men left the community for work in the city; there was hardly any place to get lunch and just a few restaurants for dinner; women spent time working on behalf of the Temple sisterhood, Hadassah, and National Council of Jewish Women. Few social problems intruded on the rhythms of the suburban world: there appeared to be no racial unrest, no problems of divorce, and hardly any single-parent families. Nonetheless, for this deeply thoughtful, modest, and caring young rabbi, Great Neck held out promise as a liberal outpost and suburban center of social concern. It was a place where Davidson could develop into an outstanding religious and community leader.

While the immediate objective of Jewish education concerned children, there was a secondary effort to inform those who had grown up without any Jewish learning and to deepen the knowledge of those who came from learned families. Within the Beth-El community there were two routes to learning that the congregation promoted as models for other communities. One was the development of adult education programs in the temple itself. The other was the continuing, informal meeting of a study group, which had started in the mid-forties, with Bernard Thomson, a lawyer; Margerie Hess (whose father was a Reform rabbi in Chicago); Norma and David Levitt; Jacob Arlow, a psychiatrist; Rabbi Rudin; and later Rabbi Davidson. The self-motivated members designed a stimulating and constructive program focused on Jewish ideals, thoughts, and history.

A participant remembered that the group fostered, "a deep bond of mutual identity and interest. People made a sincere effort over many years to come to terms with basic texts and concepts."[40] The group became a training ground for leadership in national Jewish life: Earl Morse became the chairman of the board of the Union of American Hebrew Congregations; Norma Levitt, who wrote numerous innovative confirmation services for Temple Beth-El, also became president of the National Federation of Temple Sisterhoods, the first female officer of the Synagogue Council of American, the Union of American Hebrew Congregations, and the Union of Progressive Judaism; and Margerie and Nat Hess founded a synagogue in Sands Point and established a biblical garden in Jerusalem.

Temple Beth-El could barely expand fast enough, despite additions to the original building, to accommodate all those who wanted to join. With the encouragement of Beth-El board members, especially Josslyn Shore, a group decided to organize Temple Emauel as Great Neck's second Reform Temple. The effort was not only about numbers but class and style. For some members of the Jewish community, Beth-El was too big and top heavy with wealthy and influential people. "These were the people," according to Hilda Frank, a member and critical observer of the new congregation, "whose names and pictures appear regularly in the local newspapers, who serve on the boards of Federation, the United Jewish Appeal and various hospital and community organizations. Their monetary contributions are announced in the American manner at fundraising dinners where they serve to inspire those who can match them and to embarrass those who cannot." The author conceded that Beth-El's "prestige" was also due to its strong rabbi and educational programs. "Nevertheless," she concluded, "the dominant associations which arise at the mention of its name are bigness and wealth."[41]

The seventy-five families who formed Temple Emanuel in 1953 wanted a more intimate, less conspicuous congregational life. In comparison to the Beth-El members, the initial Emanuel members were younger, less well-to-do, and more often professional people such as dentists and lawyers. The congregation met first in the Community Church, as had Beth-El members in the late 1920s. Two years later, with over 200 families, the new temple hired Walter Plaut as its full-time rabbi and moved to a house set on a large property. A refugee from Germany, an intellectual and social activist, Plaut found himself the leader of a sometimes contentious congregation which reflected Great Neck's many different types of people and divergent views about religion and social change.

Some were intellectuals. Some, in welcoming a black minister from the NAACP to speak frequently to the congregation, wished to show their concern for discrimination against blacks. Others, according to Hilda Frank's critique, sought to be identified by their "external symbols" such as "income, style of life, often beyond their actual means, housing, clothing, the seat at the opera, in short—conspicuous consumption." In 1957, after an unsuccessful attempt to depose the rabbi, the temple grew stronger. Two years later, Emanuel dedicated its new and permanent home. Plaut's passion for social and moral exhortation invited another test of strength when he was among the first group of clergymen from the North to join a Freedom Ride in 1961. When some in his congregation objected, 1400 people came to a meeting to support his actions. Sadly, he died at the age of forty-four just a few years later.

Under Rudin's strong leadership, Beth-El never experienced the divisive tensions that beset Emanuel: the tug of war between those wanting a particular intellectual and spiritual orientation and those who demanded less from their religious experiences. Nor did Beth-El openly question

Rudin's strong sermons in support of the Civil Rights movement in the 1950s and 1960s. His authority, unquestioned within the congregation, was augmented by his connections to the local Gentile clergy and his leadership in the national Reform movement. In the 1950s, as the ideal representatives of the ecumenical approach desired by many in the community, Rudin and Beth-El maintained their dominant roles as the voices of Jewish Great Neck.

Nonetheless, without any direct challenge to Beth-El's leadership, another model of Jewish life gained strength at Temple Israel, under the leadership of Rabbi Mordecai Waxman. In 1947, Waxman had taken the risk of leading a Conservative congregation with only one hundred members in a Gentile community accustomed to Reform Jews. He had come because he found Great Neck people to be "interesting" and because Great Neck was on the "doorstep of New York and in the heart of Jewish organizational and intellectual life." Ever the political science teacher manqué and the unannointed professor who could not, because he was a Jew, make a career in the academic world, Waxman taught the young Great Neck residents in his congregation about Judaism. They craved Jewish knowledge as well as the means of making a traditional, ever-expanding, Jewish community in the suburban world. "The assumption was," according to Waxman's wife, Ruth, who also pursued an independent career as a professor of English literature at Adelphi College and was an astute observer of Great Neck sociology, "that if you lived in Great Neck, you came from someplace else." These were people in their thirties who were ready for new associations, reaching out to build new organizations. This, she observed, was a dynamic "new community that was bursting out. You knew that the community was going to grow. Everyday, somebody else moved into the community."[42]

Waxman quickly recognized that there were social and religious currents at work in the suburban culture that shaped his challenge and benefited his ambitions. The suburban community fostered cohesiveness through its religious structures. In the 1940s and 1950s, if one wanted to belong in a suburban community, one had to be part of a religious institution. For suburban Jews, the only local source of a religious connection was the temple or synagogue. Several decades before the state of Israel and the memories of the Holocaust became critical indicia of Jewish identity, a transformation that accelerated after the Arab-Israeli war in 1967 and the trial of Adolf Eichmann, the synagogue was the critical fount of Jewish attention and association. Ruth Waxman remarked that the "level of affiliation was very high since the pattern was set by the non-Jews. You had to establish your own community. That pattern was church-going." She and her husband referred frequently to the gas station syndrome in which the well-supported and established synagogues were like gas stations where "non-affiliated Jews could come in and gas up when they wanted."[43] A key to the synagogue's strength was that Jews, such as those from the labor movement or Yiddishists—people who wouldn't have been connected to a synagogue in an urban Jewish setting—felt compelled to be associated with synagogue life in the suburb.

Great Neck was virgin territory for observant Jews from cosmopolitan Jewish backgrounds, such as the Chicago world that both Mordecai and Ruth Waxman had grown up in. In the city of their youths, there were impressive Jewish religious and academic institutions and there was, with the density of the Jewish population, a Jewish folk culture that lived off of the immediate traditions, habits, and knowledge of Jewish life in Eastern Europe. Waxman, assured and, at times, even arrogant in his convictions and knowledge of Jewish subjects, commanded his congregational troops. As a young rabbi with a rich urban background, he brought the right tools for making a vibrant Conservative Jewish life in Great Neck: rich learning in Jewish theology and history; a fascination with everything Jewish; intensity of concern with Jewish observance; the eye of the political scientist who relished the dynamics of a community in the making; the insight of an historian who understood that Jewish life in the 1950s was framed by the tragedy of the Holocaust and the promise of the young Israeli state; and, not least, the ambition of a man who wanted to make his mark, and that of the congregation, on the Conservative Jewish world. Waxman became a rabbi and not an academic because there was no assured future for a Jewish professor in any discipline in practically any academic institution. His ambitions were shaped by that reality.

Waxman accepted the paradoxical needs of people in Great Neck and elsewhere who were attracted to Conservative Judaism. Without identifying Great Neck, his editor's introduction to *Tradition and Change: the Development of Conservative Judaism*, described the conflicting demands of his Jewish community-in-the-making:

> People who labored on the Sabbath could not bring themselves to discard their hats in the synagogue. Men and women who stayed away from the synagogue throughout the year wanted the *shul* they stayed away from to be a *shul* where people *davvened*. People who came to services only on the

High Holidays wanted to feel a sense of warmth and belonging and to hear
the cadences of Hebrew liturgy which they rarely understood, but which
rang in their ears from their early youth. Men who rode on the Sabbath
and had discarded the dietary laws wanted to belong to a synagogue which
said that these things were important, and to have their rabbis observe them.
When they faced the death of a father or mother, these same people wanted
to observe mourning in a traditional way and then to gather with a *minyan*
to recite the *kaddish*. With total inconsistency, people who violated the dietary
laws the year around desired to be sumptuously observant on Passover.
When a son was born, they wanted the services of a *mohel,* rather than a
doctor, a modern up-to-date *mohel,* it is true, but a *mohel.* When their son
attained the age of thirteen, they wanted him to chant a *haftorah* in a synagogue on the Sabbath, even if he had to cram it down at the last moment
by rote. When marriage came, at length, to their children they wanted the
ceremony performed under a *hupah* even if it consisted only of flowers, and
to stand by its side.[44]

Waxman took in those who half-heartedly joined the Conservative
movement and built up its ranks. He worked hard to capture the interest
and engagement of those who would make a real commitment to Temple Israel. He frequently cited Disraeli, who was criticized for talking
above people's heads. His response was one that Waxman followed: "I am
talking to where the heads ought to be." Temple Israel could not be, in
Waxman's view, a replica of the urban Conservative synagogue. It was,
instead, a pioneering venture, the central institution, for promoting a
demanding new affirmation of Jewish knowledge, ritual observance, and
community.

While Rudin was deeply hospitable to the growth of a Conservative
synagogue, it was clear that Waxman's view of assimilation in America
differed markedly from Beth-El's. Waxman, as part of the Conservative
movement, staked out the territory—in a non-Jewish community that
had gained much of its identity by church affiliations—between Reform
and Orthodox. He was not indifferent to Gentile life around him, although
in his early years he did not always go out of his way to make non-Jews
feel comfortable in the synagogue. In time, however, he developed a strong
relationship with the Methodist church in Great Neck and belonged to a
group of clergymen which included all but the Catholics, who were not
encouraged to participate in ecumenical activities until Vatican II. But
when interacting with Great Neck's Reform Jews, Waxman insisted on

observing Jewish traditional practices, most notably, Jewish dietary laws and Sabbath and holiday observance. He strongly objected to attending Hadassah and Federation gatherings when ham and cheese sandwiches were served. Jacob Arlow, a psychiatrist who had once belonged to Temple Israel but later joined Beth-El and its informal study group, observed that Waxman was "dyed in the wool of the old tradition and comfortable there."[45]

As the confident teacher, spiritual leader and social magnet for his congregation, he shaped the young, prosperous, and highly intelligent congregation to his vision. In the beginning of his term the goals were modest. The first building, a conventional, red-brick structure in the same style as the high school completed in 1949, was called a "refugee" from Williamsburg, Virginia. It was designed by a group of 200 families for a congregation of only 300 families. In the initial equalitarian stages, everyone paid $35 a year. Following the tradition of the public schools, initially, the Sunday and Hebrew schools were free for anyone in the entire community. The idealistic experiment didn't last long. When the membership was sufficiently large, Waxman started the first after-school Hebrew high school on Long Island for boys and girls from the second grade up. The school, for six hours a week, was conceived as a complement to education in the public school system. For the adults, there were Waxman-inspired discussion groups, lectures, and sermons. At one time, Waxman ran three groups that met every other week. Through this intensive interaction, he found the leaders of the synagogue, such as Martin Burell, George Schwartz, Hincky Finklestein, and Jack Stein, and writers for *The Light,* a publication of articles on Jewish history and thought. The magazine came out ten times a year and set a national standard for a synagogue publication, especially because of Waxman's editorials.

Ruth Waxman proudly recalled the impressive qualities of those involved in study: "many with European backgrounds . . . top-notch exciting people who had pulled themselves up . . . people with whom one could talk . . . people who appreciated Jewish learning," and people in sufficient numbers who could "staff a university"[46] and pay the costs of the Jewish organizational life. This was the place where many wealthy and middle class people gave money to their schuls and religious schools. Some sardonically opined, however, that the ritual of "calling cards" at fundraising events for Jewish causes was more binding and celebrated than the observance of any holiday, including Yom Kippur. (Calling cards in the Jewish context meant calling out the names of those present at a fundraising event and asking for a public response as to the amount of a donation. The purpose was to let everyone know what the others were giving to the cause. The expected big donors were always called first to set the pledging in high motion.) By the mid-fifties, Temple Israel could afford to expand as well as give generously to the Jewish Theological Seminary—the seat of Conservative education in New York—and other Jewish causes including the United Jewish Appeal, Federation, and the Joint Distribution Committee.

In the late 1950s, Temple Israel was a full-fledged part of the Great Neck community and a force in its social and religious transformation: a vibrant, fast-growing synagogue with an effective emphasis on education for the children; a breeding ground for national leadership in the Conservative movement; and a center of support for Israel. Waxman was the omnipresent, indefatigable, erudite president, provost, dean, and professor of a mini university dedicated to Jewish learning and activism. (The Waxmans were also the hosts, every Saturday afternoon, for any who wanted to visit them.) His students, both parents and children, spread Waxman's influence far beyond Great Neck's borders. When the children went away to college, many developed careers, especially in the rabbinate and Jewish education, which brought further recognition to the congregation.

Waxman perceived the synagogue as a significant element in the Americanizing process of the immigrant or second-generation Jewish population. "There was," he wrote, "a clear double process going on: the acculturation of the synagogue to the American scene, and the synagogue as an agency for the acculturation of the first or second generation of American Jews to American life."[47]

EDUCATIONAL ASCENT

"I am an American, Chicago born," Saul Bellow wrote in the boastful opening sentence of *Augie March*. A Great Neck Jewish student, on the verge of leaving home for college, could easily have adopted the same exuberant voice: "I am an American, Great Neck born! I am an American, Great Neck educated! I am an American, the child of a suburb connected to America's greatest cultural and intellectual center!" This was Great Neck's claim to belonging and entitlement in America. Education was the golden signature of the thriving community of 30,000 people. From teachers to real estate agents, Great Neck's population had a stake in building a high-quality educational system to meet the needs of an expanding population.

The synagogues performed one part, but hardly the major part, of the educating, confidence building, and assimilating work in Great Neck. The public schools did the biggest job. Residents measured the schools against the standards of the best public and private schools in the country. While Temples Beth-El, Israel, and Emanuel attracted Jewish families to the community, they were the lesser part of the double draw that promised mobility and success for parents and children alike. College entry was the reward for striving and the measure of achievement as students pressed for admissions to the finest schools.

The Great Neck graduates constituted a significant part of what one Ivy League college administrator called the "bagel around the city," the hard-to-digest pressure of too many qualified but socially and religiously undesirable students. The witty epithet actually connoted a serious problem for colleges, especially for the Ivy League schools, and for Jewish students. Highly qualified Jewish applicants from outstanding public schools, such as those in Great Neck, stormed the bastions of Gentile collegiate institutions. Their aspirations were part and parcel of moving on and moving ahead.

House pride, school pride, and local civic pride made Great Neck attractive and prosperous. Gaining entrance to the schools was the primary reason for Great Neck's growth, especially among the school-age group in the 1940s and 1950s.[48] Year after year, in pursuit of excellence, residents approved higher and higher budgets for the educational system. Although Great Neck administrators in the late 1940s anticipated a student body of no more than 6,000, it nonetheless built enough facilities by the early 1960s—three for kindergarten to third grade, five schools for grades three to six, a junior high school, and a second high school—to accommodate 10,000 students out of a population of 48,000. In addition, the system expanded its adult education programs to enroll 8,000, ran summer and Saturday programs, and established a new administrative center on a former Phipps estate.

John L. Miller, the superintendent of schools from 1943 through the 1960s, succinctly stated his justification for the vast and successful undertaking: "Let us remember that we are building for a future we can hardly envision but which will hold us accountable."[49] The schools provided the training ground for entrance to a college or university, the true prize of educational accomplishment and the mark of accountability for the system.

In 1945, 50 percent of the high school graduates went to college. In 1960, the figure had shot up to 85 percent. Acceptance at a good college, especially the Ivy League schools, was the real measure of the system's success. In the spring the crucial count was made: how many students got into Harvard, Yale, Princeton— the best colleges and universities in America. And how did Great Neck rank against Scarsdale, Shaker Heights, and the private schools in New York? This was the test. The Great Neck public school system had to deliver and it did.

The community's investment in securing an adequate number of schools, fine teachers, and strong administrators could not have come at a more promising time. Great Neck was building its stock of qualified students at the start of what Louis Menand termed the Golden Age of higher education. Despite the continued existence of quota systems for Jews at many of the finer institutions, entering the college of one's choice was increasingly within reach of Great Neck students by the 1950s. The GI Bill, the Servicemen's Readjustment Act, Diane Ravitch wrote, was that bold "experiment in mass higher education." It was the basis for a revolution in American education. "Nothing else," Ravitch stated, "had so dramatic an effect on the way the public thought about the issue of opportunity for higher education."[50] Millions of men, but far fewer women, used government support to obtain college and graduate school educations. Universities and colleges expanded due to rising expectations and the influx of adequately financed undergraduates and graduates. "In the Golden Age," Menand observed, "between 1945 and 1975, the number of American undergraduates increased by almost 500 percent and the number of graduate students increased by nearly 900 percent. In the 1960s alone enrollments more than doubled."[51]

New York City, along with academic institutions throughout the country, produced an unprecedented level of educational and cultural vitality in the late 1940s and 1950s. Great Neck profited in its educational and cultural pursuits from its close connections to the city and its outburst of artistic, theatrical, and literary excitement. Proximity was important, but ambitions and attitudes mattered more. Great Neck viewed New York, with its rich enticements of culture and an educated population, as a special extension of the schools and of Great Neck's spirit. The community shared an appetite for learning and culture that was expressed in the pages of *Horizon,* a magazine devoted to art, history, and thought, first published in 1958. "We came along, of course at a most appropriate moment, in the midst of the much-heralded 'cultural explosion,' that sudden, mid-century outburst of interest in the arts which has resulted from the unprecedented spread of education, wealth, and leisure." *Horizon*'s credo was "to open the door, and serve as a guide . . . to the long cultural adventure of modern man."[52]

Great Neck was the very personification of that wealthy, education-oriented, intellectually concerned, leisure-seeking population. As a community, it, too, had its own deep interest in education and culture: American culture, Western and Oriental culture, history, music, and art. It had its own symphony orchestra in the 1950s and 1960s. Many Great Neck residents, as well, were collectors of museum-quality Chinese, Egyptian, American, and European paintings and sculpture. Some of their collections, such as the Chinese holdings of Earl Morse and Egyptian works amassed by Norbert Schimmel, would become significant additions to the holdings of the Metropolitan Museum of Art. In the early 1950s, when the Great Neck Education Association needed to raise money, Great Neck collectors displayed their holdings. For those who came from homes that were not as richly endowed, finding art treasures on the walls and tables of their friends was an education in itself.

The interest in a rich cultural heritage was not only founded on the triumph of American democracy after World War II or in defense of American values against Communism. For Great Neck in the late 1940s and 1950s, there was an added dimension to the triumphs of American life. It was bound up with the knowledge that Jewish immigrants and their children were transforming American culture. Great Neck proudly identified with Jewish success in America. Philip Roth, growing up in Newark, wrote about the infectious "assertive gusto that the musical sons of immigrant Jews—Irving Berlin, Aaron Copland, George Gershwin, Ira Gershwin, Richard Rodgers, Lorenz Hart, Jerome Kern, Leonard Bernstein—brought to America's radios, theaters, and concert halls by staking their claim to America (as subject, as inspiration, as audience) in songs like 'God Bless America,' musicals such as *Oklahoma!* and *Show Boat,* and classical compositions such as Aaron Copland's 'Appalachian Spring.'"[53]

For Roth and other children of immigrant Jews, the reality of success for the popular and classical composers inspired the spirit of possibility in other fields. Writing for Roth—and Saul Bellow's writing in particular—meant entering the realm of belonging in a new country. "This assertion of unequivocal, unquellable citizenship in free-style America . . . was precisely the bold stroke required to abolish anyone's doubts about the American writing credentials of an immigrant son like Saul Bellow." The exuberant Augie March says: "Look at me, going everywhere! Why, I am a sort of Columbus of those near-at-hand." He was, Roth wrote, "going where his pedigreed betters wouldn't have believed he had any right to go with the American language. Bellow was indeed Columbus for people like me, the grandchildren of immigrants, who set out as American writers after him."[54]

Great Neck's children, like Roth, were ready to go where their "pedigreed betters" didn't necessarily want them to be. Great Neck students ambitiously planned for college educations that would lead to careers, not just as writers, but also in business, academia, the arts, science, and medicine. But first came the basic preparatory education. Public education, nearly a community-wide obsession for parents, children, and educators, was the critical resource for mobility. A newcomer to Great Neck, such as Rabbi Jack Stern in the early 1950s, upon arrival recognized "a level of educational energy that vibrates in the community."[55] In its collective educational campaigns, Great Neck established a highly valued, integrated education culture that joined students, teachers, and parents. An extraordinary rapport developed between the schools and community because education was of prime importance. (The spirited drive to improve public education was hardly affected by the private schools in the community: St. Aloysius for Catholic elementary school children, and Buckley Country Day, a 1923 spin off of the Buckley School in the city, for Protestant children.)

A plethora of committees and advisory boards brought teachers, administrators, and laymen into working forums within the classroom and without. Membership on the school board bestowed status comparable to being a bank president. Parents, through their participation in school-board elections (sometimes contentious and nasty) and numerous committees, demanded superior educational programs and discipline. Administrators and teachers, meeting the challenge through superior teaching materials and supports, thrived on the engagement in learning and the respect proffered to them by the community. Great Neck, although consisting of many villages and incorporated areas, formed a collective identity through its educational interests. The Great Neck Education Association, started in 1943, became more influential than each of the school's PTAs.

Great Neck's high educational standards and concerns set it apart from the dismal state of primary and secondary education in most of the country. The suburb's sense of privilege, for which it worked hard, was real. According to Benjamin Fine, a journalist for the *New York Times*, American schools were in deep crisis once again. In the late 1940s there were too few teachers, too many who were poorly educated, too many with an average pay of $37 per week, too much turnover, too many buildings in dreadful condition, and too many inequalities among schools throughout the country. America was spending less on its schools than Great Britain or Russia.[56]

Paradoxically, while Great Neck soared above the bleak national educational scene, the community nevertheless benefited from many positive traditional attitudes and expectations towards the schools. Diane Ravitch succinctly described them in her study of American education in the mid-twentieth century. "In the 1940s, few teachers belonged to a union; strikes were uncommon; administrators were powerful within their school building or their district in hiring, promoting, and assigning teachers. Though their pay was low, teachers had more education than did the parents of their students and commanded the respect that went with the authority they wielded. Teaching attracted a number of gifted women, for whom other career opportunities were limited."[57]

Residents measured the system's success in many ways: national rankings; admissions to the most privileged colleges and universities; strong, infectious, public participation in school governance; and a continuing flood of new home owners who were drawn to the community by its educational reputation. In 1957, *Time* magazine noted a survey of thirty-five of America's outstanding secondary institutions. The article described the findings of an Illinois school board president which identified American high schools that had frequently produced twenty or more national merit scholars in one year. He then corresponded with the principals of the schools to see what made them good. Great Neck was one of six such schools in New York—along with the Bronx High School of Science, Forest Hills High School, Midwood High, Erasmus Hall High School in Brooklyn, and Regis High in Manhattan.[58]

Publicity was another gauge of success. In 1952, Great Neck basked in a ten-page *Life* magazine spread on the Saddle Rock Elementary School. The author of the article had looked for a public school that featured progressive education. "Great Neck's brand of teaching," she wrote, "revolves around what is called the 'interest-centered' classroom, which is really another name for progressive education—a term educators shy away from using because of the controversy it always arouses. This method is based on the fact that a child who is interested in what he is studying will understand it better and remember it longer. It is the teacher's job to get the student interested in what he is supposed to learn. If she cannot arouse any interest, she will have to devise a way of teaching it to him anyway."[59]

The *Life* magazine author followed Grace Warner's sixth grade class at the newly opened school on Saddle Rock land that Mrs. Eldridge had donated. Impressed by the discipline in Warner's class, the author and photographer spent three weeks building their story. The pictorial profile was buttressed by a positive set of facts: "good teachers, good equipments, relatively small classes and an actively interested community." The article reported that half of Great Neck teachers had M.A.s in education, were paid between $3,100 and $7,200 and that they worked in "one of the best systems in the state."[60] Through pictures and text, Warner was shown giving close attention to the individual needs and learning patterns of each student. She also made clear that she maintained a strong connection to the parents, depending upon them, through interest at home and expectations of proper discipline, to reinforce her goals and commitment to teaching.

This is exactly what Great Neck residents were paying for through a $10,000,000 bond issue voted over the previous five years. Nothing could be better than national recognition for Great Neck's aspirations and achievements: praise for the teachers and the community of parents; accolades for a gifted teacher giving lots of attention to children; and a plethora of pictures showing the world a young, engaged woman teaching serious suburban Jewish children.

The article narrowly focused on the progressive method of teaching and not on the broader educational philosophy that infused the Great Neck system. No reference was made and no hint was given to the special social and political dynamics that infused the educational life of the community. Had the writer so desired, she could have described a set of principles, initially formulated at curriculum conferences in 1946 and 1947, that defined and guided the system's educational objectives. These principles read:

The staff of the Great Neck Public Schools believes that:

1. Wholesome social living demands organization.
2. Democracy is the best 'way of life' for our society.
3. Democracy implies equality of opportunity for all people.
4. A democratic society respects the worth of the individual.
5. Each individual participates in different ways in the society and must assume responsibility for making his best contribution to it.

6. Each individual grows at different rates, and varies from every other individual in abilities, interests, and potentialities.

7. Individuals come from varying social and economic backgrounds.

8. The more inner resources an individual possesses, the more adequately he can adjust to life situations.

9. An individual (or a civilization) reaches the highest level of development only when working in harmony with a Spiritual Force.

10. Changes in both the physical and social environments are inevitable.

The purpose of education in the Great Neck Public Schools is to help the individual develop his own capabilities and be an effective citizen in a democracy.

Such an individual is:

1. One who develops his interests and abilities so that he may participate intelligently and with personal satisfaction in an ever-changing democratic society.

2. One who, possessed of sound physical, emotional, and mental health is, as a self-disciplined person, able to meet adequately and with suitable composure the problems imposed by living in modern society.

3. One who can think clearly, communicate thought, make relevant judgments, and discriminate among values.

4. One who realizes the necessity of social control and the importance of subordinating himself to this control.

5. One who, recognizing his prejudices, but believing in equality of opportunity and appreciating the contributions made to society by varying groups, works for better human relationships among all peoples.

6. One who develops moral, ethical, and spiritual attitudes.[61]

Additional formulations dealt with self-expression balanced by self-control, recognition of individual differences, the need for self-evaluation, education that encompassed more than academic achievement, attaining skills that would lead to satisfactory vocational and professional work, recreational instruction, and transmitting "our cultural heritage." The declaration of beliefs reflected the ideas that mattered most to Great Neck: equality of opportunity, the worth of the individual, respect for a variety of social and economic backgrounds, the power of spiritual forces, relating education to the larger community, and public participation and citizenship.

Lest it be assumed that family didn't matter in the over-all formulation of Great Neck's educational philosophy, the administration sponsored another set of principles. *Home and Family Living in the Elementary Schools, Great Neck Public Schools*, was published sometime in the 1950s. Presented as a model for other schools, the publication described the responsibilities of both boys and girls and "a total home and family living program plan from kindergarten through the sixth grade . . . to reflect . . . that good family living is the most vital basis of education in the elementary school."[62] The topics included family relationships, personal appearance, social graces, nutrition, cooking, sewing, consumer education.

The principles were not just pieties but represented educational, political, and social possibilities that were within the reach of Great Neck residents—parents, teachers, and children alike. The changing local milieu, shaped and invigorated by ambitious residents, was a grass roots phenomenon. The vigor for change was enhanced by the vigor of local participation. In the small residential community where just about everyone, except for Mrs. Eldridge, came from somewhere else in the not-too-recent past, new associations, organizations, and opportunities were the norm.

Local life was the training ground for building organizations and making changes, but it did not represent the end of the horizon. New York was always at hand, always offering opportunities beyond the immediate suburban world. Great Neck thrived on dual attractions: the intimacy and malleability of the small town—under pressure from the educational demands of its parents and the educational receptivity of its students—and the great city. This blend of possibilities was as important for teachers who came from New England as for the residents who were within one generation of the urban Jewish ghettos.

Gertrude Buffington Pingree, for example, became a renowned sixth grade teacher in Kensington School. She had been educated at Keene Normal and worked as a teacher and principal of an elementary school in Manchester, New Hampshire. In the late 1930s, after a divorce, she, her young son, and father moved to Great Neck where, as a teacher, she could better support her family than on a New Hampshire salary. Great Neck, however, provided more than a satisfactory income: it was safe ground for a divorced woman from a New England city. Her fellow teachers and others in the community, always respectful of her privacy, never inquired as to why she was a single mother.

Pingree enjoyed the high status that Great Neck bestowed on its teachers. The community provided a strong base for her to educate and discipline her students. For most of her time in Great Neck until she retired in 1964, she could also take deep comfort from the town's Republican majority. It satisfied her family, one that never allowed mention of FDR's name at home. Literature was her passion, but civic action and public awareness were her missions. Great Neck was her training ground. One of her classes in the late 1940s mounted a yearlong campaign to force public officials to eradicate the pervasive spread of poison ivy. Another class in the early 1950s was told to scour the windows of every store on Middle Neck Road to find one spelling error on one sign. She mixed tradition and innovation, warmth and firm authority. She relished her bright students, the generous parents (many of whom gave her lovely gifts), the trips to New York for courses at Teachers College, and visits to its museums with her family.

There were many other teachers like Pingree who thrived on the vigorous community in transition. Dorothy Hicks, who came to Great Neck in 1936, was once asked if she noticed the change from a predominately Gentile student body to a Jewish one. "How could you help but notice it!" she shot back. From her perspective, when Jews started moving in, there was a remarkably smooth transition. She and other teachers recognized that the new residents in the community were deeply interested in education and supportive of the teachers and schools. Many came precisely because of the strong schools. The challenge, from her perspective, was to absorb the remarkable growth without compromising academic standards.[63]

Hicks grew up in the Hudson Valley, graduated from college in 1931, and planned to work in a school system outside of Albany. Her contract stipulated that she would lose her job if she married. Before actually teaching there, she took a job in Spring Valley. After working there as a teacher for five years, her contract was renewed with only a $25.00 raise. Insulted and furious, she went to New York to an agency that placed teachers. Kensington had an opening. She was hired immediately with a salary that was 50 percent more than her previous job. Hicks characterized the teachers like Pingree in Kensington, under the strong direction of the longtime principal Margaret Johnson, as exemplifying kindly forcefulness and a strong ability to cooperate with each other. Through the years, they became formidable, sometimes intimidating figures, especially Hicks, who ran the program that monitored student behavior; served as president of the Teacher's Association; and was an active figure in the Great Neck

Education Association, which brought teachers and parents into close co-operation. Her strengths in building teachers' organizations allowed her to thrive in the Great Neck community that she found uniquely liberal, tolerant, and respectful of the educators' work. She, like many of the teachers, including her sister, with whom she lived, never married. The community afforded her safety as well as access to the city. By train she would go to the opera and then return, confidently walking home from the train station to her apartment at night.

Teachers such as Pingree and Hicks prospered in the stable system under John L. Miller's stewardship as superintendent of schools. The Miller regime, which lasted over twenty years, however, could present distinct challenges for those whose creativity and innovative goals differed from the powerful superintendent's. Jack Fields, who came to Great Neck in 1951 to teach English in the high school, was one whose educational values clashed with Miller and his administration. Fourteen years after coming to Great Neck, the tensions between Fields, the beloved English teacher, and Miller, the entrenched and respected administrator, broke out in public dispute.

Fields was an exception to Great Neck's typical New-England-born, normal-school-trained teacher. He grew up in Philadelphia, gravitated to New York City, went to New York University for a few terms, and then worked as a journalist from the age of nineteen to twenty-three. In 1942, he was drafted into the Army and began to write for *Yank* magazine. Eventually he became the editor of the Manila-based Far Eastern edition. After the war, Fields joined with several Army journalists to start *Salute*, a general magazine for veterans. It survived for only two years because national advertisers thought it too liberal and radical. He tried public relations for a short time and then went back to NYU in the School of Education and started work on a Ph.D. In 1952, he was hired to teach English at the Great Neck High School. Shortly before he started the job, John L. Miller asked him to fill the public relations position for the school district. Fields insisted on teaching but agreed to take on the additional responsibility. His salary went from $2,500 for teaching high school English to $5,000 to organize the district's public relations operation. Among many other efforts, he successfully arranged for the *Life* article on Grace Warner and her class at Saddle Rock School.

Fields soon developed into an exceptional English and creative writing teacher. "From the moment I started to teach," he remarked, "I had made up my mind not to lecture to the kids, but to raise questions and have them respond." His classes reacted with excitement and dedication to the dual disciplines of reading great literature and expository writing. Fields made immense efforts not to teach "at" his students but to relate to them and "take them personally and let them know that I cared about them." It worked over his many years of teaching. "Jack Fields taught me everything I needed to know to succeed in college," one student wrote. "In fact, what I imbibed subsequently at Harvard pales in comparison to what I learned in his tenth-grade journalism class and under his guiding hand on the staff of our student newspaper. Mr. Fields taught us how to investigate and report—to get the 'gist and pith' of a story and write it in spare, sparkling prose."[64] Unlike Dorothy Hicks, however, Fields's observations did not extend to the particular nature of Great Neck's ethnic and religious complexion. The well-being, creativity, and accomplishments of his students came way ahead of his interest in Great Neck's sociological make-up. Although Fields recognized that not all of his students had college-educated parents, he understood that they valued education and wanted their children to be responsive to learning. Great Neck's growing Jewish population and the fact that there were few Jewish teachers in the system, however, made almost no impact on him.

In 1965, Fields's values clashed openly with Roul Tucker, the principal of Great Neck South, and John L. Miller. For several years, Fields, as a representative of the teachers union, had struggled with the administration over higher salaries and better working conditions for teachers in terms of the size and numbers of classes. But it was his views on academic freedom and experimentation that caused a public dispute. Fields had served as the teacher advisor to the *Guidepost,* the newspaper of Great Neck High School and then for the *Southerner* at Great Neck South. In the fall of 1965, several students published articles in the *Southerner* about their experiences in the South, the previous summer, as part of the Civil Rights campaign. Tucker thought the articles inappropriate and told Fields not to allow similar subjects to appear again in the paper.

Fields objected and immediately resigned as the paper's advisor. His students were alarmed and offended. The issue turned into a confrontation between the parent and student supporters of Fields's position, on one side, and Tucker and Miller, on the other. Public pressure led to Fields being reinstated, but the administration exacted a high price: Miller and Tucker retaliated by depriving Fields of many privileges normally granted to a teacher of his standing. He resigned again, but this time from teaching as well as from the paper. Supported by parents and students in the community, Fields once again confronted Miller and the administration. In a public forum, the Board of Education devised a compromise that Miller opposed and Fields reluctantly accepted: he would take a one-year leave of absence from Great Neck South and teach in a private school in Cambridge, Massachusetts. Upon his return, Miller assigned him to teach in Great Neck North. Ten years later, Jack Fields retired for good. His legacy, cultivated in his creative classrooms, is still treasured by many of his former students. At the latest count, in 2005, over forty of them have published books in fields including anthropology, law, English literature, Sanskrit, poetry, and journalism. Among the most prominent Fields students are Francis Ford Coppola and Talia Coppola Shire, famous for their films, and the Sanskrit scholar Wendy Doniger.

The Fields controversies revealed some of the tensions embedded in a community that often promoted a progressive image in its educational goals, although the image was sometimes at odds with a strain of conservatism and strict administrative control over creative, experimental teachers. The controversies reflected, as well, the continuing, deep involvement of parents who supported the teachers in their efforts to improve the educational system. In truth, the assertive and confident spirit of teachers such as Pingree, Hicks, and Fields was enhanced through the activism of Great Neck's residents.

So many of these residents, such as Joe and Hilda Liff, who moved to Great Neck in 1939, came from backgrounds that were completely different from those of the Great Neck teachers. Newly married, potential homeowners, they were the ambitious children of Jewish immigrants, breaking away from Jewish New York. Joe Liff went to Brooklyn Law School at the same time that he worked for a law firm as well as the *New York Morning World* as a police reporter. In 1931 he got a job as a law clerk in an office, eventually making $5 a week. Hilda Liff graduated from Hunter College in 1933 and worked at three jobs: every weekday as a teacher at the Lexington School for the Deaf; Saturdays at Arnold Constable modeling beach pajamas and selling silk underwear (despite the fact that advertisements for such work frequently stated that no Jews or Catholics should apply); and during vacations at a bookstore. She and her husband lived with Hilda's family in the Bronx for the first two years after they married, then moved to a small apartment for $68 a month. When she became pregnant and needed more room they moved to Great Neck at the suggestion of the parents of a blind child whom Hilda taught. Their rented house cost $65 per month. Five years later they bought a house for

$7,000. Although for several years Hilda commuted to work at the Lexington School, driving into the city every day with her husband, who was practicing law, her attention was more and more focused on educational and political issues in Great Neck.

Believing, in the late 1940s, that the schools needed to be substantially improved, Hilda Liff threw her organizational skills and energy into planning and carrying out the Teachers College survey. Block by block, she and others worked to raise money for the study and then to undertake fieldwork for the two-year investigation. Year by year, they saw results through an infusion of taxpayers money, strong and responsive administrative leadership, a diversified teaching staff, and the unrelenting attention of school-watching activists. As for Liff's other grassroots involvement, the Democratic Party, there were lots of efforts amid increasing frustrations with all too few electoral achievements. Great Neck was overwhelmingly Republican country, as was almost all of Nassau County except for a handful of Democratic enclaves scattered among a few towns. Soon after Joe and Hilda Liff moved to Great Neck a representative of the Republican Party came to call on them. Two things became quite clear to these two urban Democrats: leaving nothing to chance, the Republicans had committeemen in every election district; leaving nothing to the Democrats, only enrolled Republicans got the county government to act, from a stop sign to a variance. The message to all newcomers was clear and convincing: power and prestige lay with the local town, country, and state Republican Party.

The political facts of life, both present and future, hardly discouraged Joe or Hilda Liff. They began the long, difficult process of infusing liberal Democratic ideas into Great Neck's political life. It would take decades before Great Neck became known as a firm Democratic base, faithfully supported by liberal Jewish voters. In the early 1940s, however, the Liffs discovered only a small coterie of Great Neck Democratic stalwart troops that were used to defeat. Judge Stanish, a Southern-born and faithful Democrat was one; Danny Dugan, a bright, small Irishman and the essence of the Democratic Party in Great Neck was another. In 1941 and 1942, Joe proposed to give new life to the paltry organization. Meetings were held in the Liffs' house, which essentially became the Democratic headquarters. Sometimes, in a fit of optimism, they rented the firehouse room on Northern Boulevard for $10.

Their enthusiasm notwithstanding, nothing much happened until early 1952 when Joe and Hilda returned from a trip in Europe. When they got

to the dock in New York, Danny Dugan was at the pier with a great surprise: "Hi Joe," he called out, "you're running for Congress."[65] If Joe had
been around for the nominating meeting, he would have put the finger
on someone else. Nevertheless, he accepted the designation and built a
strong campaign that profited from growing interest in Adlai Stevenson's
presidential campaign. While right next door in Manhasset, Tex McCrary
and Jock Whitney plotted big things in terms of money and publicity for
Eisenhower's presidential campaign, Joe and Hilda Liff scrounged around
for publicity, endorsements, and funds. From friends, new and old, such
as Lou Baker, George and Maxine Schwartz, Jean DeMosquite, Robert
and Jean Benjamin, and Beti and Alvin Kaplan, the Liffs raised money
and organizational support to make the run. Joe ran and lost as Great
Neck again voted Republican, especially after 5,000 people cheered Eisenhower when he visited Great Neck in a motorcade. Liff's only victory
came when he debated with his Republican opponent in the high school
and won 69 percent of the vote. This was the first Democratic victory ever
in Great Neck. (In 1962, he won a seat on the State Supreme Court.)

Stevenson's next presidential campaign in 1956 brought an influx of people into Great Neck's Democratic ranks. The campaign generated a frenzy
of interest among many in the high school who joined the Taskforce—
Teenagers for Stevenson and Kefauver. As Hilda Liff recalled, the kids,
more active than the adults, provided the best political experience that
Hilda ever had. Many students developed a strong interest in politics because of the Stevenson/ Liff campaign. They starting working within the
system, in contrast to the 1960s when the Vietnam War and Civil Rights
movement turned many students against the political system, and their
schools and parents. The highpoint of the 1956 Democratic campaign was
Stevenson's appearance at the High School, which Joe arranged despite the
initial hesitation of John L. Miller, a Republican and superintendent of
schools. It was the biggest and best gathering that the Democrats had ever
had in Great Neck. When Hilda Liff picked Stevenson up at the airport,
he was still working on his talk, editing notes on a little piece of paper. She
recalled it was a great speech in which each word counted. The next day,
Newsday devoted the entire front page to the story, with a picture of Liff
and Stevenson. Of course, Great Neck went for Eisenhower once again.

From 1952 on, the Liffs worked with some wealthy, well-connected
Democrats who remained faithful to their former urban political predilec-
tions and resisted the dual conversion to suburban life and the Republican
Party. In many ways, Robert Benjamin, an immensely successful lawyer,

movie executive, and philanthropist, was the most influential of this group. He grew up in Brooklyn a few years after his parents had left Russia and Poland for the United States. After graduating from high school at fifteen he went to City College at night and worked for the New York Film Board of Trade as an office boy. It was the beginning of a career that married the necessity of making a living with a love for movies. In 1931 he graduated from Fordham Law School, which he also attended at night. During law school he began to work at his uncle's law firm, Phillips and Nizer. This association would provide the base for his professional success. The firm, small and hardly well known at the time, employed Arthur Krim as the second associate assisting Lou Phillips, who represented Paramount Pictures, and Louis Nizer, who was beginning his career as a trial lawyer. Within a few years, Benjamin made valuable acquisitions of film companies and became a partner of the firm. He served in the Army during the war, using his legal skills and knowledge of the movie business to assist the army in effectively filming training information as well as images of D-Day. At the end of the war, he became president of the J. Arthur Rank Organization and director of Universal Pictures. In 1951, Mary Pickford and Charlie Chaplin sold United Artists to Benjamin and Krim; Benjamin continued his dual career as lawyer and businessman.

When Benjamin moved to Great Neck a year after he married Jeanne Kortright, an English woman who had worked at the American Embassy in London and at the Nuremberg trials, he reconnected Great Neck to the movie world. He wasn't a celebrity like Eddie Cantor, but he was a big figure in the movie industry who knew the stars and Hollywood world. That was enough to impress people in Great Neck. What made Benjamin unique was the range of his interests and accomplishments. In 1952 he signed on as the co-chair of the North Shore Citizens Committee for Stevenson. After meeting Eleanor Roosevelt, when she visited Great Neck, he began his long-term support for the United Nations, still in its infancy, as did Jeanne Benjamin, who became the chair of the Great Neck chapter of the American Association of the United Nations. Within the next few years, he became a major figure in programs involving the UN, finance committees of the Democratic Party, Carnegie Hall, the American-Israel Cultural Foundation, the Anti-Defamation League of B'nai B'rith, the Corporation for Public Broadcasting, the Eleanor Roosevelt Memorial Institute, Brandeis University, and Temple Israel of Great Neck. He used the community as the prosperous, well-known base from which to reach organizations in the New York City and beyond.[66]

Robert Benjamin, the strongest link to Great Neck's theatrical past, epitomized many of the community's confident, successful businessmen, professional, and civic leaders. The son of immigrants, he established a respected presence in legal, business, political, and philanthropic circles, without ignoring his local civic and religious interests. He was a successful American, who could have used Augie Marsh's voice of awe and amazement at how far he had come: born in Brooklyn, educated in city schools, engaged in the legal profession and movie industry, and comfortably settled for most of his adult life with his family in Great Neck. A Jew who moved with comparable ease in both Jewish and Gentile circles, with national and city politicians, international diplomats, musicians and educators, he personified how much Jewish Great Neck had changed since the 1950s.

When the Benjamins moved to Great Neck in 1952, the community, taking care of its own needs, was already successfully engaged in building two hospitals, expanding its religious institutions—especially Temple Israel and Beth-El—and maximizing its educational capacity and quality. But its concerns were not insular: the city remained the focus of professional, business, and cultural life; the UN, temporarily located in Lake Success, and its many employees provided the community with an international flavor. Thirty years after Eddie Cantor and F. Scott Fitzgerald had touched down in Great Neck, it had evolved into a distinguished community—not just beautiful and convenient—but fortified by an impressive array of institutional services.

And yet, the ambitions that transformed these local medical, educational, and religious institutions made for contradictory results. Having left urban centers for a different style of life, Great Neck residents needed assets that were the product of urban concentration. Desiring a community that would be more mixed than the ethnic, religious ghettos of the city, Great Neck Jewish residents, propelled by their fierce drive for improved schools and an intense religious life, overwhelmed their Gentile neighbors and altered the Christian nature of the community. Ironically, the escape from the ethnic ghettoes of the city to the Great Neck suburb developed into a new form of social and religious isolation, in a suburban configuration, of an overwhelmingly Jewish community.

When the stunning work of institution building was done it might have seemed to the world at large that nothing out of the ordinary had happened in the well-known suburb. In fact, much had changed within and without. By the end of the 1950s, Great Neck had established the foundations for existing as its own little city, detached from its former urban orientation and international concerns. Physically, the community began to look a bit like a small city, with newly constructed middle-income apartment houses, in addition to the few fancy ones built in 1920s. In addition to the Miracle Mile in Manhasset, started in the mid-1940s, the Great Neck–based developer Sol Atlas built a 50,000-square-foot department store for John Wanamaker right across from the railroad station.

In 1951, when the United Nations moved from New Hyde Park to its permanent site on the East River in the city, Great Neck lost some of its cosmopolitan character. Great Neck began to assume that it didn't need to promote its close connections to the city. The writer Peter Hall, in his *Cities and Civilization,* has speculated that urban greatness and innovation came from people who felt that they were outsiders or marginalized in the city. New York in the early decades of the twentieth century was the quintessential city for outsiders: for immigrants, who landed at Ellis Island, millions of whom stayed in the city; and for those born in America who migrated from rural communities and small cities to the city seething with opportunities.

The city that made itself different from the rest of America with its outsider populations nonetheless imperiously tried to make its markets, values, and aspirations the center for the rest of the country. Great Neck men who worked in the city were enriched by the boundless opportunities of the city's mass market in clothing, housing, entertainment, and advertising. By the mid-1960s, however, Great Neck was ready to abandon the city that loomed as an ominous place of racial tensions and to protect its suburban residential assets of homes; school; and the safe, idyllic life. Commercial Great Neck started to take form as office buildings rose that dwarfed the traditional retail establishments situated on Middle Neck Road, the commercial spine of the community.

By the late 1950s, Great Neck was a cliché in the making: reputedly a population of spoiled, wealthy, demanding, and ostentatious individuals and groups. For some who lived in Great Neck and some who saw it from outside, the community evoked contempt and embarrassment. For others, both within and without the community, Great Neck was a rare mix of ambitious, striving people, led for many years by John L. Miller, Rabbis Rudin and Waxman, and lay leaders such as Hilda Liff and Robert Benjamin, who forced their community to excel. Whatever one's view, it was clear by the early 1960s that many Jews from the city were moving beyond Great Neck's promised land in the relentless pursuit of finding somewhere better, some place more like the rest of America, somewhere less developed. "New money moves on" was the way that an English social critic described the basic phenomenon of wanting something better.[67] A Great Neck era had passed and with it, the unique experience of living in a community that moved out of mediocrity and suburban provincialism into the exciting world of promise, opportunity, and the reconfiguration of the American dream.

5

The Price of Achievement

FAULT LINES

In 2003, Great Neck's image and reputation changed dramatically. On top of the general impressions of being a wealthy, materialistic, ostentatious, and Jewish community—layers of impressions cultivated over many decades—a new one emerged. Great Neck was unsafe for its children. The former clichés, those cultivated from the 1920s through the 1960s, in retrospect convey a quality of innocence. They mattered, certainly, in terms of who moved into or out of the community and why people found it either attractive or undesirable. But 2003 produced something altogether new: Great Neck was the scandalous setting for a powerful documentary about incest, pedophilia, and deep suffering in one family's life. *Capturing the Friedmans* presented the history of a husband, wife, and three sons confronting accusations, indictments, criminal prosecution, and convictions. The Nassau County attorney, drawn to the family by a trove of pornography, brought charges against Arnold Friedman and his son Jesse. The cases were based on accusations, gathered by the prosecutor's office, of students who attended computer classes in the Friedman house in the late 1980s. The documentary, a dark, claustrophobic view of one family, depicts Great Neck as the background for perversity, community shame, and crack up. The story could have happened anywhere, but Great Neck added a special degree of notoriety and a bonus for the directors.

It is hard to imagine that any political or financial scandal could have been worse for Great Neck's identity. What greater violation could have taken place than a Jewish teacher abusing children and fracturing the emotional and physical safety of the house and home? What other set of events could have so besmirched the standing of the community that had such strong local organizations and institutions? Unquestionably, the documentary was about a family of modest means and not about the rich community where it lived. The film's major theme asked what actually happened among the father, son, and students, given an era of hysteria and allegations, aggravated and exploited by prosecutors and the troubled history of abuse in the Friedman family. But the community—because it was Great Neck—was the secondary subject, with frequent allusions to its wealth and a harsh competitive spirit among its students.

The documentary used Great Neck but showed little footage, except for incidental overhead shots, of the lush residential community. There were no images of the schools, village, religious institutions, and social organizations. No references to the community building and aspirations in Great Neck that involved the efforts of so many people and so much money in the 1940s, 1950s and 1960s. Finally, in 2003 Great Neck was again part of the movie world but this time, unlike in the 1920s, the stories and stars were sinister and shameful.

Of course there were communal fault lines in Great Neck based on psychological, social, cultural, economic, and religious instability below the changing surface of day-to-day life from the 1940s to the 1980s. These were, however, hardly ones of sexual perversity and family disintegration, although there were horrible cases hidden within the impenetrable walls of family privacy of which the community took little note. From the perspective of Great Neck's Gentile population, the first upheaval occurred between the 1920s, when the community attracted a few hundred Jewish families, and the 1960s, when Jews constituted the majority of the vastly expanded population. The demographic transformation affected basic community dynamics of leadership, church membership, organizational activities, and even educators. Finally, in the 1950s, Jewish teachers, including Annette Lillianthal, Richard Benjamin, and Karl Seitz, were invited to join the junior high school and high school faculties. Without a staunchly embedded Gentile establishment in place, Jewish residents asserted themselves with increasing confidence. While Gentile teachers made a deep impression on many Jewish students, they did not grow up deferring to the power of Protestant privilege. (The lack of deference may have contributed to the insufferable aura of conceit that some Great Neck students took out into the larger world.) On the other hand, for Gentiles who remained in the community, it was often uncomfortable, sometimes even shocking, to find themselves as the outsiders in an increasingly confident

Jewish and highly competitive Great Neck world. That transformation was most noticeable in the schools. In the graduating class of 1952, for example, approximately 60 percent of the students were Gentile. By the late 1950s, the figure was significantly reversed.

The fault lines of the 1960s, however, went far deeper than the critical ethnic and religious differences that had determined Great Neck's changing identity in the previous decades. In the Kennedy and Johnson eras, seismic trends and events throughout the country challenged racial segregation, traditional roles and expectations of women and men, the assumptions of family cohesiveness, the entitlements and sexual behavior of youths, and the primacy of cities over the suburban upstarts. The challenges presented themselves through the Civil Rights movement and the Great Society legislation; in the feminist revolt, exemplified by such publications as *The Feminine Mystique*; the pill; student strikes in schools against the Vietnam war; the busing of minority children from the cities to the suburbs; and a surge in intermarriage rates between Gentiles and Jews.

Ironically, Great Neck's strengths in achieving its collective goals and national reputation in the 1940s and 1950s were founded upon a set of opportunities, expectations, obligations, habits, restraints, and inequities that could not withstand the demands of the 1960s. Great Neck had thrived on the strong economic, social, and cultural connections between the suburb and the city. Great Neck had come of age when there was still a relatively balanced mix of Gentile and Jewish populations within the community. This was a period before the claims of diversity, affirmative action, and multiculturism overtook subtle adjustments and the primacy of belief in the melting pot and ecumenical harmony under the sway of an increasingly tolerant Christianity.[1]

The 1940s–1950s was also a period in which business profited from discrimination: William Levitt, the largest residential builder in America after the Second World War, in fact, had built homes that he wouldn't sell to his fellows Jews. In the Levittowns, his epochal developments, he would not sell to blacks. Levitt had the dubious honor, in 1953, according to the sociologist Alan Wolfe, of having developed on Long Island the "largest town in America with no black residents." Seven years later there were still only fifty-seven black residents in Levittown.[2]

In addition to these distinctive patterns of the 1940s and 1950s, Jewish Great Neck, in particular, had maintained close connections to its immigrant family and religious roots in the city. And finally, in terms of leadership, the Great Neck of the 1920s, which had originally gained fame and éclat through the presence of celebrities such as F. Scott Fitzgerald and Eddie Cantor, was different from the Great Neck of the 1930s to the 1960s, which gained stability from the longevity and distinction of its leaders: from Rabbi Waxman, as senior rabbi for over fifty years, and Rudin, as leader of Beth-El for over thirty years, who provided two different models of Jewish adaptation to the suburban world; school leaders such as John L. Miller and Margaret Johnson; and lay leaders such as Willie Cohen, Josslyn Shore, Hilda Liff, Saul Epstein, Max Rubin, David and Norma Levitt, Jack and Ethel Hausman, and Robert Benjamin.

In the mid-decades of the century, why did people choose Great Neck over other suburban destinations? Some came because they had friends or family, family clans in some cases, already in residence. Others, knowing no one, took a chance on the good reputation of the schools. Others came because the community was known to be hospitable to Jews, those who wanted a religious affiliation and those who simply wanted the ambiance of a suburban Jewish culture in the making. "Jewish Americana" was the way Leni Reis, who graduated from the high school in the 1950s, described it.[3] There were economic and geographical advantages. Before the war, when the Liffs moved in, the rents were cheaper than in the city. For the Arlows, Westchester was out because it was too far from Brooklyn and the family. When the Barzuns came to the States as refugees from Belgium, they were directed to the community by their Gentile bankers at the Chase Manhattan Bank in the city. For Sylvia Pechter, the reason was far less rational. On a train to the South Shore to buy a house since she was expecting a child, she sat across from a woman who had an epileptic fit. Remembering her mother's superstition about avoiding, at all costs, anything scary during pregnancy, she fled the train, returned to Penn Station in a panic and took the next train out to find some other place to live. It was Great Neck, where she knew no one and where she immediately bought a house.

For its Jewish residents in particular, Great Neck was a family-based frontier of upward mobility. It was palpably away from, out of, different from the urban background. The community offered new organizations, friends, and activities to consume the energies of ambitious families. Not bound to the house by incessant hard work, married women in Great Neck, with few exceptions, lived lives of leisure with time to devote to husband and children. (One male "wit" described the period as a time when women put their minds to work at home.) Along with others throughout the country, Great Neck women rose above the mundane through fantasies spun by the fashion and entertainment worlds. According to Eleanor Dwight, the chronicler of Diana Vreeland's mastery of the world of high chic and society, "in the 1950s, fashion magazines portrayed women as objects of worship, who could present themselves through artifice as other-worldly and perfect."[4] The aura of perfection mysteriously blended with the Rodgers and Hammerstein dream world of order, romance, and the superior needs of men. From *The King and I* and *Allegro* the lyrics resonated with a message of wifely sacrifice to preserve marital order, bolster the ego of the husband, and support him—right or wrong, strong or weak.

The stage ideal was often far different from the reality of marriage and family life. Women in the Hammerstein era had few choices but to live the image. Not many had college educations, few had careers, and fewer could support themselves. In fact, the postwar period, according to historian Lizabeth Cohen, intentionally or not, narrowed economic and professional possibilities for women. The government, she wrote, "buttressed a male-directed family economy by disproportionately giving men access to career training, property ownership, capital, and credit, as well as control over family finances, making them the embodiment of the postwar ideal of purchaser as citizen and limiting their wives' claim to full economic and social citizenship."[5]

Furthermore, the national tax structure favored a male-centered married family, which made it financially imprudent for women to work.[6] National economic policies, Cohen wrote, "rewarded the traditional household of male breadwinner father and home-maker mother, thereby making women financially dependent on men at a time when the transformations of depression and war might have encouraged alternatives."[7] Even in religious institutions, where women spent enormous time and effort, there were no rewards in terms of real status. (It wasn't until 1953 that Temple Beth-El elected Lillian Fink as the first women to its board of trustees.) A woman's goals were to find a man with a good job, a good future, and a nice or not-too-difficult family; have children and educate them well; enjoy life; move to a house in the suburbs; join the golf club, the church or temple, and other organizations.

KEEPING THE FAMILY TOGETHER

And finally, in the Great Neck setting, these goals included finding a maid or housekeeper who probably wouldn't get paid too much—a black maid from the South, to help hold the house and family together. Most maids lived in the home, worked every day but Thursday and every other Sunday, watched the children, cooked and did all the housework. The maids stayed home while the wives went to community organizations: the PTA, the hospital volunteers programs, the temple sisterhoods, or, in a few instances, to work, usually in the city. The black maids had no options other than to work as domestics in white communities far from their own families, even their own children, who were left behind in poor areas of the South. In Great Neck, black women with the most limited opportunities allowed white women to expand theirs. The presence of black women was accepted easily, especially because there were few black children and even fewer black men. The black women didn't bring their children with them, nor their husbands or boyfriends. The exceptions were those men who worked as taxi drivers or handymen. Blinded by America's dominant, white, family-oriented, recreation-driven, consumer-hungry spirit in the 1940s and 1950s, few Great Neck families acknowledged the degrading conditions of the black population within its midst. Tied to the city's vibrant economy, Great Neck residents also profited from cheap black labor in the home. In this regard, it was no different from any other white suburb.

Few white employers knew or cared that many black maids on Thursday evenings and Sunday evenings went to the area called the Boat around Steamboat Road and the Boulevard on Spinney Hill. The Boat was a small, contained black neighborhood in Kings Point, an exception to the generally grand expanse of impressive Great Neck homes. By contrast, Spinney Hill, three miles away from the Boat, existed at the edge of Great Neck's most modest residential and commercial area. Black men from the city, along with black maids from Great Neck, went to Spinney Hill bars, clubs, and hotels such as the Hotel James. Tommy James, the owner, made it part of the Chitlin Circuit for black musicians where extraordinary rhythm and blues musicians—Maxine Brown, Etta James, Ruth Brown, Baby Washington, and Pops Moore, among others—played. In the all-black establishments on Steamboat Road and Northern Boulevard, the maids were known (to others and themselves) as "kitchen mechanics." They told stories of humiliation when their employers called them "my girl" or "my jewel of a maid," and when white men pursued them while their wives were out of the house.

Black women could achieve little more than serving as maids. In many cases, the relationships between the maid and family brought unexpected enrichment and affection to both. Poorly schooled but immensely competent black women entered the homes of accepting, educated white families. They heard the cadence of Southern dialogues—expressions, rhythms, and ideas that mixed in with the Yiddish and urban-inflected language of so many of the Jewish families. Black women with strong characters and moral rectitude gained respect from the families for whom they worked. In strong families, the black women added to the richness of the white family's life. In other, less-fortunate homes, they came to relieve the children, who in the words of Zora Neale Hurston were "sucking sorrow."[8] Away from the poverty and violence of Southern black life, white against black and black against black, these black women earned money to send home to their families as well as a degree of independence, especially if they had apartments in Harlem. Separated from their own families still in the South, they shared their affection with the white children for whom they cared.

Lucy Andersen came from Durham, North Carolina. She was young, without a high school diploma, boisterous, bright, once married (to "this no good," she said) but without children. When she came to interview at Mordecai Waxman's home, Lucy took one look at the house and said, "I am going to like it because there are lots of books here."[9] Since she had not had access to public or private libraries in the segregated South, the books in the Waxman home constituted an unexpected treasure. Over time, she took courses and finished high school. Getting the diploma satisfied her ambition, she said, having no further interest in going to college, accumulating much money, or living anywhere else but with the Waxmans. Part of the highly literate Waxman family, she knew best where all the books were. On Sundays before the family came down for breakfast she had already finished the *New York Times* crossword puzzle. She became an expert on kosher laws. She did everything in the house, they joked, but become a good housekeeper. She was "definitely part of the household," part of all family weddings and bar mitzvahs. She took responsibility for the children and they took care of her when she was dying of lung cancer. They went down to Durham for her funeral.

For Beti Kaplan, one of the few women who worked in the city, while her children were growing up, Ruthie Helen Palmer made "everything possible."[10] While Beti assisted in her husband's advertising firm, Ruthie ran the house, took care of three generations of Kaplans—including two grandmothers, Beti and Alvin, and their two sons. Twenty years old, she arrived in Great Neck in 1937, a few months after leaving home in

Frankfort, Kentucky. For the next twenty-one years she lived full-time with the Kaplans, making a profound impression on all the family as a forceful, caring and intelligent woman. She maintained an apartment in New York that she used on her days off to see friends in Harlem. Never married, she essentially committed her life to the Kaplans. Almost fifty years after they met, Beti said that Ruthie had kept peace in the house— she "saved me" and was "my heart and soul."[11] In the first ten years of living with the Kaplans, she had a two-week vacation. After that it was open-ended: Beti told her to come back when "she was ready." She never stayed away for more than three weeks, although Beti's mother would proclaim after ten days: "you see, she isn't coming back, she's gone." This fear would be repeated every day until Ruthie "inevitably returned." Zora Neale Hurston, the black author who would sometimes work as a maid when she needed money, observed, "I have been amazed by the Anglo-Saxon's lack of curiosity about the internal lives and emotions of the Negroes."[12] But the ties between Ruthie and the Kaplans were deep and deeply unusual. When Ruthie developed cancer, Beti nursed her until she died at the age of forty-one. The family was devastated by her death.[13]

For Chassie Lee Burr, working for a family in Great Neck provided a measure of pride and accomplishment. She was born in 1902 into a large family in Cabarrus County, North Carolina, where her father was a farmer. With little education, a failed marriage to a man who drank too much, and a daughter left with her family in the South, she came to New York to work and live. When she died, at the age of ninety-four, the short obituary in her "Homegoing Service" in Harlem simply stated: "She worked as a housekeeper. Chassie went to work for Kate & and Meyer Stein in 1943. This employment lasted for thirty or more years. Within those years, she became a loving, devoted member of their family. She left her granddaughter, grandsons, greatgrands and 'Chassie's very special family Judy Goldstein, Susannah Hadorn, Jon Stein and a host of relatives and friends.'"[14] As the Stein children grew up, she set the rules of their behavior, enforced discipline, commanded respect, enforced devotion to her New York Yankees, and dispensed her love to them. Her employment as a housekeeper enabled her to earn a living, remarry, live in Harlem, and adopt a comfortable white family, some of whom suffered from emotional illnesses. Patient and dignified, she kept her own hurts, at the hands of her employer, and her own family wounds to herself. Sadly, Chassie's work in Great Neck kept her from the intimacy of bringing up her daughter before she died in her thirties from heart disease.

Were Ruthie Palmer, Chassie Burr, and Lucy Andersen the exceptions—memorable for their affection and commanding roles in three white families—to the general condition of black maids in Great Neck? Unfortunately, the answer is most probably yes. While the black housekeepers were ever-present in white households, there was little awareness of black life, the histories, emotions, hopes, and frustrations, beyond the immediate needs of the employer's home. Even in 1950, when Ken Sidon and Moreson Kaplan, two high schools students, made an exposé in *Newsday* of the scandalous living conditions in Spinney Hill, it made little impact. On behalf of eighty members of the Inter-Faith Fellowship of the Great Neck Youth Center, Sidon and Kaplan took inventory of the living conditions of residents in fifty Spinney Hill homes. They discovered that 60 percent used outdoor toilets, 85 percent had no hot water, and "several hundred people live in tumble-down firetraps."[15]

Unpleasant conflicts between the demands of the white employers and the work of black maids aired in the *Great Neck Circle* in May 1951. Appearing several times over a two-year period, the glossy publication presented profiles of well-known Great Neck figures that boasted about Great Neck's unique and interesting population. The editors, however, didn't shy away from controversial feature articles. In one, "Psychiatry in the Suburbs," the author declared: "Great Neck is not in an emotional class by itself," nor filled with more neurotic people than those found in Greenwich, Beverley Hills, or New Rochelle.[16] In the same vein, an anonymous author wrote: "I was psychoanalyzed: A Great Neck Housewife Pleads Tolerance for your Neurotic Neighbor." She found little sympathy or knowledge about emotional or mental illness. In fact, she wrote, her friends ignored her after discovering that she was ill and in treatment. "The second by-product," she wrote, "was the realization that, despite all the conversational facility with Freudian terms which exists, emotional disturbances are still not accepted as casually as physical disease."[17]

"Why Great Neck Maids Don't Stay," authored by an anonymous maid, was another hard-hitting, personal declaration that punctured Great Neck's rosy facade. The tone was indignant and blunt, although the author now worked for people whom she very much liked. In her ten years in Great Neck, she had known some good employers and some awful ones. From the start, the job interviews were one-sided: "when a prospective employer asks me for *my* references, I often feel like asking her for *hers*," including questions such as: "is the family a happy one, how long did the previous maid stay, do the employers think of other people's feelings?"[18]

She came from a small Southern town as a widow with two children to support. She had never been a maid before she took a job in Great Neck. "I have never known a housewife," she wrote, "without help who worked from 7 am until the dishes were done at night without stopping at least once during the day to read, primp or just plain relax, yet that's what some employers expect us to do." Fifteen minutes for lunch or dinner was all the time maids were supposed to take off. "Remember, to earn her $40.00 weekly salary, the average maid must spend more than 120 hours in the confines of your home, subject to your every whim and command. If she is shut off from the outside world, your home, richly furnished and carpeted as it is, becomes nothing more than a luxurious prison. In this environment, your maid will be irritable, frustrated or neurotic—and finally quit!" She has no place to entertain her friends. She must answer the door and be on call all the time. Often she was given no desk or chair to read and write. The worst frustrations, she wrote, involved the children. The most common reason for maids leaving was that they found the children insufferable. The kids hit, spit at, and called maids names. "Many of them have little respect for their mothers and none at all for the maid," she wrote. "Although some mothers can't control their own children, they forbid anyone else trying, especially the maid, even though she may have children of her own who love and respect her, as I do."[19]

It is not surprising that this anonymous author put so much blame on the children in the 1940s and 1950s as part of her focus on Great Neck families. Maids often knew better than most what parents and children were like and which families lived in destructive discord. Without question, children were at the center of individual family concerns and Great Neck's collective aspirations, as they were throughout the country. That focus was a blessing for some and a painful burden for others. As the children grew up, many suffered from the wounds of family secrets, conflicts, hidden divorces, parental neuroses, and mental illness. Some children would become emotionally disabled: some committed suicide; the more fortunate ones spent years coming to terms with their turbulent pasts. But the author's harsh and dismissive judgment against the kids should not be taken as the last word or assessment of Great Neck children.

Nice or nasty, well-behaved or out of control—and there were more who were decent and disciplined than mean, spoiled, or disturbed—the children were the *raison d'etre* of suburban existence. The welfare, education, and advancement of Great Neck children constituted the community's social veneer, fixation, and major ambitions, particularly Jewish ambitions for upward mobility. It determined the character of the community and the cause of its transformation from an ordinary North Shore suburb into America's most outstanding postwar Jewish suburb.

What did all of those expectations, opportunities, and religious differences mean to the children growing up in Great Neck's suburban frontier? How did Great Neck affect them and their futures? What kind of impressions did the place make upon them? For some children, the town was blissful; for others, a torment. Some, such as Max Tannenbaum, felt that they belonged to the place: a small, safe, walkable, friendly, intimate, beautiful, and, in parts, still rural place that one could put one's arms around and embrace. Others, who lived on the social periphery, were excluded for being different or repulsed by the materialistic, competitive, and mercurial social groupings of adolescents. The rejected ones would have to wait until they were adults to find acceptance and respect from others. Some who came from modest families felt the sting of rich show-offs in fancy clothes and cars; others never felt that money determined who was popular or not. Some thought the education first-rate; others found the education unstimulating and routine. (David Baltimore, a future Nobel laureate in science, remembers nothing distinctive about the science education in Great Neck, although his parents moved there solely to give their children good educations.) The increasing emphasis on educational success was hard on late bloomers, slow learners or those with average or below average abilities. The focus on college preparation slighted the vocational needs of many students.

In the fluid atmosphere of a changing population, questions of identity filled the air: were you a Yankee or a Dodger fan? A Gentile or Jew? Did you go to Saddle Rock, Kensington or Arrandale School? One innocent child, when asked if she was "Jewish" answered that she was "Kensington," the elementary school that she went to. The ethnic/religious splits were not just amusing but for real. In the late 1940s and early 1950s, the Jewish kids went to Stefans, an ice cream store, and the Gentiles to Gilliars. The social distances between Jewish and Gentile kids grew gradually through high school when religious differences made their mark, especially through exclusionary fraternities and sororities that divided along religious lines in the late 1940s and early 1950s. (The exceptions involved the muscular and therefore popular Jewish football players, of whom there were many. They dated Gentile girls who were referred to as the "shiksa goddesses.") It didn't occur to Alfred Appel, in the class of 1952, until thirty years after he was in high school that a girl he wanted to date would not go out with him because he was Jewish. One kid said to him the day after he had been absent for the Yom Kippur holiday: "I didn't know you was Jewish." Alfred said he had been out sick and the kid said, "I knew you was all right."[20] The social patterns of students firmly reflected the low rate of intermarriage for Jews. Nationwide in 1940, it was only 3 percent. Some originally mixed couples lived in Great Neck, but they were mostly Gentile women who later converted to Judaism and raised their children as Jews.

The ascendant Jewish culture made some children feel completely at home; others, particularly among the diminishing number of Gentile students, felt left out by the strangeness of Jewish religious holidays and other religious observances, highlighted by the flood of bar mitzvahs. By the 1960s, some non-Jewish kids even tried to pretend that they were Jewish: they were the ones excluded from parties given by Jews and isolated since there were so few Gentile kids to mix with. The community was especially difficult for Catholics, according to Bruce Bent who graduated in the mid-1950s, since the smartest Catholic students went to private school, leaving the impression that the rest, many of whom came from working-class backgrounds, were not capable or smart.

Religious education made a strong impression on many children, especially those who went through Temple Israel's intensive after-school programs. For many Jewish children, however, enrollment in religious classes meant going through the motions of affiliation without any real meaning, except to please their parents and grandparents. In fact, by the late 1950s and 1960s, the community was so at ease with its Jewish population that formal connections to Jewish institutions were superfluous for those families that just wanted the atmosphere of Jewish culture through the superficial, albeit satisfying, verbal and social insignia of a common immigrant background. Many Great Neck Jewish parents of the 1940s and 1950s took for granted or neglected their own ethnic identities formed in Eastern Europe and American urban ghettos. Thus, many Jewish children, despite the ritualistic Sunday visits from grandparents, knew little about Jewish observance, history, or even their own family backgrounds.

The connection to the culturally rich and heterogeneous city, not to their urban immigrant and religious roots, made a deep impact on many Great Neck students. Alfred Appel, Jr. for example, often went to the city, most memorably with Mrs. Hubbard, his French teacher, who took him to the Museum of Modern Art. *The Art of Celebration*, Appel's book about art and a subtle autobiography, was about his infatuation with New

York City. The son of a lawyer, he became a prolific writer on Vladimir Nabokov, jazz, and modern art. Appel was one of a multitude of Great Neck students who rushed to the city on the weekends to go to theater, concerts, and museums and break through the limited suburban horizons. Among them were students with a broad array of interests that led to accomplished careers: Barbara Stoler Miller and Wendy Doniger, who became two of the leading Sanskrit scholars in America; Stephen Albert, a future composer and Pulitzer Prize winner; and Bernard Pomerance, a playwright who won a Pulitzer for *The Elephant Man*.

Visiting New York City was only one of the many extraordinary opportunities that made Great Neck children the beneficiaries of one of America's golden ages. As children of the suburban, white, middle and upper class, they grew up in a time of postwar wealth, government-encouraged consumerism, subsidized higher education, and home ownership. Vast numbers of parents, including immigrants and the children of immigrants, for the very first time had the means to become educated, prosperous, and confident of giving their children unequalled opportunities, especially in a time of diminishing anti-Semitism. In Great Neck, parents worked hard at insuring that they grasped all that they could of the good life, the American way of life, and the American dream. Spending money on homes, cars, clothing, and entertainment, according to Lizabeth Cohen, was a postwar patriotic duty: insurance against recession and the assertion of the superiority of western capitalism.[21] Whether from patriotic or other motives, Great Neck did it with splendid zest.

From time to time, the sustained binge brought unwelcome notoriety in the press. In November 1956, the *New York Post* featured "Suburbia, L.I., the Intimate Story of Great Neck." The account dug deep into the Great Neck's psyche and ethos: its residents were "lunging for success;" Great Neck women were "narcissistic and too conscious of themselves sexually;" the children were "over-stimulated."[22] Among others, the editors of the high school newspaper came to the community's defense, challenging the barrage of accusations. "Surely," it proclaimed, "Great Neck, like most American communities of 45,000 and over, has its share of neurotics, malcontents and ostentatious people. It also has (unlike many communities), a better than average share of people who are genuinely interested in the schools, in charities, their children and in community affairs." And next to the editorial, a spoof titled "Absurbia, L.I. Minks and Analysts Vie for Pie in The G.N. Sky" challenged the *Post* some more. "If one is lucky enough to maneuver his sleek Cadillac down Northern Boulevard,

and make that left turn, he finds himself in a never-never land" where
the sun shines, the maids smile and clean children play in the streets. Great
Neck is a "town where cherubs cavort unmolested in the sky, shooting
arrows through dollar signs."[23]

Consuming and showing off were endemic, despite the price of ridicule,
but children were Great Neck's fixation as well as its valued product by
means of education and community building in the 1940s, 1950s and early
1960s. Despite its most recent stigmatization, Great Neck's legacy should
not be viewed through the darkened lens of the documentary *Capturing
the Friedmans*, about one tormented Great Neck family and its trove of
filmed family secrets. Nor is that legacy to be found in the machinations
of the community's rebellious, alienated sons of the 1960s as described in
Great Neck, a novel by Jay Cantor. One should look instead to the achievements of its children who became the musicologists, composers, authors,
doctors, law professors, anthropologists, journalists, scientists, film makers,
lawyers, businessmen, educators, historians, poets, politicians, photogra-
phers, and political activists: Francis Ford Coppola, the movie director;
Jean-Claude Van Itallie, playwright; Bob Simon, the television journalist;
Richard Zeckhauser, Ramsay Professor of Economics and Political Economy at the Kennedy School of Government; Neil Zaslow, the musicologist
and Cornell professor; Judith Friedman, authority on French history and
professor at Hunter College; Peter Camejo, the Green candidate for governor of California in 2003; William Tucker, professor of psychology at
Rutgers; George Segal, actor; Carl Seitz, cellist; Louis van Amerongan,
investment banker; Bruce Bent, businessman and politician; Wini Shore
Freund, community activist on Long Island; Alfred Appel, professor of
literature at Northwestern and author; Wendy Doniger, Mircea Eliade
Distinguished Service Professor at the University of Chicago and Sanskrit
scholar; Stephen Albert, composer; David Baltimore, scientist and president
of Cal Tech; Joseph Lane, orthopedic surgeon and head of the Hospital
for Special Surgery in New York; Mark Soloman, poet and businessman;
Peter Schuck, Baldwin Professor of Law at Yale Law School; Barbara
Stoler Miller, professor of Asian studies at Barnard and Sanskrit scholar;
Larry Poons, artist; Alan Miller, director of documentaries on music;
Daniel Stern, doctor and authority on infant psychiatry; Enid Schildkraut,
former chair of the Department of Anthropology and curator for Africa
at the American Museum of Natural History in New York; Richard Taub,
professor of sociology, University of Chicago; Nancy Meckler, theater
director; Paul Cohen, professor of Asian history at Wellesley College;

Nadine Ullman Brozan, *New York Times* journalist; Peter May, a mathematician at the University of Chicago; Barbara Paul Robinson, lawyer and first female president of the Association for the Bar of the City of New York; Jay Bernstein, professor of philosophy at the New School; Jay Cantor, author and professor at Tufts University; Ann Laura Stoler, anthropologist at the New School; Ralph Austen, professor of African history at the University of Chicago; Michael Schwartz, litigator and jazz pianist; Louis Uchitelle, a *New York Times* economic writer; Dr. Karen Hein, a specialist in adolescent medicine; Richard Shweder, anthropologist at the University of Chicago; Neil Flax, a professor of comparative literature who would become an expert on nineteenth-century art criticism in France; Sue Bernstein, a philanthropist of cultural and educational institutions; Robert Friedman, foreign editor of *Fortune* magainze; Dale Rosengarten, author; and Barbara Finkelstein, professor and director of the International Center for Transcultural Education at the University of Maryland.

For some people, Great Neck could be viewed, in yet another vein of disparagement, as the perfect manifestation of Lizabeth Cohen's consumer republic.[24] Although she didn't write about Great Neck, in the minds of many she could have used it as the quintessential example of self-serving spending and offensive pride that deepened America's postwar racial, class, and gender inequalities. She might have entitled her book: *The Consumer Republic: Great Neck and Other Atrocities.* Cohen harshly judged the reign of residential suburbia in which "the mass of Americans shared less and less common physical space and public culture" in their favored realms of private space.[25]

Many who grew up in Great Neck shared the same sense of dismay. They felt the tension between the values of Great Neck's intellectuals and artists, mostly of modest means, and those of the consuming and ostentatiously successful businessmen and their families. The tension drove many children to flee the high-living suburb after graduating from high school. For others, the disenchantment emerged later in their lives. Alfred Appel, Jr., who loved Great Neck when he was growing up there, was ashamed of the changes he perceived by the 1970s. Neil Kurk, chairman of the Finance Committee in the New Hampshire House of Representatives, refused in any official publication to reveal that he grew up in Great Neck.

Great Neck was an epicenter of excess in material things and self-satisfaction. It imparted to its privileged families and, particularly, some of its children, the sharp weapons of entitlement. To those who came from cities and towns where wealth was more established and impressed more sensitively into relationships between the many diverse parts of a community, Great Neck was an affront. Other negatives were hard to miss. Many Great Neck students entered colleges and universities on a wave of aggressive academic superiority. The level of teaching in the high school sometimes exceeded what students found in first-rate colleges. The arrogance of youth crowned the confidence of an education-oriented community. At best, teachers such as Jack Fields had listened carefully to his students' ideas and encouraged many to claim future rewards in the fields of journalism, academia, literature, and the arts. And why not? Many smart students were eager to learn. Their parents wanted them to succeed, if only to get into a good college. Although not all parents were educated or cultured—far from it—they all shared the values of learning, educational success, and the hunger for mobility through their children from secondary school to college.

Beyond college, however, different perspectives often emerged between children and parents. Children who wished to go into academia or the arts envisioned opportunities beyond their parents' dreams. Wounded by the Depression and discrimination against Jews in numerous fields, some parents could not conceive of success and security beyond business in the garment trade, real estate, or small manufacturing pursuits. The struggle between the parents' fears and the children's confident ambitions could be intense. Family ties weakened and sometimes temporarily dissolved under the pressure of competing expectations. Parents could see America opening up to them in the suburb, but not beyond. Once out of Great Neck, the next generation, especially Jewish men, moved into a new world where the anti-Semitic prejudices of the educated elite began to succumb to new financial and programmatic needs of the academic institutions. As Jewish students made their way through college and graduate school in the 1950s and 1960s, the system opened up. In the process, the children lost some of the arrogance but not the drive to succeed that had been generated in Great Neck.

Ultimately, the community should be known more for its substantive achievements and community experiments rather than for brash airs of educated superiority and the habit of gaudy consumerism. From the 1940s through the 1960s, Great Neck created a common democratic culture: a grass roots culture of aspiration through heavily funded public education, a culture of suburban Jewish life, a culture of urban connections, a culture of generous institution-building for its local social, artistic, educational, medical, and physical needs.

There was failure as well, but failure that deserves serious recognition. The vigorous adventure to create a new suburban version of the American melting pot did not hold: the balance of Gentiles and Jews disintegrated under the ethnic and religious pressures of an assertive Jewish presence and Protestant and Catholic flight. Today, the Great Neck community of 42,000 is an ethnoburb with a stunning variety of immigrants from Asia, South Africa, and the Middle East; a recognized center of suburban Jewish life, with thousands of members in Temples Israel and Beth-El, but conspicuously Orthodox and thus sorely divided and contentious; a consumer paradise par excellence; a demanding workplace for women as well as men; an exhausting place for working mothers; a fiercely competitive cauldron for its children learning in fine schools; a magnet for medical care through its merged North Shore Hospital and Long Island Jewish Hospital; and, as always, the frequent target—sometimes well deserved—of ridicule and denigration for its self satisfied suburban attitudes. In the past few decades, Great Neck, this exemplary symbol of the suburban American Jewish dream, has faltered and waned along with the American dream itself.

Buried beneath the restless, ever-changing nature of suburban life, and American life in general, are the currents that once charged Great Neck, particularly Jews in Great Neck, with energy, pride of place, community, and accomplishment. From the 1920s through the 1960s, Great Neck was a luminous spot in itself and, in America's unrelenting tradition, as a place on the way to somewhere else. John Higham, the great historian of American immigration history, thought that the covered wagon and the Statue of Liberty were America's most important symbols. "They both mean," he wrote, "opportunity grasped by moving on."[26]

The Promised Land in America has always been a moving target, inexorably pushing its population on to something seemingly more desirable in terms of individual fulfillment, landscape, social geography, illusive and real possibilities. For a glorious few decades Great Neck was the place to be for ambitious Jews on their way out of the city into the country, away from their immigrant pasts into the territory of Gentile America. Great Neck was perfectly poised at the center of converging aspirations, possibilities, collective myths, and realities: a wealthy community that paid handsomely for its preeminent public education system; a well-located community that tied itself tightly to America's greatest city and center of Jewish life; an integrated community of Jews and Gentiles that provided the foundation for mobility for its finely educated youth; a "celebrity" place that claimed connections to Fitzgerald, Cantor, and Whitney; a suburban community that proudly exemplified America's shifting population; and a community that resonated with confidence drawn from American postwar prosperity and power. Just a few miles from Broadway, Seventh Avenue, Wall Street, and Greentree, a critical mass of ambitious second generation Americans poured their hunger for education and success into their children and community.

In those years from the 1940s through the 1960s, Great Neck transcended the panache and poignant, ephemeral shallowness of Gatsby's place. It defied the strong odds, as predicted in *The Great Gatsby*, of going from "nothing to nothing." It was Great Neck, in Fitzgerald's poetic words, that prompted a pure vision of what America promised. Before departing the spot, Nick Carraway took a last look at the Sound: "And as the moon rose higher the inessential houses began to melt away until gradually I became aware of the old island here that flowered once for Dutch sailors' eyes—a fresh, green breast of the new world." It was in this place that people found a special way to hope and build, a new way to make themselves known. Decades after Gatsby's time, it wasn't Gatsby's way. Great Neck's way was through its children. It was they who bore the promise and succeeded in making meaningful contributions—suburban-bred contributions—to the betterment of American life.

Epilogue

In the summer of 2005, much of Great Neck looks as it did forty years ago. It remains lushly residential despite an obvious increase in the number of houses, apartment complexes, condominiums, stores, and corporate buildings. Educational excellence remains a priority as Great Neck's two high schools continue to rank high in the United States. Civic interest and participation is strong, especially in regard to the individual villages, public parks, and library. North Shore Hospital and Long Island Jewish, now joined, constitute an outstanding medical center. Real estate prices have never been higher. With 43,000 residents, the peninsula is thriving.

There is, however, a strong current of uncertainty about Great Neck's future. Trends that began in the 1970s have reached a new stage of uncertainty. Many wonder if Great Neck is reinventing itself and tipping once again. The first years of the twenty-first century could constitute a defining period in the succession of changes that have marked Great Neck's history since the 1920s. Although there is a significant increase in middle- and upper-class Asian residents from Korea, India, and China, mainly settled in Lake Success, as well as a growing Hispanic population, it is clear that the demographic forces within the Jewish community mean that Great Neck might recreate itself once again.

Adjusting to the growing numbers and types of Orthodox Jews is cutting deeply into Great Neck's Jewish identity and the identity of the community as a whole. The differences among the secular, Reform, Conservative, and the many different types of Orthodox Jews position Jew against Jew.

Starting in the 1950s, Orthodox Jews established a secure place for themselves, centered on the Great Neck Synagogue, despite the initial discomfort of many long-time Reform and Conservative Jewish residents in the community. By the 1980s, tolerance was harder to come by when hundreds of Sephardic Jews, mainly immigrants from Iran, settled in Great Neck. (The other favored spot was Beverly Hills.) The Persians, as they are popularly referred to in Great Neck, brought tightly held family and religious traditions. These differed drastically from those embodied in the majority of second- and third-generation Jews who arrived in Great Neck via Eastern Europe and the Lower East Side, Brooklyn, Queens, and the Bronx.

Endowed with wealth and large families, the first generation of Iranian immigrants quickly established their own institutions. Not wanting to venture beyond their familiar family, social, and religious worlds, they had little need or inclination to defer to the interests and mores of the established Great Neck Jewish population. The long-time residents reacted with embarrassment, annoyance, and even dismay: unpleasant stories circulated about the Iranians negotiating and quibbling over prices in the supermarkets and stores; consternation developed over the lavish architecture of Persian homes; resentment grew over Middle Eastern habits of separateness. Among the long-established Jewish population there was little inclination to wait for the transforming effects of American life to modify the ways of second and third generations from the Middle East. The general reception towards the new immigrants was characterized by dislike and suspicion, despite the efforts of Reform and Conservative religious leaders to interact with the Sephardic Jews.

The particular tensions between Great Neck's Ashkenazi and Sephardic Jews provide rich and intriguing material for future works of fiction and nonfiction alike. One eagerly awaits historians, sociologists, and novelists to approach the subject. The interactions between the two groups are fascinating, yet they may prove to be of secondary importance in Great Neck's history. Of greater significance is the fact that the Iranian presence in Great Neck may have provided the opening wedge for a greatly expanded Ashkenazi Orthodox presence—one characterized by varying degrees of observance and religiosity. From the 1980s on, the Iranians developed a number of Orthodox synagogues, day schools, kosher restaurants, and shops that provided the religious and tradition-based infrastructure for a greatly expanded Orthodox community. In the mid-twentieth century, Reform Jews had followed other Reform Jews to Great Neck. Today, Orthodox Jews follow other Orthodox Jews to Great Neck. Their needs and expectations present a basic challenge to Great Neck's suburban connections and ethos, which began to develop in the 1920s and reached the pinnacle of success in the 1950s.

Twenty-five years ago, the future seemed very different. *Ethnicity in Suburbs: the Long Island Experience*, published in 1980, featured chapters about many different ethnic groups in Long Island communities. For Great Neck, the subject was the Jews. According to the report, there were 1,300 families that belonged to Temple Beth-El; 650 to Temple Emanuel, the second largest Reform temple; 1,300 to Conservative Temple Israel; 450 to the Great Neck Synagogue and forty-five to Young Israel, the two Orthodox centers.[1] Dr. Jay Schulman, author of the concise history, presented several positive conclusions: Jews in Great Neck were "not an endangered ethnic species";[2] the distinctions between religious and ethnic identity were not important, since both secular and religious Jews successfully identified as Jews in their own different ways; Great Neck's dominant liberal Jewish beliefs and mores were alive and well. "Acting upon civic-minded impulses," Schulman wrote, "Jews have enriched the cultural life of Great Neck, exerted a salutary influence upon the schools, and contributed generously of their time, talents, and substance to the health and welfare agencies of the community."[3] His assessment continued in this laudatory and optimistic vein: "Though the Jewish presence has been extensive, there is no trace of ethno-centrism or separatism in it. In spirit and practice the Jews of Great Neck subscribe to a pluralistic and an integrated community."[4] The long-term leadership of Great Neck's rabbis, including Jerome K. Davidson, of Temple Beth-El; Mordecai Waxman, of Temple Israel; and Robert Widom, of Temple Emanuel—all dynamic and confident practitioners of integration—undoubtedly contributed to Schulman's conclusions.

Today, in 2005, community concepts of pluralism and integration are in dispute. The tensions—perceived and real—between separatism and integration involve Great Neck's streets, public spaces, public institutions, and commerce. Zoning fights constantly erupt over the building of new synagogues and religious schools, by Chabad and others, in residential areas. Large numbers of children now attend Young Israel and the North Shore Hebrew Academy, instead of going to the public schools. Once modest areas around Steamboat Road, many formerly owned by blacks, have become valuable properties since they are within walking distance of many Orthodox and Persian synagogues. The numerous kosher restaurants and stores owned by Orthodox Jews—butchers, delicatessens, hairdressers, pharmacies and clothing stores—strictly follow Orthodox rules. Countless people conform to a traditional Orthodox appearance: women wear wigs and long skirts; men wear kippas, broad hats, and tallitim. Of late, many Orthodox gather in small learning centers, known as *stiebels*, which proliferate in houses or stores. Political issues are contested with a new ferocity. Many Orthodox Jews, who vote Republican in support of conservative social and political views in America and Israel, outspokenly object to Great Neck's established liberal, Democratic proclivities.

For some long-term residents, Middle Neck Road, the commercial center of Great Neck, has become a strange, eerie land on the Sabbath: quiet during the day, boisterous and busy after sunset. In a place that no longer feels like an extended home for people sharing a common set of values, the sense of unease is not confined to the twenty-four hours of the Sabbath. Instead, the discomfort of many goes to the essence of past and present expectations of what Great Neck was and would remain. Living in a new Great Neck can be a deeply painful and jarring experience.

Questions abound, while answers are uncertain. Is visibility—simply seeing traditional Orthodox Jews fulfilling traditional Orthodox practices—the irritant and the issue? Or, is there pressure for Great Neck, in its public life, to conform to traditional and often extreme Orthodox mores? Will support for the public schools change because significant segments of the community choose parochial religious educations? How will Great Neck promote its collective goals and identity if it can no longer rely upon widespread interest in its public schools? Will the suburb, defined since the 1940s by a common commitment to educational excellence, now take on the ethos of a diversified city with its amalgam of interests? Will stores owned by non-Orthodox be forced to close on the Sabbath, under pressure from some members of the Orthodox community? Will Jewish leaders in Great Neck find a common meeting ground that transcends the petty personal annoyance of what people look like, as well as the substantial differences over basic religious values and practices? Do the many different types of Orthodox want to engage with a larger and somewhat diverse American society, or do they want Great Neck to conform to traditional Orthodox way? Will Great Neck look inward and become a golden *shtetl*?

For centuries, Jews have challenged each other with different forms of Jewish religious practice and education, different concepts of Jewish identity, and different ideas about community, integration, assimilation, and survival. For centuries, Americans have made and remade their communities. Although no longer recognizable as Fitzgerald's West Egg, Great

Neck is still prosperous, ambitious, and inventive. No longer envious of the North Shore to the east, Great Neck is still a largely Jewish community. But Great Neck continues to face challenges of diversity, as it did from the 1920s on, which are deeply meaningful to American life. The community remains a conspicuous place where pluralism is under pressure. The issue is not Gentile versus Jew, as it was in the past, but religious freedom versus the demands of secularism and religious differences about public institutions and civic responsibility. Great Neck's tensions will be played out on its unique suburban stage, but they are unmistakably part of searing national and international forces that affect us all.

Notes

INTRODUCTION

1. Theodore Rosengarten and Dale Rosengarten, eds., *A Portion of the People: Three Hundred Years of Southern Jewish Life* (Columbia: University of South Carolina Press, 2002).

2. Paul Johnson, *A History of the Jews* (New York, Harper & Row, 1987), 373.

3. Russell Baker, "Out of Step with the World," *New York Review of Books,* September 20, 2001, 10.

CHAPTER 1. ON THE MAP

1. Eddie Cantor, *My Life Is in Your Hands* (New York, Harper & Brothers, 1928), 292.

2. Ibid.

3. Ibid.

4. Ibid.

5. Ibid.

6. Lurten Blassing, Anne, "Type Model," *New Yorker*, January 27, 1927, 23.

7. Ibid.

8. *The Most of John Held, Jr.*, Forward by Marc Connelly, Introduction by Carl J. Weinhardt (Brattleboro, Vt.: Green Press, 1972).

9. *This Is Great Neck,* The League of Women Voters of Great Neck, (Great Neck, NY, 1995), Introduction.

10. Frederick Lewis Allen, *Only Yesterday; an Informal History of the Nineteen-Twenties* (New York: Harper & Brothers, 1931), 82.

11. Ibid., 83.

12. Ibid., 92.

13. Ibid., 97.

14. E. J. Kahn, Jr., *The World of Swope* (New York: Simon and Schuster, 1965), 292.

15. Allen, *Only Yesterday*, 115.

16. Kahn, *The World of Swope*, 292.

17. Allen, *Only Yesterday*, 81.

18. Kahn, *The World of Swope*, 293–294.

19. Ruth Gordon, *Myself among Others* (New York: Atheneum, 1971), 160.

20. Allen, *Only Yesterday*, 101.

21. Gordon, *Myself among Others*, 168.

22. Ibid., 169.

23. Ibid., 170.

24. Swope Collection, Jan 20, 1928.

25. Allen, *Only Yesterday*, 110.

26. Ibid., 128.

27. F, Scott Fitzgerald, *The Great Gatsby* (New York: Collier Books, 1975), 9–10.

28. F. Scott Fitzgerald, *All the Sad Young Men* (New York: Charles Scribner's Sons, 1926), 1–2.

29. Ibid., 5.

30. Fitzgerald, *The Great Gatsby*, 7.

31. The Fitzgeralds lived at 6 Gateway Drive in the Great Neck Estates. James R. Mellow, *Invented Lives: F. Scott and Zelda Fitzgerald* (New York: Houghton Mifflin, 1984), 166.

32. F. Scott Fitzgerald, *The Crack-Up*, ed. Edmund Wilson (New York: New Directions, 1945), 29.

33. Alfred Kazin, ed., *F. Scott Fitzgerald: the Man and His Work* (Cleveland: World Publishing Company, 1951), 64.

34. Matthew Bruccoli and Margaret M Duggan, eds., *The Correspondence of F. Scott Fitzgerald* (New York: Random House, 1980), 11.

35. Ibid., 135.

36. Ibid., 246.

37. F. Scott Fitzgerald, "How to Live on $36,000 a Year," *The Saturday Evening Post,* April 1924, 90.

38. Ibid., 91.

39. Ibid., 94.

40. Ibid., 95.

41. Ibid.

42. Fitzgerald, *The Crack-Up*, 29. Fitzgerald also took with him bad memories and debts from the Great Neck days. There were complications relating to his possessions in the Great Neck rented house. He appealed to his editor Maxwell Perkins for help with the furniture. "As Ring has gone and my others [*sic*] friends there are drunk and unreliable, I am going to ask you to send the enclosed to

some reliable warehouse. . . . This is a hell of a thing to ask anybody but I don't know what else to do as everybody in Great Neck is either incapable or crooked." Bruccoli and Duggan, eds., *The Correspondence of F. Scott Fitzgerald*, 146.

43. Ibid., 174.

44. Kazin, *F. Scott Fitzgerald: the Man and His Work*, 88. This review could hardly have pleased Fitzgerald, especially because he identified with Gatsby. John Peale Bishop responded to Fitzgerald on this point: "I can't understand your resentment of the critic's failure to perceive your countenance behind Gatsby's mask. To me it was evident enough. . . . The point is that you have created a distinct and separate character, perhaps the first male you have ever created on the scale [. . .] a novel, whom you have filled, as is inevitable, with your own emotional life. But to ask people to see you in Gatsby seems to me an arrant piece of personal vanity; as an artist it should flatter you that they did not see it." Bruccoli and Duggan, eds., *The Correspondence of F. Scott Fitzgerald*, 175.

45. Kazin, *F. Scott Fitzgerald: the Man and His Work*, 91.

46. Fitzgerald, *The Great Gatsby*, 187–188.

47. Ibid., 113–114.

48. Ibid., 73–74.

49. Ibid., 78.

50. Ibid., 179.

51. *The North Hempstead Record and Long Island Globe*, July 8, 1925, 5.

52. *Great Neck News,* April 11, 1925, 10.

53. Ibid.

54. Jonathan Yardley, *Ring: a Biography of Ring Lardner* (New York: Random House, 1977), 259.

55. *Great Neck News*, April 4, 1925, 10.

56. Ibid., October 24, 1925, 10.

57. Ibid., December 12, 1925, 10.

58. Ibid., July 24, 1926, 7.

59. Ibid., March 28, 1925, 10.

60. Ibid., May 7, 1927, 30.

61. *Great Neck Record*, September 23, 1925, 1.

62. *Great Neck News*, December 18, 1926, 26.

63. Ibid., December 11, 1926, 7.

64. Ibid., January 23, 1926, 11.

65. Ibid., January 20, 1926, 10.

66. Ibid., March 13, 18.

67. Ibid., September 22, 1928, 15.

68. Ibid., November 24, 1928, 9.

69. Ibid., April 13, 1929, 18.

70. Cantor, *My Life Is in Your Hands*, 297–298.

71. Fitzgerald, *The Great Gatsby*, 189.

2. Preparing the Ground

1. Kenneth T. Jackson, *Crabgrass Frontier: The Suburbanization of the United States* (New York, Oxford University Press, 1985), 4.

2. Ibid.

3. Lewis Mumford, "The Wilderness of Suburbia," *The New Republic*, September 7, 1921, 44.

4. Lewis Mumford, *The City in History: Its Origins, Its Transformations, and Its Prospects* (New York: Harcourt, Brace and World, 1961), 487.

5. Jackson, *Crabgrass Frontier*, 99.

6. Richard L. Bushman, *The Refinement of America: Persons, Houses, Cities* (New York: Alfred A. Knopf, 1992), xvii.

7. Ibid., 302.

8. Ibid., 407.

9. Dennis P. Sobin, *Dynamics of Community Change: The Case of Long Island's Declining 'Gold Coast'* (Port Washington, NY: Ira J. Friedman, Inc., 1968), 4, 49.

10. Robert B. Mackay, Anthony K. Baker, and Carol A. Traynor, eds., *Long Island Country Houses and Their Architects, 1860–1940* (New York: Society for the Preservation of Long Island Antiquities, 1997), 11, 13.

11. Mrs. John King Van Rensselaer, *The Social Ladder* (New York: Henry Holt, 1924), 5.

12. Bushman, *The Refinement of America*, 420.

13. Ibid., 419.

14. Van Rensselaer, *The Social Ladder*, 35.

15. Ibid., 213.

16. Ibid., 200.

17. Ibid., 210.

18. Ibid., 280.

19. Mumford, *The City in History*, 485–486.

20. Richard A Winshe, *Historic Structure Report, Saddle Rock, Grist Mill, Saddle Rock, NY,* 1978.

21. Michael Ballentine, "Putting on the Dog with the Cavalier King Charles Spaniel," *Town and Country*, March 1981, 188.

22. All efforts to identify Knapp have been futile. The lack of information about him leads to the possible conclusion that Knapp, this legendary figure in Eldridge family lore, was not as prominent or legitimate as the family and press thought.

23. Ballentine, "Putting on the Dog," 129.

24. *Great Neck News*, January 22, 1927, 28.

25. Sobin, *Dynamics of Community Change*, 100.

26. *Kansas City Star*, July 3, 1931.

27. *Great Neck Record*, November. 27, 1936, 8.

28. *Great Neck News*, January 26, 1927, 4.

29. *Great Neck News*, December 8, 1933, 7.

30. John Lahr, "Light Fantastic," *New Yorker*, May 31, 1993, 56.

31. Jesse Green, "The Song Is Ended," *New York Times Magazine*, June 2, 1996, 6.

32. Cantor, *My Life Is in Your Hands*, 15.

33. *New York Times*, January 25, 1998, 17.

34. Ibid., 114–115.

35. Eddie Cantor, *Take My Life* (Garden City, NY: Doubleday, 1957), 66.

36. Cantor, *My Life Is in Your Hands*, 186.

37. Ibid., 187.

38. *Long Island Country Houses and Their Architects*, 179.

39. Johnson, *History of America: The American People*, 70.

40. Ibid., 718.

41. Cantor, *My Life Is in Your Hands*, 173.

42. Robert Miller, "The Long Island Motor Parkway: Prelude to Robert Moses," in *Robert Moses: Single-Minded Genius*, ed. Joann P. Krieg, Long Island Studies (Interlaken, NY: Heart of the Lakes Publishing, 1989), 152.

43. Edwin Palmer Hoyt, *The Vanderbilts and Their Fortunes* (Garden City, NY: Doubleday, 1962), 347; Miller, "The Long Island Motor Parkway," 156.

44. Robert A. Caro, *The Power Broker: Robert Moses and the Fall of New York* (New York: Alfred A. Knopf, 1974), 328–329.

45. Ibid., 277.

46. Ibid., 301–302.

47. Cantor, *My Life Is in Your Hands*, 172.

48. *Great Neck News*, May 11, 1929, 25.

49. Eddie Cantor, *Caught Short!: A Saga of Wailing Wall Street* (New York: Simon and Schuster, 1929), 12.

50. Ibid., 26.

51. Ibid., Foreword.

52. Eddie Cantor, *Between the Acts* (New York: Simon and Schuster, 1930), 69.

53. *Great Neck News*, February 1, 1932, 14-15.

54. *Great Neck News*, August 18, 1933, 5.

55. *North Hempstead Record*, June 12, 1930, 4.

56. *Great Neck News*, August 9, 1928, 1.

57. *Great Neck News*, September 18, 1930, 4.

58. Temple Beth-El, *Notes*, September 5, 8.

59. Temple Beth-El, *Notes*, October 11, 1927.

60. *Great Neck News*, April 13, 1929, 8.

61. *North Hempsted Record*, September 18, 1930, 1.

62. *North Hempstead Record*, April 2, 1931.

63. Lewis Mumford, "Towards a Modern Synagog [*sic*] Architecture," *Menorah*, 1925, 225.

64. *Great Neck News*, December 8, 1933, 10.

65. Address by Josselyn M. Shore, "The Term Long Time Members Evokes Some Interesting Connotations," 2.

66. Idem.

67. Idem.

68. Josselyn M. Shore, *Shades of Chariots of Fire* (Privately printed), 13.

69. Ibid., 14.

70. After Baltzell's death in 1997, Art Carey wrote in the *Philadelphia Inquirer* about Baltzell's high standards and trenchant and unsparing views of the demise of America's Protestant leadership. "He revered WASP values, traditions and contributions, but Baltzell was contemptuous of the upper class for losing its self-confidence, abdicating its responsibility to lead, squandering its moral capital, and violating its Christian principles by indulging in anti-Semitism, racism and mindless snobbery." *Philadelphia Inquirer*, January 5, 1997, Section E, 3.

71. William H. Zinsser, *Family History*, 1962, 6–7.

72. Ibid., 7.

73. *Great Neck News*, July 24, 1926, 7.

74. William K. Zinsser, *Inventing the Truth: the Art and Craft of Memoir* (Boston: Houghton Mifflin, 1987), 3.

75. Martin Lenn, ed., *Five Boyhoods* (New York: Doubleday, 1962), 117.

76. Art Carey, "A Look Back at a Gentleman and His Life," *Philadelphia Inquirer*, January 5, 1997, Section E, 3.

77. Ibid.

78. *Great Neck News*, June 16, 1939, 16.

3. WAR AND RENEWAL

1. Jacob Philip Rudin, *Very Truly Yours* (New York: Bloch Publishing Company, 1971), 234.

2. Ibid., 237.

3. Ibid.

4. Ibid., 238.

5. Ibid., 239–240.

6. Ibid., 198.

7. Ibid., 198-199.

8. Michael A Meyer, *Response to Modernity: A History of the Reform Movement in Judaism* (New York: Oxford University Press, 1988), 306.

9. Nathan Glazer, *American Judaism* (Chicago: University of Chicago Press, 1972), 81.

10. Meyer, *Response to Modernity*, 296.

11. Glazer, *American Judaism*, 105.

12. Temple Beth-El, *A Family of Families: Temple Beth-El, 1928–1978* (Great Neck, NY, 1978), 10.

13. Ibid.

14. Boorstein moved to Manhasset soon after finishing the thesis.

15. Paula Boorstein, "The Decision to Live in the Suburbs: An Analysis of Fifty Great Neck Families" (Master's thesis, Columbia University, 1936), 8.

16. Ibid., 10.

17. Ibid., Appendix A. 1930 Census.

18. Ibid., 20.

19. Ibid., 22.

20. Ibid., 12.

21. Ibid., 13.

22. Ibid., 113.

23. Ibid., 20.

24. Ibid., 15.

25. Ibid., 24.

26. Ibid.

27. Ibid., 84.

28. Ibid., 52.

29. Ibid., 26.

30. Ibid., 46.

31. Ibid., 33.

32. Ibid., 44.

33. Ibid.

34. Ibid., 65.

35. Ibid., 85.

36. Ibid., 58.

37. Ibid., 96.

38. Ibid.

39. Ibid., 66.

40. Ibid., 98.

41. Ibid., 100.

42. Ibid., 102-103.

43. Ewing Walker, *Vignettes* (Privately published), 54.

44. Doris Kearns Goodwin, *No Ordinary Times: Franklin and Eleanor Roosevelt: the Homefront in World War II* (New York: A Touchstone Book, 1995), 23.

45. Ibid., 313.

46. Jacob Rudin, *The Aleutian Story Itinerary* (Cincinnati: Jacob Rader Marcus Center of the American Jewish Archives, Hebrew Union College Jewish Institute of Religion, May, 1943).

47. Ibid., 29–30.

48. Ibid., 3.

49. Boorstein, "The Decision to Live in the Suburbs," 103.

50. Paul Johnson, "Schools: God and the Americans," *Commentary*, January, 1995, 34.

51. Ibid.

52. Richard Match, *Lucky Seven: Union Free District 7* (Great Neck, NY, 1964); *Great Neck News*, May 13, 1938, 1. Undoubtedly, this was a moment of social unrest. A month before, Great Neck Plaza passed a clothing ordinance—disallowing residents to "unnecessarily expose or reveal any part" of themselves. No shorts or bathing suits would be allowed in the commercial section (Ibid., April 29, 1938, 1.).

53. William Max Wise, "Developing a Guidance Program through Social Process" (Ed.D. dissertation, Teachers College, Columbia University, 1948), 61.

54. Interview with John Miller.

55. Albert Gordon Peterkin, "The School-Community Relations in Great Neck" (New York: Teachers College, 1954), 69.

56. Interview with Hilda Liff.

57. Peterkin, "The School-Community Relations in Great Neck," 63.

58. Ibid., 66–67.

59. Ibid., 67.

60. Ibid.

61. Ibid., 199.

62. *Yakar Le'Mordecai: Jubilee Volume in Honor of Rabbi Mordecai Waxman*, ed. Zvia Ginor (Great Neck, NY: KTAV Publishing House, Temple Israel of Great Neck, 1998), 2.

63. Interview with Ruth Waxman.

64. Ibid., 3.

65. Amos Oz, *A Tale of Love and Darkness* (New York: Harcourt, 2003), 358.

66. *New York Times*, December 28, 1997, 23.

67. Wise, "Developing a Guidance Program through Social Process," 15.

68. Lecture by Kenneth Jackson.

69. Zora Neale Hurston, *Mules and Men* (Philadelphia: J. B. Lippincott, 1935), Introduction.

4. THE QUINTESSENTIAL JEWISH SUBURB

1. Peter Hall, *The City in Civilization: Culture, Innovation, and Urban Order* (London: Weidenfeld & Nicolson, 1998), 746.

2. Everett L. Perry and Ross W. Sanderson, *Nassau Country, Long Island: Social Change and Church Trends, 1910–1948 Report to the Nassau Country Christian Council*, December 31, 1948, 5.

3. Malvina Reynolds, "Little Boxes," *Malvina* (Schroder Music Company, 1968).

4. Lizabeth Cohen, *A Consumer's Republic: The Politics of Mass Consumption in Postwar America* (New York: Alfred A. Knopf, 2003), 123.

5. Thomas Hine, *Populuxe* (New York, Alfred A. Knopf , 1986), 23.

6. Ibid., 18.

7. Ibid., 3.

8. Ibid., 3–4.

9. Interview with David Levitt.

10. John C. Miller, *Interview*, 2, Quoted Material Courtesy of David S. Taylor Archives at the North Shore–Long Island Jewish Heath System.

11. Ibid.

12. Ibid., 3.

13. A.S.G. Butler; with the collaboration of George Stewart & Christopher Hussey. *The Domestic Architecture of Sir Edwin Lutyens* (Woodbridge, Suffolk: Antique Collectors' Club, 1989), 14.

14. E. J. Kahn, Jr. *Jock: the Life and Times of John Hay Whitney* (Garden City, NY: Doubleday, 1981), 108.

15. Ibid., 110.

16. Ibid., 176.

17. Interview with John L. Miller.

18. Richard Kluger, *The Paper: The Life and Death of the New York Herald Tribune* (New York: Vintage Books, 1989), 512.

19. Steven M. L. Aronson, "Tex Rex," *Town and Country*, August 1993, 148.

20. Interview with David Levitt.

21. John Reagan McCrary, January 24, 1992, 23, *Interview*, Material Courtesy of David S. Taylor Archives at the North Shore–Long Island Jewish Heath System.

22. Interview with "Tex" McCrary.

23. *Analysis and Plan: North Shore Hospital Fund, Inc.* November 23, 1949, 2.

24. Interview with David Levitt.

25. Ibid.

26. Dr. John Miller, *Interview*, April 2, 1991, 11, Quoted Material Courtesy of David Taylor Archives at the North Shore–Long Island Jewish Heath System.

27. *Memo: Identifying data concerning the Long Island Jewish Hospital . . . ,* 2, Quoted Material Courtesy of David S. Taylor Archives at the North Shore–Long Island Jewish Heath System.

28. Dr. Israel Strauss and Dr. Joseph S.A. Miller, *Yesterday, Today and Tomorrow*, 2.

29. Ibid., 1.

30. *Memories & Milestones* [Department of Archives Newsletter, Long Island Jewish Medical Center] (Winter 1997), 2.

31. LIJ *Reporter*, June 1953, 2.

32. Ibid., 11.

33. Ibid., 11.

34. Ibid., 6.

35. *Great Neck News,* October 30, 1953, 4-H.

36. Interview with Dr. Jacob Arlow.

37. Ibid.

38. Interview with Rabbi Jerome Davidson.

39. Ibid.

40. Interview with Dr. Jacob Arlow.

41. Hilda Frank, "Concepts and Conflicts in the Synagogue," January 12, 1965, 1–2.

42. Interview with Mordecai Waxman and Ruth Waxman.

43. Interview with Ruth Waxman.

44. *Tradition and Change: the Development of Conservative Judaism*, ed. Mordecai Waxman, Introduction (1958, Rabbinical Assembly of America), 17.

45. Interview with Dr. Jacob Arlow.

46. Interview with Ruth Waxman.

47. Zvia Ginor, ed. *Yakar Le'Mordecai*, (New York: KTAV Publishing House, Inc., 1998), 20.

48. Peterkin, *School-Community Relations in Great Neck, New York*, 56.

49. Match, *Lucky Seven: Union Free District 7*, 46.

50. Diane Ravitch, *The Troubled Crusade: American Education, 1945–1980* (New York: Basic Books, 1983), 12.

51. Louis Menand, "College: The End of the Golden Age," *New York Review of Books*, October 21, 2001, 44.

52. *Horizon*, I, 1958, 2–3.

53. Philip Roth, *Shop Talk: A Writer and His Colleagues and Their Work* (New York: Vintage International, 2001), 142–143.

54. Ibid.

55. Interview with Rabbi Jack Stern.

56. Ravitch, *The Troubled Crusade: American Education*, 7.

57. Ibid., 323.

58. "What Makes Them Good," *Time*, Oct. 21, 1957, 52.

59. "The Sixth Grade," *Life*, November 17, 1952, 147.

60. Ibid.

61. *Statement of General Educational Philosophy*, Great Neck Schools, Great Neck, N.Y. 1962.

62. *Home and Family Living in the Elementary Schools, Great Neck Public Schools.*

63. Interview with Dorothy Hicks.

64. Interview with Dale Rosengarten.

65. Interview with Hilda Liff.

66. *Robert S. Benjamin: a Citizen's Citizen* (New York: 1980); Interview with Jeanne Benjamin.

67. Butler, *The Domestic Architecture of Sir Edwin Lutyens*, 118.

5. THE PRICE OF ACHIEVEMENT

1. Susan Jacoby, *Freethinkers: A History of American Secularism* (New York: Metropolitan Books, 2004). Writing about Norman Vincent Peale, Jacoby observes: in the late 1940s and 1950s, "before the first stirrings of American ecumenicism, Peale would probably have specified Protestant rather than Christians as God's American anointed; a few years later, as Christians became more sensitized to the feelings of Jews, he would likely have used the more general 'religious' or 'God-fearing.' At any rate, all that was required for Peale's countrymen to claim the happiness and success that was their birthright as Americans was to acknowledge the power of God." 303.

2. Alan Wolfe, "Buying Alone," *New Republic*, March 17, 2003, 30.

3. Interview with Leni Reis.

4. Eleanor Dwight, *Diana Vreeland* (New York: William Morrow, 2002), 89.

5. Cohen, *A Consumer's Republic*, 137.

6. Ibid., 144.

7. Ibid., 146.

8. Valerie Boyd, *Wrapped in Rainbows: the Life of Zora Neale Hurston* (New York: Scribner, 2003), 14.

9. Interview with Mordecai Waxman and Ruth Waxman.

10. Interview with Beti Kaplan.

11. Ibid.

12. Boyd, 402.

13. Interview with Beti Kaplan.

14. "Homegoing Service for Chassie Lee Burr," January 30, 1996.

15. *Newsday*, March 27, 1950, 3, 62.

16. Lynn Halperin, "Psychiatry in the Suburbs," *Great Neck Circle,* Summer, 1951, 44.

17. Ibid., 9.

18. "Why Great Neck Maids Don't Stay," *Great Neck Circle*, May, 1951, 18.

19. Ibid.

20. Interview with Alfred Appel.

21. Cohen, *A Consumer's Republic*.

22. "Great Neck Guide Post," November 21, 1956, 2.

23. Ibid.

24. In the latest variation of blaming the suburbs for the ills in American life, the *American Journal of Public Health* and the *American Journal of Health* blamed obesity and hypertension on suburban sprawl (*New York Times,* September 4, 2003, 12–13).

25. Cohen, *A Consumer's Republic*, 254–255.

26. *New York Times*, September 18, 2003, A17.

Epilogue

1. Salvatore J. LaGumina, ed., *Ethnicity in Suburbia: the Long Island Experience* (Papers from a Symposium on Ethnic Group Life held at Nassau Community College, 1980), 63.

2. Ibid., 74.

3. Ibid.

4. Ibid., 75.

Bibliography

Archives and Unpublished Works

Boorstein, Paula. "The Decision to Live in the Suburbs: An Analysis of Fifty Great Neck Families." Master's thesis, Columbia University, 1936.

Boyd, Melody Victoria Isobell. "Black Population of North Hempsted, 1830–1880." Ph.D. dissertation, State University of New York at Stony Brook, May, 1981.

David Taylor Archives, North Shore–Long Island Jewish Health System. Analysis and Plan: North Shore Hospital Fund, Inc. Nov. 23, 1949.

———. LIJ *Reporter*, June 1953.

———. *Memories & Milestones*. Long Island Jewish Medical Center Department of Archives Newsletter, Winter 1997.

———. Strauss, Dr. Israel, and Dr. Joseph S. A. Miller. *Yesterday, Today, and Tomorrow*.

Frank, Hilda. "Concepts and Conflicts in the Synagogue." January 12, 1965.

Herbert Swope Collection, Howard Gotlieb Archival Research Center, Boston University.

Herzig, Helene. "A Family of Families: Temple Beth-El, 1928–1978." Great Neck, NY: 1978.

"Home and Family Living in the Elementary Schools." Great Neck Public Schools.

LaGumina, Salvatore J., ed. *Ethnicity in Suburbia: The Long Island Experience*. Papers from a symposium on Ethnic Group Life held at Nassau Community College, 1980.

Perry, Everett L., and Ross W. Sanderson. *Nassau Country, Long Island: Social Change and Church Trends, 1910–1948. Report to the Nassau Country Christian Council,* December 31, 1948.

Peterkin, Albert Gordon. "School-Community Relations in Great Neck, New York." Ed.D. thesis, Teachers College, Columbia University, 1954.

Rudin, Jacob. "The Aleutian Story Itinerary." Cincinnati: Jacob Rader Marcus Center of the American Jewish Archives, Hebrew Union College Jewish Institute of Religion, 1943.

Shore, Josselyn M. *Shades of Chariots of Fire*. Privately printed.

Walker, Ewing. *Vignettes*. Privately printed.

Wise, William Max. "Developing a Guidance Program through Social Process." Ed.D. thesis, Teachers College, Columbia University, 1948.

Zinsser, William H. *Family History*. 1962.

BOOKS AND ARTICLES

Allen, Frederick Lewis. *Only Yesterday: An Informal History of the Nineteen-Twenties*. New York: Harper & Brothers, 1931.

Aronson, Steven M. L. "Tex Rex." *Town and Country*, August 1993.

Baker, Russell. "Out of Step with the World." *New York Review of Books*, September 20, 2001.

Ballentine, Michael. "Putting on the Dog with the Cavalier King Charles Spaniel." *Town and Country*, March 1981.

Boyd, Valerie. *Wrapped in Rainbows: The Life of Zora Neale Hurston*. New York: Scribner's, 2003.

Bruccoli, Matthew, and Margaret M. Duggan, eds. *The Correspondence of F. Scott Fitzgerald*. New York: Random House, 1980.

Bushman, Richard L. *The Refinement of America: Persons, Houses, Cities*. New York: Alfred A. Knopf, 1992.

Butler, A.S.G., with the collaboration of George Stewart and Christopher Hussey. *The Domestic Architecture of Sir Edwin Lutyens*. Woodbridge, Suffolk: Antique Collectors' Club, 1989.

Cantor, Eddie. *Between the Acts*. New York: Simon and Schuster, 1930.

———. *Caught Short!: A Saga of Wailing Wall Street*. New York: Simon and Schuster, 1929.

———. *My Life Is in Your Hands*. New York: Harper & Brothers, 1928.

Caro, Robert A. *The Power Broker: Robert Moses and the Fall of New York*. New York: Alfred A. Knopf, 1974.

Cohen, Lizabeth. *A Consumer's Republic: The Politics of Mass Consumption in Postwar America*. New York: Alfred A. Knopf, 2003.

Condit, Carl W. *The Port of New York: A History of the Rail and Terminal System from the Beginnings to Pennsylvania States*. Chicago: University of Chicago Press, 1980.

Dwight, Eleanor. *Diana Vreeland*. New York: William Morrow, 2002.

Fitzgerald, F. Scott. *All the Sad Young Men*. New York: Charles Scribner's Sons, 1926.

————. *The Crack-Up*. Edited by Edmund Wilson. New York: New Directions, 1945.

————. *The Great Gatsby*. New York: Collier Books, 1975.

Ginor, Zvia, ed. *Yakar Le'Mordecai: Jubilee Volume in Honor of Rabbi Mordecai Waxman*. Great Neck, NY: KTAV Publishing House, Temple Israel of Great Neck, 1998.

Glazer, Nathan. *American Judaism*. Chicago: University of Chicago Press, 1972.

Goodwin, Doris Kearns. *No Ordinary Times: Franklin and Eleanor Roosevelt: The Homefront in World War II*. New York: Touchstone, 1995.

Gordon, Ruth. *Myself among Others*. New York: Atheneum, 1971.

Green, Jesse, "The Song Is Ended," *New York Times Magazine*, June 2, 1996.

Hall, Peter. *The City in Civilization: Culture, Innovation, and Urban Order*. London: Weidenfeld & Nicolson, 1998.

Hine, Thomas. *Populuxe*. New York: Alfred A. Knopf, 1986.

Horizon 1, 1958. Foreword, 3–4.

Hoyt, Edwin Palmer. *The Vanderbilts and Their Fortunes*. Garden City, NY: Doubleday, 1962.

Hurston, Zora Neale. *Mules and Men*. Philadelphia: J. B. Lippincott, 1935.

Jackson, Kenneth T. *Crabgrass Frontier: The Suburbanization of the United States*. New York: Oxford University Press, 1985.

Jacoby, Susan. *Freethinkers: A History of American Secularism*. New York: Metropolitan Books, 2004.

Johnson, Paul. *History of America the American People*. New York: HarperCollins, 1997.

————. *A History of the Jews*. New York: Harper & Row, 1987.

————. "Schools: God and the Americans." *Commentary*, January, 1995, 25–45.

Kahn, E. J. Jr. *Jock: The Life and Times of John Hay Whitney*. Garden City, NY: Doubleday, 1981.

————. *The World of Swope*. New York: Simon and Schuster, 1965.

Kazin, Alfred, ed. *F. Scott Fitzgerald: the Man and His Work*. Cleveland: World Publishing Company. 1951.

Kluger, Richard. *The Paper: The Life and Death of the New York Herald Tribune*. New York: Vintage Books, 1989.

Lahr, John. "Light Fantastic." *New Yorker*, May 31, 1993.

League of Women Voters of Great Neck. *This Is Great Neck*. 1995.

Lenn, Martin, ed. *Five Boyhoods*. New York: Doubleday, 1962.

Mackay, Robert B., Anthony K. Baker, and Carol A. Traynor. *Long Island Country Houses and Their Architects, 1860–1940*. New York: Society for the Preservation of Long Island Antiquities, 1997.

Match, Richard. *Lucky Seven: A History of the Great Neck Public Schools, Union Free District 7*. Great Neck, NY: Great Neck Public Schools, 150th Anniversary Committee, 1964.

Mellow, James R. *Invented Lives: F. Scott and Zelda Fitzgerald*. New York: Houghton Mifflin, 1984.

Menand, Louis. "College: The End of the Golden Age." *New York Review of Books*, October 18, 2001. 44–47.

Meyer, Michael A. *Response to Modernity: A History of the Reform Movement in Judaism*. New York: Oxford University Press, 1988.

Miller, Robert. "The Long Island Motor Parkway: Prelude to Robert Moses." In *Robert Moses: Single-Minded Genius*, ed. Joann P. Krieg. Long Island Studies. Interlaken, NY: York Heart of the Lakes Publishing, 1989. 151–158.

The Most of John Held, Jr. Brattleboro, VT: S. Greene Press, 1972.

Mumford, Lewis. *The City in History: Its Origins, Its Transformations, and Its Prospects*. New York: Harcourt, Brace & World, 1961.

———. "Towards a Modern Synagog [*sic*] Architecture." *Menorah*, 1925. 225–236.

———. "The Wilderness of Suburbia." *The New Republic*, September 7, 1921. 44–45.

Oz, Amos. *A Tale of Love and Darkness*. New York: Harcourt, 2003.

Ravitch, Diane. *The Troubled Crusade: American Education, 1945–1980*. New York: Basic Books, 1983.

Robert S. Benjamin: A Citizen's Citizen. New York: Privately published 1980.

Rosengarten, Theodore, and Dale Rosengarten, eds. *A Portion of the People: Three Hundred Years of Southern Jewish Life*. Columbia: University of South Carolina Press, 2002.

Roth, Philip. *Shop Talk: A Writer and His Colleagues and Their Work*. New York: Vintage International, 2001.

Rudin, Jacob Philip. *Very Truly Yours*. New York: Bloch Publishing Company, 1971.

Sobin, Dennis P. *Dynamics of Community Change: The Case of Long Island's Declining "Gold Coast."* Port Washington, NY: Ira J. Friedman, 1968.

Statement of General Educational Philosophy. Great Neck, NY: Great Neck Schools, 1962.

Van Rensselaer, Mrs. John King. *The Social Ladder*. New York, Henry Holt, 1924.

Waxman, Mordecai *Tradition and Change: the Development of Conservative Judaism*. Rabbinical Assembly of America, 1958.

Winshe, Richard A. *Historic Structure Report, Saddle Rock, Grist Mill, Saddle Rock, NY*.

Wolfe, Alan. "Buying Alone." *The New Republic*, March 17, 2003. 28–33.

Yardley, Jonathan. *Ring: A Biography of Ring Lardner*. New York: Random House, 1977.

Zinsser, William K. *Inventing the Truth: the Art and Craft of Memoir*. Boston: Houghton Mifflin, 1987.

Index

About the Author

Judith S. Goldstein is an historian who received her B.A. from Cornell University and M.A. and Ph.D. from Columbia University. She is the author of *Crossing Lines: Histories of Jews and Gentiles in Three Communities* and *The Politics of Ethnic Pressure*. She is the founder and executive director of Humanity in Action, an international educational program.